Respecting Children:
Social Work with Young People

Respecting Children: Social Work with Young People

Margaret Crompton

 SAGE PUBLICATIONS   Beverly Hills

First published 1980 by
Edward Arnold (Publishers) Ltd
41 Bedford Square, London WC1B 3DQ

Published in the United States of America   1980
by Sage Publications, Inc.
275 South Beverly Drive
Beverly Hills, California 90212

ISBN 0-8039-1544-6 (cloth)
ISBN 0-8039-1545-4 (paper)

Library of Congress Catalog Card No. 80-5820

Printed in the United States of America

To John

Acknowledgements

My grateful thanks are due to Allen Lane (The Penguin Press) and James MacGibbon for permission to quote the poem by Stevie Smith, 'Not waving but drowning'. I would also like to acknowledge the generous cooperation of the Association of British Adoption and Fostering Agencies, the Family Service Units, the British Society for Music Therapy, the Save the Children Fund and the Northorpe Hall Trust.

Margaret Crompton

Contents

Introduction

This book is my masterpiece – a statement not from conceit but in humility, for a masterpiece was, orginally, the work offered by an apprentice who hoped to be accepted as a new master craftsman, that is, a mature and competent practitioner and member of his guild. I have for some years been writing my apprentice pieces in the form of articles; now I have put all I have in a book.

For this book is also my life-work; it has grown from and includes philosophy and experience drawn from my love of literature, work in a settlement and children's department, teaching in two universities, passionate concern for the respect towards and care of children and slow-growing but now firm convincement by and commitment to the Religious Society of Friends (Quakers).

Quakers encourage liberty of thought and attention to the voice inside each individual and every Quaker holds firm the belief in 'that of God in every man'. This book is a declaration of my belief in that of God in every child. In order to grow in health into a whole adult capable of giving love and earning trust, every child from the moment of birth, even of conception, must be regarded as a separate individual of personal worth, able to form opinions, to give and receive love, to accept responsibility for his own responses and behaviour. Every response and action is the result of a choice and the responsibility of the caring adult is to offer models for making such choices and to help the child understand the possibilities and the constraints which relate to each choice he makes, whether this is a decision about moving to a foster home or whether or not to throw a tantrum when he is refused a third helping of pudding.

The model of human psychology and interaction I adhere and refer to is *Transactional Analysis*. There is not space to describe this in detail but my taking-from it is that all individuals, whatever their chronological age, interact with others from three possible stances, PARENT, ADULT, CHILD, derived from their own internalized perceptions of their own parents and their own development as fully healthy children and mature or maturing adults. The aim should always be to respond from an ADULT position, rejecting attitudes of authoritarianism or pettishness, over-dependence or isolation which

1

arise from the 'false' positions. The ADULT response requires straight dealing and a refusal to play those interactive games which we all know so well. This is hardly an adequate summary and if you are familiar with Eric Berne (1968) you may already be criticizing me: if you are not familiar with the model you may feel bewildered, even annoyed in case you should now read another book before you can proceed with this one. If you feel either of these responses I apologize and beg you to read on, for I hope that my philosophy and its models will unfold as the book progresses. One word more about models and influences; I refer several times to the work of William Glasser on *Reality Therapy* (1975), a model which relates always to the now and to the responsibility of the individual for her own behaviour *whatever* the traumas of her past.

I must here declare that I have no children of my own and my experience of domestic child care is all derived from my step-son and daughter. This has offered me the opportunity to learn about being a part-time substitute carer; to feel all the swings of emotion from overwhelming love and possessiveness to would-be rejection and the accompanying guilt. I hope that this experience has helped me towards understanding of the feelings of residential and foster parents, of hospital staff and, of course, other step-parents, full and part-time; this book is written out of concern not only for the children but also for those who care for them.

I hope that people having day-to-day care of children will read and enjoy this book but it is written with a primary focus on field social workers including, of course, students. This is because I was myself a child-care officer and so feel most equipped to understand the needs, problems, achievements and viewpoints of fieldworkers. But I do not intend to be exclusive and have always believed that children can be served well only if all those concerned for their welfare understand, trust and cooperate one with another. Indeed the many examples of thought and work in the book are drawn from a wide range of areas of practice including, apart from field social work, residential child care, hospitals, psychiatry and education, as well as autobiography and fiction.

One of the ideas underlying the structure and content of the book is that much writing about work with and for children is settings-orientated. While I acknowledge that the setting and reason for contact between social worker and child must influence that contact, I believe that the most important contribution in the development of real and useful contact is in the understanding that is uniquely defined by the individual personalities and interaction of each adult and each child. The book is therefore generic in its use of both ideas and examples of work, for I believe that lessons learned from one setting may be rehearsed in another, maybe, even, in *any* other.

The form of the book is eleven chapters arranged within four parts. The first part comprises two chapters which discuss problems of and reasons for direct communication with children by field social workers. The following six chapters are devoted to different kinds of communication, for example play and music. The third part comprises two chapters, one on Northorpe Hall (an Intermediate Treatment centre) and one on work with children's groups in Family Service Units; the purpose of these two chapters is to show field social workers practising what I have, in the preceding eight chapters, been preaching! And there is a Postscript.

Each chapter is designed to be read as a separate piece as well as a constituent of the whole. Accordingly you will find that some quotations appear in more than one chapter, illustrating various ideas. This is deliberate, and not because I ran out of references! I should like to think that any reader would at least glance at chapters 1 and 2 but I regard the book as a whole as a work for reference.

You will find throughout the book many quotations from other writers. I have done this for three reasons: first, it came naturally, secondly I have never liked summaries of other people's writing within a text – I prefer to read the original words and to taste the orginal author's own flavour, and thirdly, I believe that it is very difficult for students, social workers and anyone else in exacting employment to seek and then read many books or even short articles: I didn't, even as a lecturer and I don't think I'm unique; so I hope that the quotations, sometimes quite long, may help would-be but overburdened readers to choose other books by offering samples of the styles and philosophies of the authors.

I have adopted the convention that adults, unless known to be otherwise, are referred to as female and children as male; this is for ease of reading and does not reflect any feminist attitude.

I refer occasionally to an article published in 1975 under my former name of Wardle; all other work by me has been published under the name of Crompton.

It is usual to conclude an Introduction with a list of acknowledge-ments. I feel nervous about this for so many people have made this book and I fear to leave anyone out. So this list is inevitably incomplete. My first thanks go to Dr Jack Kahn whose suggestion that my first-ever lecture might grow into a book took five years to become this. Of the many friends and colleagues who have contri-buted directly to the content I must thank particularly the staff of Newcastle Family Service Unit and the Northorpe Hall Trust. Barbara Williams, John Willis, Judith Lee and the other students who wrote children's books and dissertations on various courses I have taught might not have expected to see their names in print as a result of their labours and I thank them both for the labour and the material. A number of people have ploughed through early typescripts and encouraged me and I thank them all, particularly Eileen Holgate and Tony Neill at Liverpool University and Barbara Williams and Imelda Richardson in Newcastle. I used to wonder why people thanked their typists so enthusiastically; all in the day's work, I thought. Now I know for my friend and expert typist Penny Walker turned the whole thing from a batch of bitty papers into a typescript of beauty. Elaine Harrison typed the bibliography. Noel Timms and the Department of Social Work Studies (Newcastle University) authorized and financed the preparation of the manuscript. I thank all the children and adults who have worked with me who have contributed so much to this book and sometimes allowed me to feel that I have been of service. I offer this book as my endeavour to serve them further. There is one more person to thank, John Crompton. Without him as friend and tutor not one word of this book could have been written.

I conclude this introduction in the style of the rest of the book with some quotations. First a child at the receiving end of recognizable and common adult behaviour:

> ..... they ... asked [Johann] how he liked school after the holidays. They asked it teasingly, with that curiously superior and slighting air which grown people assume towards children, as if none of their affairs could possibly be worthy of serious consideration (Mann, 1962, p. 513).

Little Johann's life is all summed up in those sad sentences. And this book is to help Johann and his brothers and sisters attain the state described by Noel Hunnybun (1965, p. 125) at the conclusion of her account of social work with a child and parent: 'David ... and his mother began to enjoy each other.'

Blackhall Mill
1979

Part One

Communication between Adults and Children

Chapter 1
Often Difficult

Not communicating with some children of the 1970s

'She seemed to have a need to be noticed – perhaps punished too. If she couldn't get my attention any other way' one of the teachers added 'she'd come and sit under my desk and pull the hairs on my legs, you know – anything to get a reaction; I remember letting her do it: I was so determined not to give in to her craving for attention' (Sereny, 1972, p. 190).

But this teacher

and the teachers at (her) later school were more than anything else sorry and sad for her. 'I often feel guilty', said the headmistress, 'I don't know – perhaps I should have seen more, noticed more' (p. 192).

This was written about Mary Bell the murderer but could it not just as well have referred to Maria Colwell the victim? And was not Mary too a victim? Gita Sereny suggests that Mary's escalating atrocities were ever bigger and more dramatic appeals for help, for notice, for *someone* 'to give in to her craving for attention'.

No doubt Maria Colwell craved attention too but

One of the sad aspects of Maria's case is . . . that it was not easy to assess her state of mind as she sat quietly in the midst of a noisy family, with a particularly noisy sister who tended to dominate the scene (DHSS, 1974, p. 77).

Mary flamboyantly seeking attention; Maria silently despairing. Both doomed.

That the tragedies of these two girls might have been averted if someone had paid proper attention and endeavoured to communicate directly with them cannot be disputed; every social worker should pray every day that her caseload will be free of such drama.

But every caseload *is* packed full of such potential tragedy. And all the more dangerous because so very often hidden, incipient and silently deadly. The Robertsons filmed *John* in a 'good' nursery, safe and well cared for and tumbling into despair (1969). Caseloads are full of children whose 'behaviour problems' cause them to be hustled through the courts and community homes, girls of fourteen seeking

7

attention and affection through sex, school 'rejects', the conforming uncomplaining isolates in the children's homes; all in a caring system apparently uncared for and unconsulted, untrusted and untrusting, laying down stores of vintage problems. Not murder, not violence perhaps, so not exposing their social workers to threats of official enquiries; but what 'deaths of the soul', what inhibitions of that abundance of life and self-actualization which are the goals of much current philosophy.

Why, if we accept that 'every child has as much right as an adult to be a client' (Moore, 1976, p. 15), does it often seem to be difficult, even impossible, to offer to work and communicate directly with the children who have need of and the right to social-work service?

In this chapter my intention is to discuss some aspects of and reasons for that difficulty; I believe that there is no point in considering reasons for and ways of communicating with children unless social workers understand the problems and inhibitions which they and/or their colleagues (including social workers receiving students under supervision) may experience. I do not suggest that *every* social worker will recognize in herself the memory or present experience of *every* conflict and problem mentioned in this chapter but I am sure that any sensitive and emotionally honest and mature person will find at least some points which will lead her to think, 'Oh, yes!'

From God or Satan? some views of children

Was Mary Bell a sick angel or an unchained devil; in need of help or hell or, at least, hobbling?

The debate about whether children are inherently good and innocent, to be protected from the potentially corrupting world, or inherently evil, to be protected from themselves and from whom the world should be protected, has characterized the philosophy and practice of education and child care and welfare in Western society for many centuries. The twentieth-century social worker may not be conscious of the debate but she must, surely, be aware of her own attitude towards children in general and whether this is based on beliefs in liberal or restrictive philosophies and notions of inherent good or inherent evil in order properly to understand her attitude towards each individual child on her caseload.

So many books have been written on so many aspects of the development of ideas, attitudes, actions and representations relating to children and childhood that it would take a huge volume to summarize even superficially; (a few are mentioned in the bibliography for further reading). The ways of approaching and considering the study and development of children are many and disparate and apparently unrelated. It is the unrelatedness which makes this section very difficult to write. For example, I have looked at *A*

Short History of Educational Ideas (Curtis and Boultwood, 1953), *Readings in the History of Educational Thought* (Cohen and Garner, 1967), and *Children in Care* (Heywood, 1978). They are all about the children of the past 250 years but the ideas and ideals of the philosophers and writers in the education books seem to have little or nothing to do with the legislation for and lives of the children of whom Jean Heywood writes. And all the thoughts and developments are given a disturbing slant by the writers in *Children's Rights* (Hall, 1971).

To be a little more precise: the prime dichotomy seems to be between the child seen as potentially good, to be respected and encouraged, offered every opportunity to develop and integrate all aspects of life, physical, intellectual, spiritual and emotional, and the child seen primarily as a potential producer requiring to be controlled and used, to be protected and educated in order to serve the needs of industry.

A second dichotomy appears to be between the notion of the child as an individual and as the possession of parents, employer and state.

Love, respect and freedom

The loving and liberal view of the care and education which influences much current work in relation to children is owed to a great extent to Rousseau, Pestalozzi and Froebel. Although written in different times and places their work is characterized by some common themes, principally respect for children and the notion that they should be not instructed, trained and forced but given support and guidance in their own learning about life and nature. (All quotations are taken from Cohen and Garner, 1967.)

> Hold childhood in reverence, and do not be in any hurry to judge it for good or ill (Rousseau, 1712–1778).

The child is weak but can be lead and strengthened by care and wisdom, not punished for wrong doing or over-instructed.

> All true education [and social work?] . . . should . . . be simultaneously doublesided – giving and taking, uniting and dividing, prescribing and following, active and passive, positive yet giving scope, firm and yielding (Froebel, 1782–1852).
>
> The whole spirit of my method is not only to renew the bond between mother and child, with the disappearance of its physical cause, but to put a methodical series of means, that is an Art, into her hand by which she can give permanence to this relationship between her heart and her child, until the sense-methods of making virtue easy, united with the sense-methods of acquiring knowledge, may be able, by exercise, to *ripen the independence* of the child, in all that concerns right and duty (Pestalozzi, 1746–1827) (emphasis added).
>
> Do you not see how children are fettered by the weakness of infancy? Do you not see how cruel it is to increase this servitude by obedience to our caprices, by depriving them of such liberty as they have, a liberty which

they can scarcely abuse, a liberty the loss of which will do so little good to them or us? (Rousseau).

They speak of 'the perfection of childhood' (Rousseau) and believe that children are people. (Although it is only fair to say that Rousseau was notorious as a parent, placing his illegitimate children in an orphanage. Pestalozzi is famous for his practical philanthropy and Froebel's ideals and methods are still followed and practised.)

The notion of learning through experience appears rather grotesquely in *Everybody's Book of Correct Conduct* (M. C., 1893, p. 29) where parents are told that

> *It is the correct thing*
> For parents to remember that the young have to buy their own experience. This is a law of nature which cannot be altered

and the book itself provides rules for every aspect of life and relationship, for example:

> *It is the correct thing*
> To remember that to be a good son or good daughter is a lovable trait, and inclines other persons to like you (p. 28).

It is a long leap from 1893 to 1975 and another kind of *Everybody's Book of Correct Conduct* but here are more rules which might, as with the earlier book, be preceded with the instruction 'It is the correct thing to remember'. Among her 'ten Child Care Commandments' Mia Kellmer Pringle (1975, p. 159) instructs:

> 1 Give consistent and loving care – it's as essential for the mind's health as food for the body.
> 7 Remember that every child is unique – so suitable handling for one may not be right for another.
> 10 Don't expect gratitude; your child did not ask to be born – the choice was yours.

At the beginning of the book the author picks up that long chain (or rather gossamer thread for it is so elusive and so precious) from Rousseau: 'Children's physical, emotional, social and intellectual needs must all be met if they are to enjoy life, develop their full potential and grow into participating, contributing adults' (p. 15).

Just as in the latter half of the twentieth-century parents are given instruction and instructions into being 'good enough', so social workers are trained and CCETSW (1978, p. 2) sets up a working party whose guidelines begin: 'The need to give special consideration to the training of staff in the social services who work with children has become increasingly evident' and end: ' . . . the focus of the work of this group is specially on work with children themselves, or with children and their immediate families' and the 1975 *Children Act* requires social workers to consult children involved in adoption proceedings about their own views: it does not however require anyone to pay attention to those views (HMSO, 1975, Sec. 3).

This neatly represents the dichotomy which I am trying to express, the distance between the thought and the act, the philosophy and the legislation. The idea is there in the Act but it is constrained, hedged round with get-outs if the child is for some reason deemed to be incapable of providing a 'good enough' opinion of his own wishes and situation, so that action need not be affected while philanthropy seems to be satisfied.

Possession and control

Whatever Rousseau, Pestalozzi and Froebel and their great English colleagues might have to say about education and the importance of development for children, until 1870 fairly few children in England had the benefit of full-time education. While Rousseau described the perfect life and education of Emile, learning naturally from nature with the aid of a tutor and uncorrupted by the city, many children were learning about life the hard way, a hard way which would become harder with the Industrial Revolution and mass child employment in pits and mills and factories and chimneys. Where was the opportunity to learn about 'the inner law of Divine Unity' (Froebel) for the West Riding girls in the mines?

> Chained, belted, harnessed like dogs in a go-cart, black, saturated with wet, and more than half-naked – crawling upon their hands and feet, dragging their heavy loads behind them, they present an appearance indescribably disgusting and unnatural (Children's Employment Commission. Mines, 1842, p. 41 in Heywood, 1978, p. 24).

That was written in *1842*, 80 years after Rousseau published *Emile* and *The Social Contract*; 40 years after the 1802 Act for the Preservation of the Health and Morals of Apprentices and others employed in cotton and other mills and only 137 years before I write now in 1979 when children are compelled to attend school from five to sixteen. 'Man is born free, and yet we see him everywhere in chains (Rousseau in Nash, 1968)', our children are free of the pit but are they, I wonder, free of the chains?

Between Sir Robert Peel's Act of 1802 and the 1975 *Children Act* stretches a huge catalogue of legislation relating to the employment, protection, education, health, punishment and emotional welfare of children. In discussion of the development of attitudes towards children it is important to ask if this legislation is the product of wholehearted interest in the welfare of the children to whom it applies. Nan Berger (1971, pp. 154–5) would say no:

> Few of the reformers had any idea about the needs of children as persons and if they did none of it was reflected in the legislation they pushed through a reluctant parliament. Some of the more far-sighted saw the need to give children education which would enable them to man more efficiently the machines of the developing industries of the future. Some

also saw the need for protecting property against destitute children who were forced into crime in order to exist at all. The employing classes – the owners of the new mills who were also the property-owning classes – saw only one aspect of children's lives: their ability to work in the mills and make profits for their masters.

In the so-called Great Debate about education in the mid 1970s senior politicians frankly talked about education as the preparation of children for work in industry. And was the school-leaving age raised to sixteen in order to provide more education for our adolescents, education in, perhaps, a Froebelian sense of 'leading man, as a thinking, intelligent being, growing into self-consciousness' (Froebel, in Cohen and Garner, 1967); or to offer more information about kinds of and opportunities for employment, a bridge from school to work; or was it to keep a few thousand new workers off the labour market?

Earlier in this chapter I mentioned the division of thought between those who consider children to be inherently innocent and potentially good and those who think of them as little devils – literally. I suggest that the legislation of the past century and a half is based on the latter view in that there is an assumption that children are weak and potentially disruptive, likely to injure themselves and society if not tightly controlled. I will not take space to develop this thought further except to suggest that the prime interest in most comprehensive schools is the maintenance of control and that these schools frequently resemble factories whose problem is that they are not sure what the end product is supposed to be. And besides the end product is not, these days, likely to be very marketable anyway since both produce and market are restricted.

I also suggest that much current welfare legislation is concerned largely with control and when not with that, with possession. Children are always being owned. Parents may lose their 'rights and powers' to local authorities. Children have no rights and powers to lose it seems. Adoption is about ownership; if it were not, where would be the point in going to a court of law, of all places, to discuss the welfare of a child? Foster parents have been increasingly concerned to establish rights to keep their foster children. Step-parents on the other hand have no rights; they are third-class parents and may legally lose their step-children if the natural parent dies or departs simply because there is no legal tie.

Society doles out rights to children like a parent dispensing sweets (not even pocket money over which the child has some control). At various ages a child may leave school, have legal sexual intercourse, join the armed services, buy cigarettes, vote, marry, be deemed to be adult, live on his own, give consent to his own medical treatment and be regarded as capable of deliberately committing a crime.

If children are regarded as the potential savages of *The Lord of the Flies* (Golding) where young boys trapped on a desert island without adults display all the worst that the Freudian id can dream up, or as weak inadequates, how can they fulfill Mia Kellmer Pringle's (1975, p. 15) injunction to 'enjoy life, develop their full potential and grow into participating, contributing adults'?

Bits and pieces

I have mentioned people who are concerned with 'the whole child' (for example Froebel and Mia Kellmer Pringle) but such thinkers are few and far between. More commonly people attend to their own particular bit of the child; for example morals, physical welfare, employment potential or delinquent behaviour; theorists, too, are frequently interested in only one aspect of behaviour and development, for example cognitive or emotional, physiological or psychosocial.

A friend* suggested that attitudes towards children at different periods might be represented by a variety of vivid descriptive titles, for example the time when the 11+ was becoming popular and IQ tests were all the rage may be called the age of 'the measurable child' while the mid 1970s may be that of 'the sensitive plant'. As I write I think that children in Britain are seen as both feeble and threatening. We admire precocity and achievement but are a little daunted by it, as we are by any child who is at all odd; children in long-stay hospitals whether for mental or physical disability are an embarrassment, poor achievers at home and school are a nuisance, delinquents are both. Legislation is apparently protective and providing but the benefits are frequently unprovidable and unprovided because resources are unavailable (in education, health and welfare services). So the feeble can only be protected and the threatening must be constrained and contained. We have not the time nor the money – nor perhaps the will – to bring our children into full health and strength and to harness into fruitful and healthful activity the frustrated energy of those who threaten.

Good or evil, possessions or free individuals, life first as people or as economic cogs; our attitudes today are coloured and conditioned by those of our predecessors. Before we can work with children we must know which of those attitudes we hold; and why.

Not communicating: some sources of difficulty

Social workers are required by law to 'ascertain the wishes and feelings' of children (HMSO, 1975). But social workers sometimes, even often, find it difficult to communicate with the children on their caseloads. Some of this difficulty may be due to the traditional philosophical conflict regarding the child's inherent nature discussed above, and some to the persistence of the notion that children

* Lesley Webb; School of Education, Newcastle University

are possessions and have no right to involvement in their own destinies and conditions of life, whatever the law says. It is important for the social worker to identify and understand her own position on these matters. Unrecognized and unresolved conflicts are wonderfully effective inhibitors to purposeful communication.

In the rest of this chapter I suggest some other possible sources of difficulty in communication between adults and children. None is exclusive to social workers but all may be experienced by some social workers at some time or another.

Looking silly and feeling rejected

I think one of the greatest influences on adult behaviour with children is the fear of looking silly. Social workers are particularly exposed. If an adult is rejecting, the social worker may try to understand the rebuff in terms of defences; the client's defences that is. Face can be saved by Freud. If a child is uncooperative with a doctor or dentist his behaviour can be understood as fear of being hurt and of the paraphernalia in the surgery. Face can be saved by function. But how can the social worker save face when a child refuses to respond to her overtures? Adults are supposed to be 'good with children' unless they have made a firm declaration to the contrary; 'Oh, I'm no good with children' does let you off, unless you are a woman and/or a member of a 'helping profession'. Social workers can't hide behind drills and thermometers and white overalls to cover their confusion: relationships are the tools of their trade.

Of course the reluctance of a child client to respond is very likely to be explained by his shyness or fear or anxiety. And equally of course, social workers usually realize and recognize that. But such recognition may be no defence against feeling that they ought to be able to manage; that the quality of understanding and communication ought to be enough to reach the child who should in turn respond.

Not all adults like all children. Not all adults like children at all. Not all social workers like children. And not all social workers like all the children on their caseloads. Further, not all social workers like all the children on their caseloads all the time. Just as, I think, it is often difficult to admit to being not-very-successful it is also difficult to talk about not-liking children in need. Barry can be a so-and-so, a pain in the neck, a bloody little delinquent, even thoroughly unpleasant but somehow this is likely to be expressed as a characteristic of Barry without reference to the contribution of the social worker herself to the unsatisfactory nature of the contact. And if Barry appears to be a reasonably ordinary little boy it is probably almost impossible to confess or justify negative feelings about him. Whether Barry is tough or not, social workers are supposed to understand.

Boredom and embarrassment

One of the best accounts of working with a child I have come across is by Robina Prestage (1972, p. 100) a social worker in a child guidance clinic:

> About 2 months had elapsed when Kim (aged nine) casually announced . . . his intention of climbing a large pear tree in the clinic garden.
> . . . This new element was discussed with the clinic team and I was given carte blanche by the psychiatrist – which wasn't exactly welcome as I could not imagine what I was going to do with this persecuted little boy. . . . For 14 long weeks he arrived promptly, acknowledged my greeting with a non-committal nod and proceeded to climb the 2 pear trees with the ease and agility of a monkey – a mute monkey.

Kim continues to climb trees for weeks, never addressing the social worker 'although I came to realize that he was communicating with me in other ways'. Eventually

> I literally began to dread this hour and to feel depressed, bored and angry. Doubtless many therapists would have successfuly interpreted his behaviour, but I required at this point to review my feelings of frustration and inadequacy because my 'food' was being rejected (p. 101).

What vivid writing and what honesty. Surely one can feel that aching boredom, the social worker imprisoned in the garden at the end of a long day (Kim came after school) waiting for that other prisoner, the small boy up his tree, and maintaining eternal vigilance in case he should offer any sign of communication, a nod or a wink or even, at last, the longed-for words: 'See you next week'.

Even if social workers are not frequently engaged in such garden vigils the feelings of depression and boredom and impatience must be familiar. Why do young children always want the same story time after time, long after the reading adult has reached a screaming pitch of boredom with the exploits of Baby Bear or Minnie Mouse? Why do teenagers play the same records incessantly, (or, perhaps, to the grown-up ear, the 'same' record under a number of different titles?) Why doesn't the child understand that everyone is doing their best for him, that he should really try to settle down in this foster home or that hostel? Why doesn't he understand that he'll end up in court if he doesn't stop thieving? He's been told again and again and again, it's all been explained to him. And it's boring and frustrating and what is the social worker going to do with those feelings?

Gill Gorell Barnes (1978, pp. 150–1) suggests that

> some people can never work very directly with children because they are not prepared to face the crudeness of comment children can make. . . . Three-year-olds talk openly and freely about sex, dirt, bodies and parts, personal likes and dislikes and other people as they see them.

The writer does not develop this point but perhaps one can

recognize the embarrassment which any child (not just a free-thinking three-year-old) may cause by clearly and noisily asking such questions as 'How old are you, miss?' or 'Are you married?' in public places.

Suspicion and hostility

Social workers may become unblushable and immune to embarrassment but I wonder how easy it is to resist some uncomfortable reaction to displays of suspicion and hostility from children. A threat of physical violence from an adolescent would have to be taken as seriously as if from an adult. But it is in children's eyes that these emotions are usually expressed. For example, John in the film of that name greets his longed-for mother after her nine-day absence with a look of such intense hostility that even the memory is searing. The child has been betrayed and he cannot easily forgive his betrayer (Robertson, 1969). Social workers sometimes betray children; they do not keep promises to visit; they force children to go to places of residence which they, the children, have not chosen and then expect them to settle down, even be happy; they encourage children to trust them and then leave. But it is unlikely that those social workers ever see the look in John's eye; they are not there to see it; but someone will, sometime.

One of the most dreadful pictures of hostile children is that in *The Midwich Cuckoos* (Wyndham, 1964). The alien hard-eyed children can cause people to commit suicide simply by looking at them and exerting their common will and they can mind-read. Such changeling stories are as old as myth. The innocent human nurtures the evil supernatural child and is in great danger of destruction by it. The force of this idea lies in the abuse and rejection of the power of parental care and the unthinkable thought that a parent might reject her 'own' child. But there may be even more force in the notion that a child, any child, can be entirely and irretrievably evil from birth. I have written above about the age-old conflict between the concepts of children as inherently good and inherently evil and I suggest that the social worker is most vulnerable to believing or at least acting in accordance with the latter when faced with the cold-eyed glare of a hostile rejecting child.

Role, function and task

Assuming that they are not in fact changelings, children may have good cause to feel suspicious of social workers particularly if they are associated with something 'bad' such as court or removal from home. And social workers may intensify such feelings by failing to convey that they have any benign intent. However hard it is to communicate this to children, it is made even harder if parents and other care-takers do not understand the role and function of the social workers. How often does the social worker hear the dreaded 'Miss X will take you away if you go on like that!' either in so many words or implied? There is little chance of a child's eyes showing trust if he does not really understand what Miss X is all about. And even less chance of Miss X's eyes showing warmth if she feels disliked and rejected by the child.

Lack of clarity about, and confidence in the role and task of the social worker is, I think, a major inhibitor in working directly with children (indeed with anyone). There are more or less clear guidelines about preparing a child for boarding out or completing C&YPA* investigations and reporting to juvenile court. In such work relationships to residential and foster-care workers, parents and police and to the child himself are to an extent defined though even here there are plenty of occasions for problems. Far more difficult are those grey areas of home on trial (from both care orders and Section 2 rights) and voluntary supervision, of supervision of the boarded-out child and of contact with the child in residential care.

When the child is living in his own home it may be difficult to convince his parents that the social worker has any good reason to communicate directly with him. Parents are very likely to feel suspicious and threatened and to have their own view of the purpose (or lack of it) of social workers. Any social worker who wants to make direct contact with a child in his own home will need to be very clear indeed just what and whom contact is for. She will also need to understand the parents' feelings and to ensure that *they* receive enough of her attention to be able to allow part of her time to be spent with their 'rival' child. (It may of course be that the social worker's time is best spent in helping the parents learn how to 'be' with their own children.)

I think that social workers often feel very diffident when other 'experts' are working with children. If the social worker is not clear and confident about her role *vis-à-vis* the child she may easily withdraw in favour of, for example, foster parents, residential workers, psychiatrists, nurses and play therapists.

Residential workers often complain that social workers go near them and their children only when a review or move is imminent. Such social workers, I suspect, do not realize that they would be welcomed in the children's home or community home, that they have a continuing role *with* and not just *for* the children there placed and that they are members of a team with definite tasks. The social worker's task is not to march into the children's home and 'get to know' the children on her caseload who live there, without reference to the residential staff; but she is responsible for making and maintaining contact with the natural families, for caring about the

* Children and Young Persons Act 1969

development and welfare of the children and for ensuring that plans are made and properly implemented and must therefore find ways of developing and maintaining relationships with the children, even if no action is immediate or imminent. Social workers not infrequently feel that they are less than welcome in foster homes and residential establishments and from both my own experience and observation and the comments of, in particular, residential staff, an unwelcome social worker is likely to be one who has failed either to understand or communicate the reason for her presence and her intentions *vis-à-vis* the child she wishes to visit and those who care for him. The social worker who is not completely clear about her role, function and task with regard to every client and every contact is deficient not only in professional competence but also in courtesy.

Confidence, experience and knowledge

Lack of confidence in role and function may derive partly from lack of understanding about relationships with parents and colleagues and of legal and moral responsibilities.

Lack of confidence in trying to communicate directly with children may also derive from lack of understanding of a particular child and his problems and current behaviour or from a sense of general ignorance about children.

A moving example of the first point is narrated in the children's novel *The Trouble with Donovan Croft*. Donovan, a ten-year-old West Indian, is boarded out with as nice a foster family as you could wish to meet but the shock of his mother's sudden departure for Jamaica and his father's subsequent apparent rejection of him causes him to freeze and become mute. The story is about his unfreezing and about the difficulty people have in understanding him. The following extract illustrates several all too familiar points. Donovan brought to the foster home by a peculiarly inept welfare officer, refuses to leave the car:

> ... Mrs Chapman felt a growing sense of defeat. ... 'What are we to do?' she asked the welfare officer. 'How did you get him into the car?'
> 'Oh, his father did that; he just carried him in while I held the door open.'
> 'Oh ... You know, if he won't even get out of the car on his own I wonder if we'll be able to cope with him here. I didn't know he was a problem child.'
> 'Well, dear, any child without a mother at home has problems, to a greater or lesser degree. But our records show this chap to be quite normal; no one's told me anything about him being particularly awkward.'
> The two women looked at one another, baffled. Had Donovan been the son of either of them he would have been out of that car in a flash, upset or not, and they would have thought little more about it. Somebody else's child was another matter, though, and they didn't know quite what to do (Ashley, 1974, pp. 14–15).

Mrs Chapman and the welfare officer are stuck because they don't know the rules for dealing with Donovan. Mrs Chapman is the successful mother of a boy the same age as Donovan but she cannot spontaneously treat her foster son in the same way as her own child. However, she can use her experience as a mother to help both her understanding of Donovan and her attempts to communicate with him. She knows a lot about children even if she feels that she knows nothing at all about this particular child.

The vignette of Donovan's welfare worker (who never appears again, much to my and I guess Donovan's relief) suggests that she has no children of her own. While one feels that *she* is no loss to motherhood perhaps she does for a second represent the many childless social workers who, whether or not they will be excellent parents in time, are for the present slightly handicapped by their sense of ignorance about flesh-and-snot 'normal' children. I am *not* saying that you have to be a parent in order to understand and communicate with children. This chapter is about how people may *feel* and I do know many childless social workers, particularly if they have grown up in small families, who feel shy of children because they think that they know too little about childhood and have not yet perhaps enough confidence to trust their intuition.

Understanding and respect

Knowledge and confidence and even intuition are not, however, enough. In 'Hippopotamus or Cow?' I wrote:

> many adults do not think of children as having the right to [or the ability for] active involvement in their own destinies and development. Sometimes adults simply don't think. The child is seen as a pupil, deprived, delinquent, an adolescent, a baby to be fostered, adopted, operated on, educated but not conversed with or taken into the confidence of the adult (Wardle, 1975, p. 430).

It seems to be very difficult for some adults to believe that even quite young children may have (are indeed very likely to have) an opinion about what happens to them. Here is seven-year-old Hugo on his first day at school:

> Interested, Hugo examines everything. He looks at the pictures and pronounces an opinion on them . . . .
> Several times the teacher opens her mouth. Then shuts it again. She looks like a fish out of water. In the end she has to interrupt Hugo to make herself heard at all. She realizes that Hugo doesn't understand, she says, but in school children have to sit still and be quiet. The teacher does the talking, and the children just answer when the teacher asks them a question.
> Hugo listens attentively to this, but looks frankly astonished.
> 'Now that's odd', he says.
> 'What's so odd about it?' the teacher asks.
> 'There's no sense in our answering, when we don't know anything. We're the ones who ought to ask the questions' (Gripe, 1962, p. 59).

It is salutary to follow that tale of Swedish Hugo with one from an American school:

> I was talking about my class to a twelve-year-old friend of mine. I happened to say that some of the children in my class had been having a conversation. At this my friend looked puzzled. She said, 'You mean these kids were talking about this stuff in class?' . . . 'Yes . . . there are lots of times during the day when kids can talk to each other if they wish it, about whatever interests them most. Don't you ever have a time in Class when you can talk to other people?' She was almost too astonished to answer (Holt, 1970, p. 75).

John Holt understands about respecting and using the spontaneity and interest and good sense of children. Without that understanding and respect even the most well meaning efforts by adults to communicate are likely to be useless:

> It was lunchtime and the children were having a cooked meal placed on their small tables. As the meal was served, the children began to sing spontaneously. Soon all the children, West Indian and English, were singing happily. The assistant in charge said kindly but firmly, 'You can sing after lunch children but not now. All your dinners will get cold and uneatable.' They ceased to sing.
> Half an hour later, the same assistant began to sing children's songs with the nursery group. She sang solo. The moment for the children had passed. . . . She turned to me saying, 'Aren't children contrary? They never do what you want them to do' (Brandon, 1976, p. 69).

The Swedish teacher who realizes that Hugo doesn't understand and this nursery assistant are both well meaning – motivated, it seems, by interest in the welfare of the children in their care; they would be hurt and astonished by the suggestion that they cared very little for the children as people and a great deal for the children as subjects for them, the adults, to organize and rule.

John Holt and David Brandon, listening to and looking at and with children, are rather rare. It may be dangerous for an adult to acknowledge that children are people with sense and opinion and the ability to see what is going on around them. Acknowledgement of that might involve adaptation of at least systems and timetables and plans and even worse, the treatment of children as 'adults'. One of the models of human behaviour which contributes to the philosophy of this book is the Transactional Analysis model of PARENT-ADULT-CHILD and I believe that people of any age can, if approached as ADULTS (which is briefly to say, with *true* respect), respond and behave in a sensitive and sensible manner and take considerable responsibility for their own learning and way of life (Berne, 1968, see Introduction, pp. 1–2). The Swedish teacher and the nursery assistant were not treating their children as ADULTS and in consequence the children were unlikely to learn much about self-reliance and true Adulthood from them; rather, the children were constantly being put down and infantilized, discouraged from taking any initiative. Of course it is necessary for chronological adults in positions of responsibility to ensure that their responsibilities are fulfilled; but their work will be infinitely more effective (and I suggest rewarding) if the individual (chronological) child is really engaged and regarded as ADULT.

But that may be difficult and threatening and most of us are under pressure. Perhaps there doesn't seem to be much time today for listening:

> It was a fine, crisp, wintry morning and nearby was a stretch of green patterned with snowdrops. The small child's eyes widened in excitement and she tried to halt her mother. 'Look, look Mummy, see those lovely flowers'. I stopped and with her tuition saw them but Mum was driven on and down through the weight of shopping bags and her fear of missing the bus (Brandon, 1976, pp. 69–70).
> In the bus queue, a three-year-old was talking animatedly to her mother. The mother stared straight ahead, silent – until suddenly she exploded, her voice furious, detonating. *'That's all I ever get from you! chatter, chatter chatter!'* The lively little girl's intelligent face changed, and she looked wary, self-conscious, off-balance and silly (Berg, 1972, p. 11).

Such example of non-accidental injury can be multiplied 1,000 times from both observation and personal experience. However much one likes Transactional Analysis and cares about communicating with and respecting children, real life irritation and rush is going to get in the way and some rather bruised child is going to wonder what he's done now. What he's done is to imagine that his interests can be of importance when some adult business such as cooking the tea or writing a book is in process.

Time for social workers and parents and teachers and writers and everyone else is always short. It is short for children too.

Enjoyment as work

When time is short the earnest adult is likely to think that it should be filled with earnest activities particularly if she has a specific task to perform such as boarding a child out or supervising under a court order. Play and enjoyment are strictly for children (and therapists) and Saturday afternoons. I am sure that there are many puritans who, like me, felt rather guilty about enjoying contact with children. If we went for a country walk I thought I should earn my pay by at least mentioning the current 'problem'. Surely it could't be right *only* to have a walk and enjoy the countryside? Gradually it dawned on me that it could be very right and that there was no 'only' about it. If the child and I could *be* together there was a good chance that we would be able to *do* together when and if we had the need of action. Nonetheless I think it is sometimes difficult to be convinced that a pleasant hour in the company of a child is as much 'work' as visiting the unattractive, uncooperative and downright difficult members of a caseload. But surely a happy social worker is able to communicate more effectively than one who is, for example, anxious or even resentful.

Collusion, merging, memory and pain

However, for some social workers it may be difficult to engage in play or other forms of 'enjoyable' activity because of their need to maintain distance from and boundaries between themselves and their clients; there may be some fear that authority will be lost if the social worker appears to communicate on any sort of equal level with a child or adolescent. There *is* in working with adolescents in particular a considerable danger of collusion and it is important to be aware of this when determining what kind of relationship is to be offered and what means of communication may be employed:

> Sometimes the social worker may set out to establish a friend-to-friend relationship with the adolescent client as a way of avoiding any problem of control: 'I'm one of the boys too you know, identify with me any you'll be OK'. . . . If the social worker is not fully confident of his own adulthood and his own position regarding control (both by and of himself) he may be tempted 'back into adolescence' (Crompton, 1978, p. 18).

If the social worker loses sight of her own chronological adulthood and her role *vis-à-vis* the adolescent she may do both herself and her client considerable disservice:

> Collusion with delinquents can be present without anyone quite knowing how this has come about. Delinquents . . . should be able to rely only on our continued concern. Involvement with them becomes merger, and once this has taken place the therapist is no longer in a position to help his client (Dockar-Drysdale, 1968, p. 86).

It may be fear of such collusion or 'merger' which holds some social workers back from really trying to reach their young clients, partly to safeguard the present adult in her position of authority and defined role.

Exposure to the feelings and pains of children may also bring the danger of recognizing similarities to the social worker's own past experience and memories, including perhaps unresolved and therefore still potentially explosive or poisonous frustrations and angers. I do not think it can be possible to be a really communicating social worker and not to have in one's memory some old scars:

> Recognition that a child is suffering exposes the adult to feeling memories of his own childhood agonies; a hint of an old terror of the dark, of being lost in an enormous buzzing store, of being anaesthetized, of losing a precious relative or animal or of meeting with fear and resentment a new sibling or step-parent. Perhaps a denial of the suffering of the child client helps to quell the shadows of our own bewildering pain (Wardle, 1975, p. 430).

In 1957 Ner Littner considered that

We are just becoming aware of the widespread implications of the presence in a Child Welfare worker's caseload of children with serious internalized emotional problems. Three ways in which the worker can be made tense by his work are:
1 the client's anxiety has a very contagious quality;
2 the client's feelings have a very contagious effect;
3 the disturbing effects of situations that re-activate childhood conflicts.
Whatever the nature of early separation experiences, the adjustment that the caseworker once made to it will tend to be disturbed every time the worker places a child. The impact upon the worker of each child's separation feelings is made by upsetting the worker's own emotional equilibrium and forces him again and again to renew and strengthen his prior defences.

Littner also suggests that caseworkers with children may be affected by unresolved feelings of anger against their own parents, sexual problems and 'experiences about being given to since no one has had every childhood need met'.

How long will it be before social workers give a lead to the rest of us by emerging from their own hurt childhoods to listen to and heal the children that need them now? (Lynes, 1976).

But when social workers can, as they do, emerge from their own painful memories (even if their childhoods were not all deeply hurt), they must, if they are truly open to the children that need them now, meet contact with the pain of those children.

A little boy with a grazed knee may be crying with shock and pain but his mother will have little difficulty in cleaning the knee and comforting the rest of the boy. His pain and injury are both slight and temporary and she need not feel or fear either. If he is severely burned she will need the experts to help both herself and her son to manage the physical and emotional pain. If she feels in any way responsible for the injury, possibly because of negligence, she will feel guilt and shame. Even if she can feel complete innocence she will probably find the pain and distress of her son unbearable. How can she help and comfort him when he may be disfigured and disadvantaged for life?

The experts who treat the little boy will meet the same feelings. 'Often they are called upon to carry out procedures which add to the child's distress' (Wolff, 1973, p. 69). If your aim is to help a child and ease his pain, whatever its source, you don't want him to see you as the cause of further suffering. How much nicer to be able to say 'There there, you'll soon be better' or, 'Nonsense, of course it doesn't hurt, don't be silly'.

Without special help to deal with their own anxieties, doctors and nurses commonly resort to methods of coping which preserve their efficiency, but at a cost. The most common solution is to adopt an attitude of clinical detachment: to split off the emotional aspects of illness and its treatment as they affect both the patient and oneself (p. 70).

To 'doctors and nurses' add social workers.

Clare Winnicott (1964, p. 43) tells us that

> To work effectively with children the first and most fundamental thing we have to know about is the strength of our own feelings about the suffering of children. All adults find it is a difficult proposition, and we are familiar enough with the ways in which other people deny or minimize the reality of the child's feelings.

It is tempting to believe that a child is not affected by what happens to him, particularly if he gives no overt and conventional response. I have noticed myself and had confirmed by residential workers that children in residential care frequently show no emotion when a worker leaves the home even when she has been popular and treated with affection while in residence. Whether the worker has been a member of staff for a long or short time and whether the children are placed for long or short stay, the gap will *apparently* never be noticed. And it is really convenient to believe that the children are heartless and unmoved; that the apparently much liked, even loved, Auntie Liz was really nothing at all to them and can easily be completely replaced by Auntie Dot. And Auntie Ann. And Auntie Pat. So perhaps no one really wants to know that the children may really be feeling betrayed, sold down the river by yet another mealy-mouthed adult who pretended that she was to be entrusted with the priceless fragile gift of a child's affection. What good would weeping do? Who would care? And if anyone showed apparent care it could not be trusted for that person would presumably depart as inevitably and carelessly as Auntie Liz. No. Better not to expose oneself to that kind of pain. Any adult facing that would have to feel guilt and anguish and be prepared to imagine if not actually experience the children's grief. Better to say they don't care and avoid feeling anything. (Especially because the staff left behind or taking over from Auntie Liz may well be feeling betrayed themselves.)

Conclusion

If social workers do recognize and acknowledge some of those painful and difficult feelings what can they do?

> . . . the needs of many of the children who come our way seem overwhelming. We are horrified at some of the experiences they have been through. . . . We can lose confidence in the relevance of our social casework techniques and abandon the attempt to reach the child's feelings because they are altogether too painful (Winnicott, 1964, p. 43).

Yet who would not risk burning his hand to pull a child out of a fire? The difference between social work and rescue from acute physical

danger is that the physical rescue must be initiated and accomplished quickly without pause to reflect on possible cost to the
rescuer. The social worker embarks on contact with a client with a
very good idea about the cost to herself and with a commitment
which may be for a long time. As she comes closer to the child and
allows the child to come closer to her she may find the price of the
contact rises (for example, a sense of impotence at being unable to
make everything come right for the child or the difficulty of
maintaining a sense of purpose in the contacts.) The burnt rescuer
will be praised and bandaged. But who even recognizes that the
social worker is in danger of pain, still less offers approval and
healing?

So perhaps one of the greatest inhibitors to *really* communicating
with children, to opening oneself to the embarrassment and
non-successes and boredom and irritation and sadness and commitment and confrontation with pain is this: that no one is prepared
to offer the social worker what she is required to offer the children;
respect, understanding, the opportunity to communicate, help to
achieve change, support to acknowledge and become reconciled to
frustration and disappointment, encouragement, recognition of
achievement, sharing in grieving and rejoicing and, fundamental to
all these, the love of one person concerned for the welfare of
another. Where agencies and establishments offer this to their social
workers I believe that the children on their caseloads too are
respected and loved.

No one could have blamed Robina Prestage if she had said no to
the team who gave her *carte blanche* to work with Kim or if she had
even ever so kindly asked Kim to remove himself from his tree.
Perhaps someone did care about her. Perhaps the team who *gave* her
the problem also *understood* the problem and recognized that she was
being asked to expose herself to all manner of strains.

I hope no one blames the two busy mums. Who is there to give *them*
time to admire snowdrops and to 'chatter, chatter, chatter'? The
children themselves, so charming to the onlooker, will be the first to
demand food, clothing, toys, attention. If no one plays with you for
your own enjoyment how can you be expected to give your precious
time to attend to the 'non-essential' demands of anyone else?

In nothing that I have written have I for a moment intended to
imply that children should be spoiled, given in to, treated as gods.
Children are *people* not *rulers*.

And here we are back with Maria Colwell and Mary Bell and two
questions must be asked – the questions that must be asked and
answered wherever and whenever a social worker sets out to
communicate with a child. Who really cared about Maria and Mary
as *people*? And: who cared about the carers; Mr and Mrs Kepple and
Miss Leese, Mrs Bell and those kind, busy teachers?

Chapter 2

Always Vital

And what of the children on your caseload?
Will some of them read this and help us?
(Holgate and Neill, 1978)

In a hard-hitting article in *Community Care* the authors challenge their readers to consider how little attention really seems to be paid to the apparently accepted notion that social workers should work directly with children. They suggest, for example, that children are often excluded from their own case conferences on the grounds that they would not fully understand or might be upset by the proceedings although the same children may well be present throughout juvenile court hearings. They also remind their readers that 'standards of practice' in relation to working with and on behalf of children including 'communicating with children' have been declared and sought after at least since the Monckton Report of 1945. Yet 30 years later the *Children Act*, exhorts:

> In reaching any decision relating to a child in their care, a local authority shall give first consideration to the need to safeguard and promote the welfare of the child throughout his childhood and shall so far as practicable ascertain the wishes and feelings of the child regarding the decision and give due consideration to them having regard to his age and understanding (HMSO, 1975, Sec. 3)

and the authors draw attention to those dynamic phrases . . . 'shall so far as practicable . . . having regard to his age and understanding'. The fact that they felt the need to ask the questions helps to convince me that in this book it is essential to discuss another question, *why should social workers communicate directly with children?* For the answer to that is, it seems, by no means as clear and universally agreed and believed as Eileen Holgate and Tony Neill and those who think like them would wish.

Just as these authors asked that the children should help us to understand more about their needs and interests and how to communicate with them, Jean Moore in 1975 suggested that 'The children themselves . . . may be able to help us to help them' (p. 15). Following these ideas I have turned to the children themselves to structure this chapter. *Who Cares?* (Page and Clark, 1977) is subtitled *Young People in Care Speak Out* and is a collection of the comments and ideas of a group of adolescents (12–16) and a few adults who had grown up in care. Chapter 6 is called *Making Sense of Care* but the comments are relevant to children and social workers in any setting and situation. The seven section titles that follow are quotations from this chapter.

To tell you the truth

> A social worker's there to help you understand and to tell you the truth (Page and Clark, 1977, p. 33).

A simple enough statement with which to begin; surely no one could disagree. Except that some of the children had experiences which suggest that at least two social workers might have debated the meaning of 'truth'.

> This is how it happens to lots of kids: One day the social worker comes round and says 'OK lads, we're going for a ride' and two and a half hours later they end up in another children's home (pp. 29–30).
> I was living with some foster parents and the social worker let me think that they were my real parents. When I was six she took me away from them and put me in a children's home but let me carry on thinking they were my parents. I'd been in the children's home a year before anyone told me that they weren't my parents (p. 34).

These social workers might not have been guilty of directly lying but they certainly failed to help their children understand and, it seems, used half-truth or suppression of any truth at all for some reasons of their own. Perhaps they did not want to upset or worry the children; but nothing more stimulates anxiety than knowing that something is in the air or discovering that you have been conned, for whom and how then can you trust? Sometimes social workers complete the placement of children in foster or residential care by slipping away while the child is occupied; the rationale is to avoid disturbing and upsetting the child; the reason is to avoid disturbing and upsetting the social worker and those who will have to mop up the tears once she has left; the result is a bewildered and cheated child. This behaviour is as much an avoidance of truth and reality as a deliberate lie.

'The therapist must always be strong, never expedient' (Glasser, 1975, p. 27). But expediency can be so attractive. The move to the new children's home will be accomplished more easily if there is no chance of rebellion or distress on the way. The small child does not need to be burdened with the difficult knowledge that his own parents do not care for, even perhaps, want him. If children are lied to by people they are supposed to be able to trust and if they are not shown trust themselves how can they ever learn to trust and be trustworthy? They can learn from such behaviour only how to deceive.

One of the most common temptations is to offer false reassurance, whether out of laziness, because facing the truth with a child (or anyone else) is a long and taxing activity, or lack of sensitivity:

> It's us too, you know. We shut the staff out. Children in homes get all kinds of depressions and have many troubles that worry them. I think we worry a lot about the past and what is going to happen to us, even when we're larking about. *It's no good patting us on the head and telling us not to worry and that kids our age shouldn't get depressed because we do* (Page and Clark, p. 32. emphasis added).

This comment stimulates a vivid visual picture of children, with life histories and anxieties which would sink a marine, larking around—perhaps because that is what children are supposed to do just as lambs destined to be served with mint sauce are supposed to gambol gaily. (At least, the lambs may not fear for the future, although since pigs suffer from terrible stress en route to market, lambs too may be gambolling to keep anxiety at bay). Those caring for these sad children see only the larking as real; they head-pat and pass on, avoiding the truth which they cannot handle and will not face for and with the children. Have they or the honest child who made the comment read Stevie Smith's poem?

> Nobody heard him, the dead man,
> But still he lay moaning:
> I was much further out than you thought
> And not waving but drowning.
> Poor chap, he always loved larking
> And now he's dead.
> It must have been too much for him his heart gave way,
> They said.
> Oh no no no, it was too cold always
> (Still the dead man lay moaning)
> I was much too far out all my life
> And not waving but drowning.

The children too are not *larking* but drowning, for lack of someone to bear the truth of their pain and because hands which might be used to hold up and rescue merely pat heads, pushing them with false reassurance further under the water. The heart can 'give way' while the body still larks!

The truth is hard and understanding can be achieved only if the truth is told. But the truth teller, the therapist must be not only strong but also loving and 'with' the child; the truth teller bears the truth with the child. False reassurance is a kind of lie but there can be true reassurance: 'The greatest reassurance we can give to children is the feeling that they are understood and accepted right down to the painful sad bit in the middle' (Winnicott, 1977, p. 8).

Clare Winnicott discusses in some detail the importance of the social worker at the time of crisis as 'someone . . . to encompass the child, to recognize that the child has feelings about what is going on, and to help him through the shattering effect of losing all that is familiar' (p. 7).

Proper care for and work with the child at the point of crisis may avoid much trouble for him later in life. Here is another vivid visual image; the social worker, who is probably the only person to have knowledge of all the vital elements of the child's life at this crucial time (his natural family, where they are, what has happened to them, what has happened to him, where he is now, where he is going), encompasses, is 'around' the child, physically perhaps but certainly emotionally. The child is held by a safe person who is trust-worthy even if at this moment it is difficult for the child to trust.

As well as encompassing the social worker confronts. That is to say, she requires and can achieve and tolerate contact with the 'real self of the child.' If this is not done, false reassurance and the development of a 'false self' are likely to result. Social workers must 'help children to remain in contact with themselves, and maintain a sense of their own unique identity and worth in relation to other people – at this moment – in relation to the social worker' (p. 8). Sometimes the social worker may be the only person in the world to believe in the worth of the child.

It's our future that's being decided

> . . . the social worker and staff will not consult the children. If they could just sit down and talk it over with us, they could come to much better conclusions than thinking for us and putting down a conclusion we might not like. After all it's our life and our future that's being decided (Page and Clark, 1977, p. 31).

Just as a social worker may be the one person who has access to all parts of a child's life particularly at some point of crisis, she may also be the anchor man in arrangements for the child's future. Whenever a move is possible, probable or in process the social worker will be responsible for the administration; for example ensuring that everyone involved knows exactly what is happening, and when, where and *why*. Although this is most obvious in relation to children moving into, within and out of care it is also of relevance to children in hospitals, for example, becoming subject to supervision and probation orders, and involved in custody proceedings. At any time during her association with a child the social worker should hold as complete a picture as possible of the many aspects of the child's life; including at the centre the child's own image and assessment of himself and that life.

The social worker is responsible to know and to care what the child wishes to happen to him. Hardly a new thought; for example in 1962

Jean Kastell (p. 232) wrote: 'The child must learn to share in what is happening to him, he must himself feel involved in whatever decisions are taken on his behalf'.

And yet in 1977 the *Who Cares?* child said: 'the social worker and staff *will not* consult the children' (emphasis added).

However, proper consultation and knowing the child's wishes are by no means guarantees that those wishes can be granted. The CQSW* does not include honorary membership of the Institute of Fairy Godmothers. It would be cruel to ask a child what he would like to happen if there was really no choice at all or if the social worker was not prepared to endeavour to achieve the wished-for future for the child. A child may have to leave a children's home because of his age or because the staff will not keep him for some reason, sometimes for purely administrative reasons a local in 1979 authority ordered the move of dozens of children in residential care from voluntary children's homes into the authority's own establishments). A child under sixteen cannot choose whether or not to undergo an operation. A child may not like the idea of a foster home but the chances are that the adults may have a greater investment in making the placement than in hearing him say no.

Perhaps this is a gloomy view of current child-care practice but while one child can be moved for financial and administrative reasons and one child can say that he has not been consulted about his life and his future, perhaps a gloomy view must be taken.

In order for a child to understand his present and contribute realistically to planning for his future he must have full and true information about his position. A number of *Who Cares?* children said that they had very little knowledge about their legal and familial situations:

> For all you know [your parents] might be dead. Like [X] said, all the time he was growing up in care he thought his parents were dead, but when he got out he found they were both alive (Page and Clark, 1977, p. 33).
> There's a girl up at our place and she's eight years old and she's been in care most of her life. She can talk for herself at eight and she wants to know why her mother doesn't want her back. Her mother's got all the other kids at home and she's just had another baby. So this girl is wondering all the time 'Why doesn't my mum want me?' And yet her social worker will not tell her why (p. 33).

Perhaps the reader is wondering too.

> Social workers don't always tell their children what a Care Order or Section 1† is. They don't say, 'Oh, your mother *can* come back any time and take you away'. They should explain what your real situation is in care (p. 30).

* Certificate of Qualification in Social Work.

† A care order made by a juvenile court under the 1969 Children and Young Person's Act gives a local authority parental rights and powers in respect of a child; Section 1 of the 1948 Children Act required local authorities to provide accommodation and care for children who are admitted voluntarily and may be returned to the care of their parents with no application to a court.

and such lack of information may lead to grave anxieties:

> I'm under Section 1 and one of the main problems I've found is that for the first three years I was in care, hints were always being dropped about me making peace with my parents. I was told that my parents wanted me back. But I didn't want to go back because when I was at home I was beaten up. . . . *I used to worry that they'd make me go home* (p. 31, emphasis added).

Of course the fact that these children lacked vital knowledge about themselves does not necessarily mean that no one ever tried to give them the knowledge. To give information does not imply that it is received or understood. Sometimes information cannot easily be received because it is too painful and the child wishes to reject and deny what he is told.

> When I was eleven my parents died. The police told me my father killed my mother but I won't believe this. *I'd like to know what happened but then again, I wouldn't.* They say my dad killed my mother on Wednesday, then hanged himself in the pub on Thursday (p. 12, emphasis added).

For that child to make any sense of his life and to be able to think hopefully about his future he must be able to believe the truth, to know what really happened and be helped to bear it. His sad statement suggests that he was told the brutal facts, shipped off to the first of many places of residence and left to get on with living. Perhaps none of the adults around him could bear the story; perhaps his ambivalence reflects that of those caring for him. Where at this time of tragedy was his social worker, in Clare Winnicott's words, encompassing him?

Information may also be too complicated to comprehend all at once particularly when it relates to the child's legal situation. Possibly the most complicated legislation to understand is that relating to custody particularly where the children, though living with one parent, have frequent and happy contact with the other. How can a child really understand the concept of *belonging* to one parent or another?

In order to help a child really be involved in planning and affecting his own future the social worker must with the child recognize and manage reality, discover and evaluate the real possibilities, work 'to reach a more considered appraisal of what is possible in the short and long term' (Holgate and Neill, 1978).

A way of starting to live

> I've looked back on all my life – life should start when you're born. But mine's been a bit of a mess, so why shouldn't it start now? A review should be a way of starting to live (Page and Clark, 1977, pp. 42–3).

The social worker has a vital role in helping the child learn about his past and present, discover who he is and think realistically about his future. The social worker is probably also helping the adults around the child (including his parents) to achieve the same tasks with respect to him. But his future will be a matter not only of moves and activities whether voluntary or involuntary. Whatever happens materially, the child must be helped to take responsibility for himself. While it may be important to the child to have information about his past (the whereabouts of his parents, why he is in care, why he is confined to a wheelchair) and to recognize and be helped to express grief, anger and anxiety, the only thing that can really help him to start to live is a strong grasp on the present and determination not to blame his past for misfortune but to make the best possible use of the future. William Glasser (1975, p. 40) goes further than this:

> In Reality Therapy . . . we rarely ask why. Our usual question is *What*? *What* are you doing – not, *why* are you doing it? Why implies that the reasons for the patient's behaviour make a difference in therapy, but they do not. The patient will himself search for reasons; but until he has become more responsible he will not be able to act differently, even when he knows why. All the reasons in the world for why he drinks will not lead an alcoholic to stop.
> Because the patient must gain responsibility right now, we always focus on the present. The past has certainly contributed to what he is now, but we cannot change the past, only the present (p. 39).

Accepting responsibility for oneself is difficult enough for chronologically mature, healthy and financially secure adults. How easy it is to say that life or the government or one's spouse has been unfair or failed to come up to expectation and that this therefore excuses the victim from making any effort to improve matters. Many people actually seem to prefer to feel hard done by since perhaps they can believe that they are thereby let off taking full responsibility for themselves and their lives. Bookshops and magazines are always full of stories of wonderful people who have grinned and borne terrible afflictions and deprivations. Stories of courage and achievement in the face of handicap, physical and mental, imprisonment and persecution are indeed important and inspiring. But I suggest that their common characteristic, that the subject whatever his physical and material situation took hold of his own life and said, in effect, 'I will use whatever I have and *live*', should be common to all human lives, that 'I am disadvantaged therefore I cannot' is no excuse for not taking responsibility.

I recently heard a group of teachers discussing what they would like to be able to do with their adolescent classes. One spoke of the need for the children to begin to take responsibility for themselves for they would soon leave school. Another said how much he wished they dared to let the children 'just talk' (the inhibition was that the headmaster might pass the room and think that the teacher was not teaching!) A third said that if children just talked they would only talk about lipstick and football; her class had a lot of 'creative discussion'. Herein I feel was encapsulated a common and large-scale ambivalence towards children and responsibility. At sixteen they are expected to be fit for work (and sexual intercourse) but at fifteen they may not be deemed responsible enough to talk about things that matter unless steered by a teacher; only the teacher can, it seems, decide what really matters and she may reject the child's choice of topic because it is not important in her own life or her perception of the life of that child. In other words the children were not trusted to take responsibility even for their own conversation. I believe that people need to be given permission and sometimes a good deal of encouragement to take responsibility for their own decisions and behaviour but that once they have understood that they have this permission for something which is both a right and a duty, they will accept the responsibility and flourish. Only trust helps one to become trustworthy. Collusion with weakness perpetuates the weakness.

Learning to take responsibility for oneself, not to blame others for one's own problems, these help the child to become stronger and to have increasing energy to spend on growth in other directions, for nothing is more exhausting than anxiety, bewilderment and anger. One part of starting to live is discovering new adventures of both mind and body, opportunities for enjoyment and achievement leading themselves to greater confidence and therefore even more capacity to accept responsibility for oneself.

One task of the social worker is to help the child find adventure by ensuring that there are in the child's environment plenty of opportunities for play, exploration of the world and education. Sometimes the social worker herself will be the agent of adventure, using the shared and often exciting experiences to develop trust between herself and the child and to increase the child's growth. There are many accounts of such work, often in Intermediate Treatment projects; here I quote from Berry's Introduction to Bob Payne's (1975, p. 4) account of Sheffield Family Service Unit:

> It is often said that one function of fathers is to act as mediator between their families and the outside world, and here it seems fitting that Bob Payne's group was literally exploring the world within easy reach – occasionally they went further afield but usually they were in the spectacular country on Sheffield's doorstep where hundreds of 'ordinary' local families go frequently, but which would be somewhat foreign to these boys.

The world may be within easy reach but surely the country is always spectacular to the true explorer. The social worker is a perpetual explorer helping those less confident than herself to climb hills in the High Peak whether they are made of Millstone grit or concrete or paper or emotion. She works on 'the assumption that small achievements gradually boost self-confidence in choosing to take "normal" risks' (p. 5) and in starting to live.

To talk about it

> I think that when you get older, one of the best things to relieve pressure is to talk about it. And you want somebody you can talk to (Page and Clark, p. 32).

Not all children are as articulate as those in the *Who Cares?* group (and maybe some of those had to struggle to put into words their feelings and thoughts). But all should have the opportunity to talk about it and often the one person who has time and understanding is the social worker. I do not wish to be lynched by foster parents and nurses and residential workers; the first responsibility of the social worker is to ensure that there is for the child a person who, whatever else she does or does not do with and for this child, is his own person to be talked to; and this person may very well be the social worker herself. When the social worker sees the child, whether in the office, his own home foster or children's home or hospital, she can be specifically and especially available for and to that child alone; she can take him out for a walk or drive, quite properly excluding the other children who may demand her attention. Whereas the parental or other professional adults may have to share themselves between several children and duties within a short space of time if not all at once. Sometimes social workers feel discouraged from trying to make direct contact with children because they think that occasional hours are of no use particularly compared to the time spent with the children by, for example, residential workers. But it *may* be easier for a child to talk about hopes and anxieties to someone who is *not* in residence so that the child does not feel constantly exposed because of whatever he has said and what is known about him. I think that children should be able to choose their confidants for some will prefer the resident, some the visitor. After all most people in 'normal' life have confidants other (and *essentially* other) than their home-sharers; it is often important to be able to give *your* version of events without fear of contradiction or retribution. Gossipping is an important human activity; children gossip to one another but they also need chosen adult gossips and I think the social worker must, if asked, accept this role (being careful, of course, to avoid collusion). Only if venom and spleen have been thoroughly vented in a good old gossip is there much chance of the point of view being modified. The social worker may be a vital safety valve.

The somebody for the child to talk to must be somebody who will listen. Social workers are often very concerned with the giving and receiving of information but it may be difficult simply to listen especially if the child is talking 'only' about lipstick or football and does not seem very interested in discussing his feelings about the forthcoming operation or move or why he broke into the warehouse. But it is, it seems, sometimes hard to make, preserve and justify time used listening with no perceptible doing.

Able to talk in your language

> Somebody who is highly educated should be able to talk in your language. But when I go to see [X] he uses this social-work jargon and it's really difficult to understand. I think he does it to impress me (Page and Clark, p. 32).

Sometimes social workers think that it is difficult to talk to children because they do not know what language to use. They want to know just what this or that word means to a three-year-old or a ten-year-old or a sixteen-year-old as if they could know what it means to a 25-year-old or a 40-year-old or an 86-year-old. It is certainly important to realize that people at different chronological ages are likely to have different ways of conceptualizing but I think it is far more important to realize that what matters most is whatever takes place between these two individual people, *not* a 27-year-old social worker and a four-year-old child.

The content of spoken language is of very little use if it is not backed by other forms of communication. I can express this most clearly by a quotation from Moustakas (1959, p. xiii):

> I saw that I must stop playing the role of the professional therapist and allow my potentials, talents, and skills, my total experiences as a human being to blend naturally into the relationship with the child and whenever humanly possible to meet him as a whole person. Thus I came to realize that one person, a direct, human-loving person, a unified personal and professional self, meets another person, a loving or potentially loving child and, through a series of deep human encounters, waits for and enables the child to come to his own self-fulfillment.

Talking in your language is not a matter of knowing which *words* to use; the social worker must become truly available to the child, both giving to and receiving from the whole other person. If the encounter is true there will be no need to worry about words for the right verbal language will grow out of the experience of and within the encounter. Clare Winnicott (1977, p. 8) says:

> In order to develop into a whole human being each child needs to be recognized and known as a person in his own right, with his own particular ways of thinking and feeling and expressing himself, and with his own special thing to say, which distinguishes him from everyone else.

'His own special thing to say' may not be said in words but it must be heard. And not only the child has a special thing to say; social workers too are whole human beings and their encounters with children depend on engaging one whole self with another: 'Can the counsellor expect openness, self-acceptance and personal freedom in the client if he himself lacks these qualities in the relationship?' (Truax and Carkhuff, 1967, p. 329).

Truax and Carkhuff summarized a great deal of research into 'some known effective ingredients in the therapeutic process'

(p. xiii). In answer to the question 'What are the essential characteristics or behaviours of the therapist or counsellor that lead to
constructive behavioural change in the client'? (p. 24) they suggest
that there are 'three sets of characteristics . . . *accurate empathy,
non-possessive warmth*, and *genuineness*' (p. 25).

> By communicating 'I am with you' and 'I can accurately sense the world as
> you construe it', in a manner that fully acknowledges feelings and
> experiences, [the therapist] facilitates the patient's movement toward a
> deeper self-awareness and knowledge of his own feelings and experi-
> ences and their import (p. 285).

The social worker who 'uses this social-work jargon' and whose child
client thought that he did it 'to impress me' was very far from
communicating 'I am with you' and still further from recognizing
that child as 'a person in his own right'. Perhaps he was intent on
doing his job, perhaps explaining something or trying to get the
child to express opinion or feeling. It looks as if the child himself felt
superfluous to the engagement.

Communication of and growing from the three characteristics is
possible only if the social worker trusts and respects the child. By this
I mean that the social worker believes that the child *is* a whole person
worthy of her attention who will himself be able to desire, contribute
towards and take responsibility for his own progress and safety.
Liking is not necessary but loving is essential. One of the prime
reasons for the social worker to communicate directly with the child
is that she may be the only person who really does trust, respect and
even love in the manner under discussion, the only person to regard
this child as whole and individually priceless. Truax and Carkhuff
(1967, p. 286) quote Ginnott (1965) who

> sees two requirements as the bases for effective communication: (1) that
> all communications be aimed at preserving the self-respect of the person
> being helped as well as the helper; and (2) that the communication of
> understanding precede any suggestions of information or advice-giving.

Communication cannot take place in a vacuum of course. Empathy, warmth and genuineness will need words as well as body
language. Social workers do not usually work in static settings and
communication is very likely to be associated with some activity. I
refer again to Bob Payne's (1975) excellent account of work with
teenage boys for he combines the philosophy of this chapter with the
practical ability and good sense of the really effective social worker:

> What the boys in the FSU group needed was not so much a club as a
> person, a relationship. In practice the offering of a relationship can only
> be made in the context of some activity. What that activity is supremely
> irrelevant, except that it must be such that it engages and involves the
> group members (pp. 27–8).

The main part of this book will be devoted to discussion of kinds of activities which can be shared by children and social workers; the use and effectiveness of those activities, whatever the intention of the social worker, will be negated if the social worker does not learn truly 'to talk in your language', to love and respect the child and above all to *be* with him:

> we should aim at being *what we are* in our human encounters – openly *be* the feelings and attitudes we are experienceing ... [come] into a direct personal encounter with a child ... which is often too rare (Truax and Carkhuff, 1967, p. 142).

What a two-year-old can understand

> When you're small you're just taken away from the family and nobody tells you why and you think it's your fault. I think little 'uns should be told why they're being taken into care.
> You'd be surprised what a two-year-old can understand. ... My mum and dad split up after my dad put my mum in hospital with two broken jaws. And my little brother was actually on the scene and saw everything going on. And the last thing he remembers is mum having a bad face and running out. For all he knows, he could be thinking that she's dead. So when he keeps asking 'Where's mummy?' you've just got to explain and keep answering the questions even though it gets on your nerves (Page and Clark, p. 32–3).

When is a person old enough to 'understand'? My question reminds me of a juvenile-court magistrate asking me, 'Is he an *average* seven-year-old?'

This society and its services are enormously age-based; starting, changing and leaving school, voting and retiring are all associated with specific chronological moments in a person's life. Other activities and experiences are more informally associated with age, for example first marriage and childbearing. There is for many people a pressure to be doing the 'right' thing at the 'right' age whether in terms of clothing, nest-building and material possessions or conforming to behaviour of, for example, old age – 'I can't remember as much as I used to', 'I can't do what I did' being perhaps statements about what I expect to be expected to remember and do rather than what I can actually remember and do.

The notion of the right thing at the right age is emphasized in the models of human growth and development which are usually taught on social-work training courses. Some are as apparently neat as Erikson's (1965) eight stages, a series of tasks to be fulfilled within certain chronological periods of life, for example in infancy 'Basic trust vs basic mistrust' and in adolescence 'Identity vs role diffusion'. Others divide large stages into numerous sub-stages, for example Hadfield suggests that adolescence itself (in his definition 12–18) can be subdivided into three phases which are themselves subdivided (1962, pp. 180–243). Piaget suggests that cognitive development occurs in precise age-linked phases (well set out and discussed in Donaldson, 1978, pp. 129–46).

The advantage of age-and-stage study is, it seems to me, that attention may be focused on important and interesting developments and characteristics which appear to be common to this or that chronologically linked group. (Sometimes the link is some experience separate from age, for example bereavement, divorce, but even here the impact and problems relating to the experience may be seen to be associated with age). When working with adolescents, for example, it may be very useful to know that people in their teens may be particularly aware of their bodies, experiencing dramatic physical developments which may cause anxiety and frustration. *Anxiety* because it is important to the individual that breasts or testicles develop to a satisfactory extent at the same time as those of the peer group, because growth is like Alice in Wonderland eating the cake and banging her head on the ceiling and losing for ever the chance of going through the tiny child-sized door into the beautiful garden, because approval is (as ever) essential particularly from the peer group and increasingly from the opposite sex. *Frustration* because the growth which closes the door on childhood does not at once open the door to adulthood, adult size seems to bring expectations of adult work (or lack of it) but not adult privilege (voting, signing hire-purchase agreements); physical development brings sexual desire but not socially accepted means of exploring and gratifying it, for although intercourse and marriage are legal at sixteen, marriage at so young an age is not generally thought to have much chance of success and sexual activity outside marriage is not likely to be encouraged by parents. Since, I understand, adolescence is the best physical time for childbearing perhaps young girls should be encouraged to have children but not required to make marriages and take prime responsibility for the care of those or other children until they and their potential partners are more equipped to manage the demands of marriage in this society. This suggestion may outrage the values of our society but I offer it for it may also exemplify the conflict imposed on adolescents by society.

But can society impose a conflict on adolescents? I question my own statement not in order to embark on further discussion of its precise content but because it is just this kind of statement which characterizes the disadvantages of ages-and-stages study. For one thing the word 'society' is in my usage here far too broad and would, to be of any use to the practising social worker engaged in work with a particular adolescent, have to be defined in terms of the individual's *own* 'society'. For another, conflict is a word too easily and loosely used. But most important within this discussion, the statement assumes agreement about what is meant by adolescents, assumes indeed that such a thing as adolescence exists. Once a concept of something such as adolescence has been suggested and accepted it is easy to accept notions about the characteristics of the phenomenon; after the film *Close Encounters of the Third Kind* I *did* expect to see beautiful space craft in the fields; accept the existence of space ships and you will begin to wonder not *if* but *how* they work. Accept the existence of adolescence and you begin to expect people aged between eleven and eighteen to behave in certain ways and enjoy or endure common experiences. And at once the ridiculousness of the notion appears for there is no more resemblance between people of eleven and eighteen than there is more than a superficial resemblance between 20 eleven-year-old boys or eighteen-year-old girls. Physical development is likely to be age linked (although, for example, size at any given age is so strongly influenced by social class and environment that this is hardly a simple statement) and children of similar age are likely to share interests and preoccupations (broadly speaking).

But surely what really matters to the social worker is the intention to understand and encounter *this* person, one of whose attributes is a certain date of birth which causes him today to be a certain age. The social worker will be concerned to know if this person's development is normal (but not average!) in that he is responsible to see that the person is not in some way disadvantaged or at risk but I suggest that the assessment of normality can be made only through experience, only working and living with and among many people and really knowing and being accessible to *this* person.

To return to my question above, 'when is a person old enough to understand?' I suggest that if that question is ever seriously asked by a social worker the answer is almost bound to be never. For one thing people who are known to social workers as clients are by definition experiencing a problem; they may be deserted or delinquent children, physically or mentally handicapped, old, ill, irresponsible. Whatever the label there is a good chance that it may inhibit the social worker from considering the client really able to understand.

To focus on children: When is a child old enough to be told that he is, for example, adopted? Here it is established that children should be told from the moment of adoption so that the word itself can never be used in any shocking way; the adoptive parents are encouraged to introduce the word, possibly with the aid of an attractive picture book, and gradually to give information about its meaning to the child and his family as he shows interest. But when should you tell a child that his father has murdered his mother? In one of the *Who Cares?* quotations above a child said that he had been told by the police, apparently at the time of the deaths and his reception into care. *Should* he have been told then and if so, by whom?

It seems to me that there can never be a 'right' time for some information. News of a pleasant surprise may be stored up to be given in some special and delightful way. News of some unpleasant experience to come may be held for a while to avoid the child being more anxious than is strictly necessary; for example, going to the dentist or hospital or the projected absence of a parent for a time need not be communicated too far in advance provided that the child is given some warning and preparation and cannot be shocked either by no preparation at all or by learning from 'outside'. But everyone has the right to full information about his own life and circumstances and to the opportunity to manage that information however terrible. It may be impossible to think of telling a small child that his father has killed his mother and then himself but the child has to know sometime and from somebody. The thing has happened and is now part of his life. The least and best that the social worker can do is to ensure that the information is given with love and compassion as soon as possible by someone who really cares about the child and who can handle the telling not only the first time but also those other tellings, the reactions spoken and otherwise, the questions.

If a child is suddenly given some information about his life relating to things that happened years ago he must surely lose all trust in all those who have misled him during those years. He will also be in danger of losing trust in himself for his self-image is based on all he *knows* about his life and environment and feelings and background and to learn that one element of his knowledge is false (whether or not it is as objectively dramatic as murder or apparently a small thing) must surely lead him to consider that the whole picture is irrevocably distorted.

If a child who has been given terrible information is then helped to manage and live with the knowledge, learning that it is he himself and not his past or the actions of his relations which matter, then he has as good a chance as anyone of becoming a whole, trusting and trustworthy person.

My final point in this section is that no child is too young to give and receive communications. Leaving aside what may or may not be experienced in the womb, a small baby can be perceived to be experiencing, for example, anxiety. A six-week-old baby placed for adoption who has already experienced three 'births' (from the womb, the hospital and probably a foster home) *knows* that he has been moved around; what guarantee has he that the relay race with himself as baton will not continue? The adoptive parents are likely to be anxious, particularly if this is their first baby, for not only must they prove themselves to themselves as good parents but also they must convince the social worker and the court. Have they much chance of remembering to convince the baby that they are not only attending to his physical welfare but aware of his equally pressing need for emotional security; can they, in other words, stop fussing about the antiseptic state of the house and just sit down and relax with him? If not has he not a good chance of growing up with the notion that he promotes anxiety in those around him and thus of becoming anxious himself?

Returning to the 1975 *Children Act*, I suggest that it should be required that the opinions of *all* children should be presented in any court proceedings; extreme youth and low intelligence or disturb ance should *never* be accepted as *ipso facto* excuses for non-consultation. Rather, social workers should be required to make a special case for every baby whose view is not given, being closely questioned by the court as to evidence for failure to present a full case.

Then we might cease to ask 'when is a person old enough to understand?' and 'what words should I use?' and instead get down to finding out how to ask *this* child 'what do *you* think and want?'

A right to know

> If we're in care – and it's our lives – we have a right to know what's going on in our lives and why our parents can't have us home (Page and Clark, p. 33).

I find the notion of 'rights' difficult and disturbing. A right should, it seems to me, be freely bestowed and generally acknowledged but rights seem to be the subject of demand, conflict and at worst bloodshed. One problem with rights movements is that they focus attention on one group of society whereas what is really needed is a true intention to achieve not Women's Lib or Gay Lib or even Heterosexual Men's Lib but People's Lib; or should that be People's Love?

Children's rights have been discussed in England for some years as evidenced by, for example, the National Council for Civil Liberties National Conference on Rights of Children (at which of the eleven main sessions only one was led by children), the establishment of the Children's Rights Workshop and such literature as the book *Children's Rights* (Hall, 1971). The end of the 1970s has seen the development of such groups as *Who Cares?* and the *National Association of Young People in Care (NAYPIC)*.

A *Social Work Today* article of January 1979 reported that

> Children in residential care are just becoming aware of the *Children Act* 1975 which gives them a right to consultation about decisions affecting their welfare. They are marching in the streets claiming their rights and some have resorted to direct action in barricading themselves in a home due to be closed. The Year of the Child is bound to strengthen the demands for legislation measures protecting children – not against environmental disadvantages in the community but against the very agencies whose duty it is to provide substitute care (Walton, p. 21).

(Children marching in the streets is not new; in 1911 children all over the country walked out of school and went on strike in support of their striking fathers.)

As I am a pacific person and believe in slow, steady, gentle and strong reform from within rather than explosive and volatile revolutions I am distressed that children should feel themselves impelled to such militant action. And I feel that the example described by Ron Walton is a severe indictment of social-work practice. How can it have taken between three and four years for those children to become aware of the 1975 Act? It may be a sign of health and strength that those children can combine to claim rights or try to prevent the closure of their home but what a terrible waste of that health and strength when those children were surrounded by people paid to ensure that they knew and received their rights and that their lives were secure and free.

I believe with Jean Moore that 'Every child has as much right as an adult to be a client' (1976, p. 15) which means entitlement to respect and trust and to the opportunity of cooperating in making and honouring a contract with the social worker. I know that 'contract' is a fashionable and problematic word in present-day social work but despite these disadvantages I think it is important and attractive. Thomas Szasz (1974, pp. 104–6) says that

> In everyday language, the word 'contract' designates an agreement between two or more persons to do or refrain from doing something.
> The analytic contract, like the legal contract, seeks clarity rather than vagueness and specifies the remedies available should one of the contracting parties fail to keep his promise.
> There are two basic principles that govern human relationships – status and contract. Relationships governed by status are simpler – legally, psychologically, and socially – than those governed by contract.

I suggest that many social work – client relationships are, whether or not under the guise of contract-based, really status-based for the reasons given by Szasz and that it may be a reluctance to relinquish the protection of 'status' which causes the adoption of 'contract' to be seen as problematic. This is particularly likely in the area of working with children who are of low status in society anyway and may be of low status in social-work interactions. Szasz suggests that children cannot be parties to this kind of contract:

> Freedom is an essential part of contract. Indeed, it is meaningless to speak of a contract between persons who are not free. This fact is significant for psychiatry and psychoanalysis because psychotherapists frequently form relationships with patients under circumstances in which one or both are not free to contract. As a result, the vast majority of encounters between psychiatrists and patients and even between many analysts and their clients *cannot* be contractual and are therefore not analytic.
> For example, the patient may be a child, a prisoner, or a person committed to a mental institution. None of these people can enter into the sort of two-person contract necessary for analytic work (p. 115).

While I am not competent to comment on the contract within psychiatric analytic work I am dismayed at the implication of this idea if applied to other kinds of helping interactive work. It is horrifying to see 'child' listed with 'prisoner' and 'person committed to a mental institution' for surely children are not subject to the same constraints on physical freedom? But this question is much broader for does it not also imply that all three types of person have constraints imposed on *emotional* freedom? And that they are incapable, indeed should not be given the chance to become capable, of freely contributing to their own development? This clashes with the philosophy of William Glasser (referred to above) but does it not reflect the actual belief of many workers in all branches of the helping professions?

Social workers are constantly in the position of making contracts with children. For example, a supervision order is nothing if not a legal contract between the child, the court and the social worker. But how often is it represented as such? Within that legal contract the social worker and child make a personal contract; this may cover only the number of times in a month that the social worker requires to see the child and the kind of behaviour expected of this child if he is not to be returned to the court. But it may be extended to particular tasks which the social workers and child will endeavour to achieve within a given time and to the kind of behaviour that they will offer each other when in each other's company (for example that neither will smoke, that the child will not swear, that the social worker will not press for information about the child's partners in crime).

A contract may be made with a child when plans for boarding-out are being made; the social worker may contract to learn and take into account the child's preferences about his future accommodation, to keep himself informed about piogress and to give the opportunity to meet and get to know his prospective foster family before any decision is made. The child's part of the contract may be to cooperate with the social worker in talking about his feelings and hopes, to give any prospective foster home a real chance and to make the move if it looks as if things might have a chance of success. Perhaps that sounds too simple to bother writing about, perhaps every social worker involved in boarding-out does all that anyway but I suspect that it is usually done without the step of deliberately involving the child in an *agreement* about what he and the social worker are setting out to do together.

One important aspect of contracts which Szasz referred to as 'the remedies available should one of the contracting parties fail to keep his promise' (1974, p. 104) is the effect on both parties of non-honouring. If a social worker fails to keep her promise, what redress has the client, particularly if he is a child? The answer is probably none, for who will know unless the effect of the social worker's failure is the injury or death of the child? But even there enquiry might show negligence but not, I suspect, the breaking of a promise because 'only' the child would know that any promise had been made and broken. If the child fails he will presumably suffer by being returned to court as refractory, moved out of the foster home, left alone by the social worker who has moved on to other tasks. When a contract is made with a child both the benefits of maintaining it and the penalties of breaking it must be made clear.

The notion of penalty leads me in passing to an interesting comment on children's rights by Morris and McIsaac (1978, p. 153) who say that

> Punishment is society's and the child's right. In a practical context this means that formal action should be taken when the delinquent commits a serious offence, action should be proportionate to the offence and decisions should be manifestly fair and just.

Their view is that social workers often do children a positive disservice by concentrating on the welfare aspect of their lives and ignoring the offence part to the extent that a child may continue to receive the services of a social worker long after he might be considered to have expiated his 'crime.' This is not the place to explore their argument further but as a contribution to this discussion of the rights of children in the context of social work it is of some importance and interest.

To conclude this section I here reproduce two lists. Each is called by its compilers 'Charter of Rights'. One is compiled by children, one by adults.

Charter of rights for young people in care
We have drawn up this charter for 'young people' because we feel it is the responsibility of the residential worker and social worker to make sure that younger kids get a good deal.
1 The right to be accepted and treated as an individual member of society. Also the right to be treated with the same respect given to any other valid member of the human race.
2 The right to know who we are. To know our parents and brothers and sisters. To have factual information about our family origins and background.
3 The right to be able to make our own decisions and to have real influence over those decisions we are sometimes considered too thick to participate in.
4 The right to privacy. We understand that in care it is not always possible to choose who we are going to live and share our lives with. But we are still human beings and are still entitled to the essential amount of privacy needed before cracking up.
5 The right to be given an insight into the use of money by handling it, using it and paying the consequences if we misuse it, e.g. being given the money in our hand to buy the clothes our clothing allowance will allow.
6 The right to choose those who will represent us whether it be legally or otherwise, e.g. social workers. Also the right to choose those whom we wish to confide in.

7 Finally, the right to be as much a part of society as the next person and not to be labelled in any way. In short, to live.

These rights can be interpreted how you like. But don't misuse them or distort them for your own devices (Page and Clark, p. 62).

Children in care: A BASW* charter of rights

Principle 1: The child in care has a right to *individual* respect and consideration, even though his rights and needs will be closely associated with those of others.

Principle 2: The child in care has a right to be looked after by skilled adults who have a commitment to the understanding and meeting of his individual needs.

Principle 3: Before a child is admitted to care an assessment of his family and home environment should be undertaken which will include the preparation of the child and his family for the admission and their participation in the plans that are made.

Principle 4: The child in care has a right to live in an environment which is conducive to his emotional, physical, social and intellectual development.

Principle 5: The child in care has a right to individual attention which shows recognition of and respect for his unique indentity.

Principle 6: The child in care has a right to information concerning his circumstances and to participate in the planning of his future.

Principle 7: The child in care has a right to administrative standards and procedures within his caring agency which will protect him and promote his interests.

Principle 8: The child in care has a right to the protection of the law (BASW, 1977, pp. 7–9).

Conclusion

Although much of the material in this chapter has been drawn from writing about children in care I believe that every comment and idea has relevance for children in any situation at all, whether in hospital or children's home, foster or own home, attendant at child-guidance clinic or psychiatric unit; indeed, whether in receipt of social-work help or not. Surely *every* child has a right to 'individual respect and consideration', to 'the protection of the law', 'to privacy', 'to know who we are', 'to live'. And where these 'rights' are not freely given and respected by the adults responsible for the care and welfare of the child, surely the child has the 'right' to the help of a social worker to procure and ensure those rights for him.

In this chapter I have considered some of the reasons why in my view social workers should regard working directly with children as of prime importance. In chapter 1 I suggested some of the reasons why I think social workers often do not so work. In the rest of the book I shall discuss some of the ways in which social workers in the field can and do put into practice their belief that in order to serve

* British Association of Social Workers

the children on their caseloads fully and faithfully they must discover the ways in which to meet each individual child in his own way and at his own pace. The social workers and others to whom I shall refer in the coming pages will be seen engaged in all manner of activities but they are linked by their common caring for the children and by their common belief in the rights of children as described by Leila Berg (1972, p. 144) in my closing quotation:

> Is it really so much a child needs – the right to have space and time for exploration so that each can grow at its own rhythm and become part of society in a natural way – to feel what they feel, to have their experiences accepted as valid, and to be responded to in their own context – to live lives that are their own, not someone else's – the right to have *happy parents, whom society accepts and values?* (emphasis added)

Part Two

Ways of Communicating

Chapter 3

Play Social Worker

... a place where a child is unable to play can be neither a Home nor a home (Ingram, 1967, p. 3).

The aim of this chapter is to suggest some ways in which social workers may encourage and facilitate play within not only Homes and homes but also hospitals and court waiting-rooms and all environments, physical and emotional, where a child may need the help of a social worker to grow, to comprehend, to live.

Providing opportunities and materials for play

Space

One could, with some truth, claim that the evils of civilization are due to the fact that no child has ever had enough play (Neill, 1968, p. 68).

Eric Ingram and A. S. Neill and the many other writers and carers for and about children to whom I shall refer in this chapter share a deep belief – that without play no child can grow into a healthy adult. Physical, intellectual, emotional and social development all depend on enough 'true' play. ('True' play is in the definition underlying this chapter the spontaneous undirected free activity of the individual where nothing is imposed from outside though others, adult or child, may be involved at the wish of the 'prime player'.)

If social workers are concerned for the healthy development of the children on their caseloads they are bound to be concerned with the opportunities for play. Yet this may be very difficult or even ignored. The word 'only' is often associated with play: 'he's not doing anything, he's only playing'. And social workers' limited time may seem to be needed for more 'serious' matters.

Granting that childhood is playhood, how do we adults generally react to this fact? We *ignore* it. We forget all about it – because play, to us, is a waste of time. Hence we erect a large city school with many rooms and expensive apparatus for teaching; but more often than not, all we offer to the play instinct is a small concrete space (Neill, p. 68).

And what space at all is there for playing when the weather is bad? Are children kept in their classrooms or allowed into the hall? Or sent out into conditions which adults would not tolerate 'to play'? Recently the kitchens of a comprehensive school were hit by a power cut and lunch could not be served. The children were sent out 'to play' for two hours in cold and rain. The staff sat in the staff room. No one thought of finding space indoors for the children. No one thought of turning the whole event into some kind of play. And that small concrete space must have turned into a prison compound to those hungry, cold, 'playing' children. The 'official play space' was abused by the 'responsible' adults because they could think no further than that the children were in their proper place doing their proper thing: playing. In consequence there was neither play nor space; merely imposed activity in a designated area. I see this as a parable of play and space and children and adults in the whole country.

If play space at school (by which I don't mean sports fields for organized games) may not be sufficient or imaginatively used, what about space for out-of-school play?

In 1974 Jack Lambert and Jenny Pearson produced a book containing descriptions of several exciting playschemes and adventure playgrounds throughout the country. But Jack Lambert (Lambert and Pearson, 1974, p. 161) says:

> The playgrounds offer a scope and freedom for development far beyond anything children can find through more conventional play and sport facilities. In saying this I am not attacking any form of play facility: obviously they enjoy roundabouts and swings, and sport is also a high priority.
>
> What I am saying is that they need more. In our towns and cities . . . space is so precious that there is virtually nowhere left free for children to shape as they like, free from adult plans and organization, doing the things *they* want to do. We salve our consciences by providing beautiful parks where they can run in their gum boots with every appearance of freedom and swings which they play on for a few minutes in passing. It is not enough.

Sometime during the 1960s a group called *Interplay* ran a month-long play scheme on a clearance site in Leeds. The children built a space ship out of anything that came to hand and then took off into space and tackled whatever adventures the stratosphere above Armley jail and its surrounding back-to-back streets presented. Perhaps outer space is the only kind of free space left. And even that is getting crowded with other people's commercialized fantasies and the products of international paranoia.

Black holes and galaxies may be reached by means of cardboard boxes and that greatest space of all, the only limitless play place, locked in a tiny bone box, imagination. Sometimes journeys into this space are hated and feared by adults. 'Don't tell lies' said a mother to her seven-year-old boy, halting his glorious tale about elephants.

Then she switched on *Tarzan* on the television and settled down to the stories in her magazine. Later on he was told, even helped, to do his homework. But of what use is that if all he learns about life is that only *other* people's stories and facts and perceptions have any value?

For many kinds of play physical space may be small but enhanced by ingenuity. Writing about play within the confines of a child-full children's home Eric Ingram (1967, p. 8) says:

> We have to provide a place which will allow the opportunity to be an individual. For the child to have not only the privacy of his own interests, and the space to develop them without undue or persistent interference from routines of meals, etc; or from younger or older children. . . . . . it is our skill to see that a child doesn't embark on a project in an unsuitable place where he is bound to be disturbed and frustrated. This may just mean the provision of large sheets of hardboard or other suitable surface made rigid so that models, etc; can be lifted straight from the table . . . . . and providing similar boards to go over the top of a bed to make a working surface with dust sheets to protect the bed-linen. Do we still think that bedrooms can never be used for such purposes?

Apart from the practical good sense, the most important thought in that extract is that the child should have the opportunity to be an individual. Wherever the space is provided the use of that space must be decided by the child.

> When we set out to provide for a child's play, we are already encroaching on his world. The type of space we provide, the equipment, the suggestions that come from our very actions will stimulate him to do things he would not have thought of by himself. But that is as far as it should go. What he decides to do with that space is not really our concern (Lambert and Pearson, 1974, p. 155).

And Jim Golcher (1978, p. 14) whose article is entitled *Child's play: A social work responsibility?*, says:

> Children find their own special places to play. To the child, play is fun and the child will play, and only play, where he sees it as fun. . . . No single 'playground' can set out to be more than one part of a child's play-map.

Before a child can play he must have space; great space for galloping, small protected space for model building, emotional space for imagining. I believe that it is often the social worker's responsibility to study the 'play-map' and ensure that all kinds of space are available:

> it helps when a child has a place he can call his own, the chance to get hold of sticks and scrap materials, and sand and water nearby. But it is best when such things are a natural part of the environment, and not too obviously 'laid on' (Shotton Hall School, 1967, p. 39).

It is encouraging to remember that many children even in this built-over busy island do still have plenty of places they can call their own in both the towns and the country. Perhaps despite television and expensive packaged toys there are still many children who could say:

> We kept to our own hillside, to the small kingdom that was our country, and there we found enough to amuse and entertain us during the long years of childhood (Uttley, 1976, p. 201).

Let us ensure that every child has his small kingdom.

Things for doing things with

> 'Have you any toys? Toys! We plays with anything, with sticks, stones and flowers, and we run about and look at things and find things and sings and shouts. We don't have toys.'
> The fields were our toyshops and sweetshops, our market and our storehouses. We made our toys from things we found in the pastures (Uttley, 1976, p. 199).

A little more of Alison Uttley's idyll, her time and kind of play, Froebelian perfection of learning about life from all things in the environment, Rousseauesque pictures of unfettered innocence. And what a good advertisement for her toys Alison Uttley is, growing up to write charming books which lead children into that countryside and its play.

> Fuzzypeg . . . made himself into a ball and rolled down the hill, faster and faster. When he got to the bottom there was no Fuzzypeg to be seen, only an enormous snowball. . . . Hare . . . gave it a kick. . . . Out came the little hedgehog eating his bread and jam. 'However did you get inside a snowball?' asked Hare. . . . 'I didn't get inside. It got round me', replied Fuzzypeg calmly, 'Can I go on your sledge now?' (Uttley, 1940, pp. 30–38).

Fuzzypeg is persuaded to settle for individual sledging on a tin tray. The best toys of Alison Uttley and her animals are natural or at least local and they don't have to be worried about. Unlike the sledge on which prickly Fuzzypeg longs to ride; it is gorgeous but it is such a responsibility and causes great anxiety when it gets lost. Fuzzypeg might have been told off if he had lost the tray (presumably his mother's) but it would not have been the near tragedy that the mislaid sledge caused.

The handsome sledge just manages to qualify as a toy or, rather, play-thing since its owners do derive enjoyment from its use. Not so the boy Kingshaw in the novel *I'm the King of the Castle*. The whole story is a picture of play perverted. At one point two boys run away and spend some time in the nearby woods. But this is not Arthur Ransome and the children are not playing at self-sufficiency. Danger and death really are very near; active play and fantasy are replaced by real-life horror and nightmare; the very things which play and fantasy seek to manage and hold at bay. Play through official play objects is perverted too. Mr Hooper, father of Kingshaw's persecutor and employer of his mother, says:

'Now I have found two things for you, this morning, I have found the draughts and a bagatelle board. The draughts are very unusual ones, very valuable, they were . . . but I daresay you will not be interested in that kind of thing, you had better find Edmund and then I will bring the things to you. There is a table in the front sitting-room, you can go there.'
Kingshaw went slowly on, up the stairs. He thought, Mr Hooper can tell us to do what he pleases, because my mother is paid to work for him, and this is not our house. I shall have to go into the sitting-room with Hooper and play draughts.
'Oh how kind of you! What a good idea!' said Mrs Helena Kingshaw, smiling eagerly, in the breakfast room. 'That is just right for a rainy morning. . . . Now they can get together over these games, and then we shall really see the friendship cemented' (Hill, 1974, pp. 50–51).

Everything is wrong. The play is imposed on the boys by Mr Hooper to keep them occupied, out of the way, in the place he determines, even on the table he specifies. Mrs Kingshaw goes one worse and imposes hoped-for meaning and result on the play. Mr Hooper selects the play-things and makes it clear that they have an intrinsic value; like the sledge they must be admired but use may endanger them. Mr Hooper will not, however, entrust Kingshaw with the full story of their value; that might have been interesting, a kind of word-play and therefore not appropriate to a mere boy. Perhaps the final insult is that the boys may not even carry the draughts to the area designated for the morning's play. They are to arrange themselves and only then will the precious objects be brought in by their custodian. Small chance of the friendship being cemented unless the cement is its shroud.

And is this not a common picture of adults' attitudes towards play and play objects?

When Pauline Shapiro (1965, p. 72) studied 'coping' and 'non-coping' families she found that

> with hardly any exceptions, the 'copers' provided for their children's play needs and the 'non-copers' did not. This does not mean merely the presence or absence of toys. On the contrary, the 'non-copers' were often extravagant in buying conspicuous objects – tricycles, prams, over-large dolls or animals – for display at Christmas. But in their homes there was a complete lack of play material for constructive and imaginative use, and, even worse, a lack of understanding or tolerance of children's play needs.

In the Beck family (with whom I worked for five years) toys were bought from time to time by the father but were locked in a cupboard to which only he had a key in a room to which only he had a key. He had been brought up in an old fashioned institution and did not know how to play; only that there were things called toys which people had and which must be respected and protected. He could not bear his children to spoil the toys by playing with them. Is there perhaps an important distinction between toys and play-things? Are toys for possessing and play-things for doing?

Many adults use the play of their children for their own ends thinking like Mr Hooper and Mrs Kingshaw that they are serving the best interests of the children. (Although I suggest that that not only those unpleasant and fortunately fictional parents but also many in real-life are deluding themselves rather than thinking.)

> David's life was over-directed. The foster parents did not want him to dig holes in the garden, or paddle through the water. They wanted him to grow up into an intelligent and well regulated being, and insisted that he played at what they considered the right level for his age, with books and pencils, and carpentry sets. They were ... unable to see that David had been cheated out of his baby play (Kastell, 1962, p. 170–71).

Not only must a child's play activity be his own but he must have control over his own play-things.

> The deprived child usually has little sense of property and will play with, lose, or destroy his own, other children's or 'the Home's' playthings without seeming to know or care which are which. His locker is empty or nearly so; and his carefully chosen Christmas present has been swopped for something worthless. It is hardly surprising, therefore, that some residential people give up the struggle, if they have ever tried to start it, and don't bother to see that the children have a decent-sized place to keep their property (Kydd, 1967, p. 28).

When Mr Beck locked his toys away he was probably remembering just the kind of enforced communism to which Robert Kydd refers and the need for strong measures to protect not only one's own property but also one's own self.

Ownership implies the right not only to protect but also to destroy (provided that destruction does not imperil other people's persons and property and that the destroyer does not then claim recompense or replacement). Kay Donley reminds us that the child who discarded and therefore emotionally destroyed her long-worked-over scrapbook actually 'had the right to deal with the scrapbook as she wished' (1975, p. 28).

Often the eventual product of play is the least important part of the play which exists in the imaginative and active creation and gathering of ideas and materials:

> our six little girls ... aged between four and ten years possess very fertile imaginations. Their 'play' begins when they arrive downstairs in the morning and keeps them busy for the rest of the day.
> They own a very large and rather grubby collection of dressing-up clothes, mainly the old-fashioned frocks and skirts that well meaning people have given for the older girls to wear. The girls must don their long frocks and put underskirts on their heads to act as veils, before they are prepared to eat their breakfast. These clothes also do duty as bedding for their dolls, or even for themselves if they decide to play houses with each other. Sometimes they are in the 'den' mood and all the dresses and skirts are draped around the edges of the playroom table to make their 'den'. The clothing seldom stays in its original style for long, someone

always gets busy with the scissors redesigning to the little girls' current fashion (Warburton, 1967, p. 59).

Miss Warburton further describes the ingenuity imployed in creating a Wendy House and paddling pool and in equipping the playroom. Nothing is wasted, everything used.

Lambert and Pearson (1974) include a description of ingenious creation on a larger scale by Edgar White and his friends who, aged fifteen, built and ran their cafe on the playground at Parkhill.

> The first cafe we built was in an old caravan. Its tyres were all punctured – perished with age. The second one was wooden. We got all the shogwood off the builders and found some old doors and corrugated iron. It got smashed too. We got fed up. We wanted to do something different – make something stronger, more lasting (p. 45).

And they succeeded.

Edgar and his mates had a large project and needed solid and large materials. Jean Moore (1976, p. 14) shows how nothing however small and unprepossessing can be without value in the right time and place and use of imagination:

> Peter ... was in the remand room at the court and was causing considerable alarm and despondancy as he was literally running up the walls and running around hitting everyone in sight. I began my interview by asking everyone else in the room to leave. ... Then I noticed on the ground a ripped copy of the *Daily Mirror* that had been left by the constable on duty. I knelt on all fours in front of the paper, which caught Peter's attention, particularly as I was obviously not dressed for this form of exercise. Then more unconsciously than consciously, I began to put the bits of newspaper together, rather like a jigsaw puzzle, I was then able to say to the now stationary Peter, 'Look, this is what the court is trying to do – to put the bits of your life together in some way, although obviously not all the bits can come together.'

In the hands of this alert and sensitive social worker the despised fragment of newspaper achieved two functions; it acted as a distraction for, and held the attention of the distressed child and it became a symbol or picture of his present position which the child might or might not accept.

It takes a good deal of imagination to make something out of a scrap of newsprint. A number of writers suggest other perhaps more conventional play materials. Eric Ingram (1967, p. 9) reminds us that

> Children enjoy using simple materials much more than elaborate toys. Offcuts of wood from the builders or joiners. Large wooden bricks for building, sand and water, clay, cardboard boxes. Old clothes from friends or the jumble sale. Nearly any material will be used by children to good purpose.

Maybe waste is something learnt from adults, not really natural to the human.

Paul Abbatt (1967, p. 19) of the famous toy-making firm says that

> Toys have to match the vitality of childhood. Children will use them upside down and the opposite way from intended. But whichever way up, and however used, the toy must not break, nor fail the child.

This sound like a prescription for parents and teachers and social workers too!

Mia Kellmer Pringle (1975, p. 45) comments that

> Choosing toys, materials and equipment which are appropriate to the child's age and level of maturity requires care and understanding. Decisions need to be made not only as to quantity but also regarding the balance between 'raw' (i.e. clay or paints), constructional (i.e. bricks or Lego) and 'finished' (i.e. dolls or trains) materials.

Ella Zwerdling's (1974, p. 8) wise words after a list of equipment are

> In general, the simpler the equipment, the less chance for trouble. It's like the dramatist, who doesn't write a dog into the script because he can't control it.

Kay Donley (1975, p. 26) advises

> A good thing to develop is a kit to carry with you. . . . I . . . include scrap-paper for drawing and crayons. . . . If you have any additional space, include something like a hand puppet as well. You can make them yourself out of a piece of fabric. Some workers have also used little human figures – the kind you can bend, which usually include a figure of father, mother and children. The figures are small and of a kind usually used by play therapists, or use the plastic figures found in Woolworth stores.

Social workers need play-things wherever they are. Small and handy boxes of dolls and books for cuddling and distraction in cars, handbags and pockets full of paper and pencils for long waits in court remand rooms, cupboards overflowing with everything possible in the department. And a teddy bear given to the department for some needy child never again left the office; he sat in the one comfortable arm chair and was cuddled by tired and distraught social workers.

Social workers are also an important source of supply of play-things for children such as those in Pauline Shapiro's (1965, p. 72) 'non-coping' families:

> The suggestion that students should take to these homes simple play-things, such as paper and crayons or plasticine, produced remarkable results out of all proportion to the equipment.

The Children's Department through me kept the Beck children supplied with paper and pencils for some years. Nothing lasted in that household for more than a week but the small gifts were looked forward to, used and valued. I also took cereal packets which at that time had masks and cut-out models on the back.

But I am being like Mr Hooper and David's foster parents and all those dreary adults who prescribe how children should play. Just as children choose what and how to play, so social workers can enjoy their professional play only if they *can* enjoy it; and enjoy the activity of choosing and using their own ideas and play-things. Which is why lists of toys are really a waste of time. For toys, play-things, are unique and spontaneous, they belong only to the finder and player herself.

So one more reference to Pauline Shapiro who takes the discussion of play material one step further:

> family caseworkers might usefully give more thought to young children's play needs within the homes of the families they visit. They should be concerned not only with the provision of simple play material and the imaginative use of household 'junk' but also with an approach to children's play needs which might involve the mother indirectly through example and interest (pp. 78–9).

Helping adults play

Non-playing captains

The child whose parents (or substitute parents) cannot play is likely to be inhibited from or even unable to play thoroughly himself. An over-anxious mother may prevent her children from gaining physical confidence because she tells them to be careful all the time, calling them down from trees and away from steep slopes. In time those children will probably either rebel, taking real risks and courting danger, or withdraw from potential cuts and bruises of both knee and heart. Such a mother is very probably a non-player enjoying neither physical nor imaginative freedom. Sex is perhaps a serious even anxious procedure for her and laughter is to be provoked only by television comedians where official permission has been given for fun to be experienced.

David's foster parents mentioned above were anxious that he should develop into an intellectual and competent man. 'They were . . . unable to see that David had been cheated out of his baby play' because they were, we might speculate, non-players themselves (Kastell, 1962, p. 171).

If a child cannot play as a child he will not play as a man. And if a man cannot play as a father his children may also not play. They may play *with* things (toys) and laugh *at* things (jokes) but how much will they create play of the body and mind?

The inability and/or reluctance of an adult to play whether with other adults or with children almost certainly derives from lack of satisfying play in his own childhood. But this may lead to other secondary causes of non-playing.

One may be simply non-thinking; maybe substituting a play-object for play-ing:

Mothers, too often, do not play enough with their babies. They seem to think that putting a soft teddy bear in her carriage with the baby solves things for an hour or two, forgetting that babies want to be tickled and hugged (Neill, 1962, p. 68).

The adult may be just not noticing that playing is happening, thinking that the child is being silly or a nuisance, not conforming to adult standards of correct behaviour:

I watched a little girl dancing, partnering her reflection in the dark shop window. She was not annoying anyone, she was well away from the queue and easily within calling distance when the bus came. But her mother yanked her and slapped her into submission (Berg, 1972, p. 12).

Leila Berg follows this sad vignette with a vivid picture of adults playing to the best of their ability, a best which has no space for recognizing, caring about or joining in the play of their child':

two young couples on the grass talking excitedly about home movies. 'Here, remember that one he took at breakfast! We was all eating cornflakes!' 'Yes – and the wind was blowing!' 'What a scream!' Hysterical choking. Followed by an absorbed, respectful assessment – 'That was clever!' 'That was a year, that was!'
Cutting into this, their unseen child calling from the distance, 'There's a tractor here!' Nobody moved. But the mother slightly turned her head to shout 'Get down!' and then father . . . jumped up and said, 'I'll get him!' . . .
Out of sight, the child, dealt with, wailed, 'Oh . .' then resilient, and quickly excited again, shouted, 'Mum! Can I stroke the dog?' And the mother, not even moving her head this time, shouted, 'No, You stroked it last year!' (pp. 12–13).

Another source of non-playing may be fear of an activity which may seem to remove the playing child from the control of the non-playing adult. And if the adult joins the play in some way she may lose control not only of the child but also of herself. Fear may also relate to the notion that playing is a waste of time, a low-grade activity, not-working rather than the stuff of life. A. S. Neill (1962, p. 69) suggests that

Fear is at the root of adult antagonism to children's play, Hundreds of times I have heard the anxious query, 'But if my boy plays all day, how will be ever learn anything; how will he ever pass exams?'

This is not the place for a full-scale enquiry into why and how adults don't play but I suggest the above few ideas because social workers helping children to play may very often need to understand why their parents are 'non-playing captains'.

Are you playing?

Social workers may find many ways of helping parents and other adults play. But social workers and other helping professionals may themselves need to be convinced that playing is a proper professional activity.

> The very small amount of staff time spent in play may surprise those unfamiliar with pre-school centres. It reflects the current educational ideology that play should be self-directed, but perhaps represents a neglect at both an intellectual and emotional level. In the case of young staff particularly, the preferred method of interacting with children is often through play. If this method is discouraged, their communication tends to be impoverished (Tizard, 1976, p. 31).

So the first step towards helping children play may be to encourage lecturers on training courses and supervising officers in social-work departments to regard it as of sufficient importance. I owe my own introduction to play as the proper occupation of the social worker seeking to communicate with a child to my supervisor on my training course in the early 1960s. My task was to get to know a little boy who had been committed to care, was in a reception centre and was during the course of my placement to be placed in a large children's home. As a young woman with no experience at all of children either personally or professionally I might well have thought that I should do the getting to know in an interviewing room. But my supervisor told me to take Philip to the Transport Museum (at the expense of the Children's Department). The success of that visit was followed by afternoons playing in the local park and visiting the Science Museum in South Kensington. I don't suppose I made much impact on Philip's long term future and happiness but we did enjoy each other's company and perhaps I did manage to help him make the transition from one establishment to another. In one great game running across a field I breathlessly introduced a fantasy game about cowboys and indians where one lot were his hostile parents and siblings and Philip was the other side. I think this was probably somewhat heavy-handed, maybe my attempt to prove to my supervisor that our playing was really purposeful. Luckily it didn't put Philip off. The point of this story is that I was free to enjoy and play with Philip because I was given permission so to do by the person whose authority was at that time of most importance to me, my supervisor. Had he disapproved of play and told me not to waste my time or said that playing was all very well but social workers had no time for such activity in real life I am ashamed to say that I should almost certainly have taken his word for it, certainly while I was a student and dependent on him for a good report. But with his strong encouragement and approval I discovered a belief which became ever more deeply rooted as I worked as a social worker and which could not, once established, be dislodged by arguments (and excuses?) about time and pressure. That belief is the one this book is about; that people who work with children must work *with* children. It gives rise to a further equally strong belief: that many people who work with children or indeed who are the parents of children, need to be given permission to join the children in their own preferred areas of activity and interest, to enjoy such work and, in short, truly to play.

As a result of Noel Hunnybun's work David and his mother began to enjoy each other. Noel Hunnybun (1965, p. 85) had allowed and encouraged David's play throughout the sessions with his mother and

> Through the medium of play and by observing my handling of David and his responses to me it became possible for his mother to discover the positive aspects of her little son, while he in turn discovered the pleasure of her approval.

Pauline Shapiro (1965, p. 79) too writes about enjoyment:

> The mothers, perhaps released from apathy by the fire-side, eased in their problems of disciplining the children and freer to do some household chores, might also come to enjoy their own children's play and in so doing, find some relief from their own pressing personal problems.

In my work with the Beck family one of my prime aims was to aid just this kind of enjoyment. The parents seemed to be locked within their own pressing personal problems without ability or interest spare for playing with and enjoying their many children. The youngest baby was always confined to a pushchair until his/her successor took over whereupon he/she descended to the floor. The house was grey throughout and reflected, I thought, the inside of its occupants. The children were uncontrollable by parents and teachers.

Starting to play took a long time. It was not easy to be accepted and playing with adults and children alike can commence only with consent from all parties. Free consent. I think it was with this family that I learned the need of parents to play. Sam came home from school full of a new nursery rhyme he had learnt. He proudly sang it to me. But 'No, said his mother, it doesn't go like that' and she sang it to me, standing beside Sam. They sang it together in rivalry and I suddenly realized that perhaps this was the first time in her life that Mrs Beck had ever sung a solo or at least a duet and been praised for her nice singing. She was not showing her son how to sing the song properly, she was singing for approval herself. If only I'd had the wit to join in after the first performance we could all have sung for enjoyment.

On very rare occasions I took Mrs Beck and the children out to a local park where the latest baby could be released from the pushchair and experience grass and the older children could run about without danger from the busy roads near their home. (One boy did run under a car and break his leg during my association with the family.) Mrs Beck could sit on a seat or even the grass, for a little while away from that grey room and the dislike of the neighbours and the harrassment of the various officials who expected a standard of coping with society beyond most well-incomed middle-class families. She *could* enjoy those usually overwhelming children. Once I took her to meet them from school and in the small park by the playground the boys had the pleasure of giving her their exercise books and receiving her shy praise. Indoors there was never space or time for that.

For a few months I was joined by a male colleague whose purpose was to offer Mr Beck the experience of social contact with another man since he seemed to be very isolated, a steady worker in a heavy job but without any social contacts and very much alone within the family. My colleague talked with passion about our local and famous football team and initiated one or two games of football with the older children. In retrospect I think we were rather tentative about this and could have sought ways to offer Mr Beck far more.

But this does not pretend to be an account of excellence; only an offering of one fumbling social worker's attempt to help a family literally to enjoy *itself*. After some years I was rewarded by seeing the family engage in some beautiful play. Mr Beck had always refused to paper the walls of the livingroom/kitchen/dining room because the owner would not plaster. The owner refused to plaster because Mr Beck would not pay the rent. Mr Beck would not pay the rent because of the disgusting state of the house structurally including the lack of plastering. Eventually the rent problem was sorted out but still no plastering. But Mr Beck decided to paper anyway and the room was enlivened with a bright paper. At this time he also painted all the elderly and shabby furniture with lively green and yellow, covered surfaces with a pretty 'Contact'. New curtains and a rug were bought from the tally man. I thought then and still think that at this time the family became undepressed and showed it in colour. But I have thought only as I write this chapter that this activity was a glorious form of play, an expression of enjoyment.

Sometimes a parent may need and wish for direct advice about playing with a child but this may be very difficult to express. Clara Claibourne Park (1972, p. 139) tells of her search for help towards understanding and working with her autistic daughter Elly. She attended a clinic:

> It should have been easy, after all, to say it: 'Look you're a professional. I need references, I need to find out about play therapy, I need to know all I can about children like Elly, because whoever else may or may not work with her, her main psychotherapist is me '

A playgroup has been arranged . . . .

It may be that the best play service a social worker can offer both parent and child is an introduction to a playgroup, nursery school or day nursery or experienced childminder. Not only can the child find space and play-things not to mention companions of similar age and concerned playing adults but also the mother (and father) can be introduced to play in a safe place with safe people. For example, Mrs McKie was not long ago the bane of her social worker's life. Her house was a slum and her children neglected in every way. Mrs McKie at 28 looked nearly 40. When a nursery school was opened near her home her younger children were among the first entrants. Both social worker and headmistress did everything they could to ensure that the children would reach school preferably on time but failing that, at all. This included the headmistress going to Mrs McKie's house to collect the family. Now Mrs McKie is a valued helper at the school. She attends regularly with the children. Moreover, conditions in her home have improved as she has learnt from the school staff and become relaxed and undepressed enough to become more cooperative with her social worker (who is highly regarded by the school).

Within the playgroup, nursery school, or day nursery, or the home of the childminder, the mother (or father) may learn confidence to play with her children and with hitherto unfamiliar materials. I once spent what felt like several weeks and turned out to be two hours in a hospital playgroup. Bravely holding the fort by the water-filled play-bath for a few minutes I noticed a mother sitting wallflower-like at the side of the room while her small son ignored her and flirted with the water. I happened to catch her eye and shyly invited her to join us. Shyly she did so. A few minutes later she was quite at home with the water and seemed to be enjoying it. I don't suppose water-play on this scale would have been appropriate in what was probably a small flat at home but perhaps the pleasure she experienced in that playroom might have helped her to find other ways of playing with her son on his return to health.

Learning about children

Learning about children cannot in real life be separated from working with and for children. All three activities must exist together or not at all. But for the purposes of this chapter I have separated one or two points regarding play as an aid to assessment.

Look at me

It is impossible to learn much about any child without understanding how he plays. Clara Claibourne Park (1972, p. 135) learned that in her tour of the clinics:

So it was over. On the whole we had been impressed, especially by their skill with Elly, who at the end of her final session with the psychiatrist had gravely tried to follow him upstairs. I was not reassured when the very last day the social worker could still ask me 'Does she ever smile?' But that was my fault. I knew that their gentle caution had missed Elly's gay side; I had wanted desperately for them to see us romping together, to watch her

delight in 'this little piggy', her laughter when her father threw her into
the air. Every day, I had determined to ask if they would watch us play.
One day I even came in an old pair of pants; in our gayest game, I would
lie on my back and lift her with my feet, high into the air. But they never
learnt the reason for my odd costume; I played no games with Elly there.
Sorrounded by that cool detachment, I just couldn't.

However at the Hampstead Clinic British social work proved itself
superior to American!

I had determined that I would not repeat my mistake of eight months
ago; whatever it cost me, I would make sure they saw me play with Elly. It
cost me nothing; playfulness was easy here. The social worker was
interested in our play; she had read my records. Knowing that, I could
elaborate on episodes I had only sketched. I described for her . . . the slow
stages in teaching Elly to turn on a tap. This is the sort of thing, I
suggested, that you can help me with. I will not forget her reply. 'I think,'
she said, 'that we will be able to learn from *you*' (p. 155).

The relaxation which had enabled Clara Claibourne Park and Elly to
play at the Clinic also led to the development of understanding and
trust between the mother and the social worker.

What does it all mean?

'Play therapy' was initiated by Melanie Klein who equipped a play
room with all manner of toys and play-things and watched.

Treatment consists of facilitating these activities, participating in them
when invited to do so but always leaving the initiative with the child.
The analyst's main task is to understand and interpret the symbolic
content of the child's play (Wolff, 1973, p. 225).

'To understand and interpret' is easily said but hard and sometimes
dangerous to do. Interpretation of any behaviour or language must
always in my view be undertaken in humility and with plenty of
hedges like 'it may be' and 'I think'; never 'it is', 'it definitely means'
or 'I know beyond shadow of doubt'. Social workers who seek to
know children must always be alert to what *may* be communicated,
deliberately or otherwise, but I think it is very dangerous to be sure
that this or that activity is bound to be associated with deep meaning:

Observe the child's play and try to understand its symbolism. Do not
probe for deep underlying meanings. Be sensitive to his wants and needs
in the play situation. . . .
Interpretation should be limited to conscious meanings and is usually
confined to what the child says and does during play, This assures the
child that he is understood and helps him to clarify what is troubling him.
Don't discover what he's thinking through play, or he'll be afraid you can
read his mind (Zwerdling, 1974, pp. 9–10).

This is Ella Zwerdling writing *The ABCs of Casework with Children* and
saying that not only play but also children must be treated with

respect. Such respect will be demonstrated both by attending to the child and giving him the opportunity to express himself and by abstaining from imposing meaning or even looking for meaning. In the next quotation Barbara Dockar-Drysdale (1968, p. 145) three times uses the word 'wonder' within two sentences. I see her use of the word as an expression of respect for she is talking about engaging her imagination to notice how a child is choosing to behave in play and then to enquire of herself what he *may* be communicating, deliberately or otherwise:

> Possibly, just because we are playing with Johnny and the others, just because we are not teaching, training, nursing, or supervising, we may be free to wonder more about the meaning of the play: for example, when a very quiet, good child becomes a savage giant when he is wearing a mask, we may wonder what hate and helpless rage may be seething inside him from behind the calm exterior he presents to the world. So that when the giant roars and rages you may find yourself saying, 'This giant is very angry about something – I wonder what made him so angry?' and perhaps the giant talking as the giant may tell you important things about himself, about his *inside* reality.

'Wonder' is a wonderful word and a sense of wonder together with the ability to engage in and enjoy play and a lively imagination are surely essential to social workers who would communicate with children.

Children playing

'It is hardly necessary to illustrate something so obvious as playing: nevertheless I propose to give two examples' (Winnicott, 1974, p. 48). In fact *I* propose to give three examples, one of them from the two mentioned by Dr Winnicott above. These examples are of adults learning with respect and wonder about the children who need their help by being with them while they play.

Edmund's mother was consulting Dr Winnicott as a psychotherapist. She brought two and a half year-old Edmund with her but he was not the patient. Nevertheless since whatever his mother felt and did must affect him he was as much as his mother in need of the help of the helping adult and Dr Winnicott was constantly aware of him and his behaviour and possible conscious or unconscious communications.

> After about twenty minutes Edmund began to liven up, and he went to the other end of the room for a fresh supply of toys. Out of the muddle he brought a tangle of string (p. 49).

The mother referred to the string in her description of Edmund's behaviour at home. Eventually

> . . .Edmund quite naturally left the toys, got on to the couch and crept like an animal towards his mother and curled up on her lap . . . . . Then he

uncurled and returned to the toys. He now put the string (which he seemed fond of) at the bottom of the bucket like bedding, and began to put the toys in, so that they had a nice soft place to lie in, like a cradle or cot . . . he was ready to go, the mother and I having finished our business. In this play he had illustrated much of that which his mother was talking about . . . He had communicated an ebb and flow of movement in him away and back to dependence. . . . What Edmund did was simply to display the ideas that occupied his life while his mother and I were talking together. I did not interpret and I must assume that this child would have been liable to play just like this without there being anyone there to see or to receive the communication. (p. 50).

Although Dr Winnicott did not interpret to either Edmund or his mother his description of this encounter is well spiced with interpretative comments. I have not included these in my quotation for I do not regard social workers as psychotherapists manqués and I think that a social worker present at this interview would have seen in Edmund's behaviour more or less what I have reproduced here; the finer points of the significance of the string would, I suggest, be too much.

Dibs on the other hand is very explicit about the inner meaning of his play in the presence of his therapist Virginia Axline (1971, pp. 160–1):

We went down to the playroom and Dibs jumped into the sandbox and began to dig a deep hole in the sand. Then he went over to the doll house and got the father doll. 'Do you have anything to say?' he demanded of the doll. 'Are you sorry for all the mean angry things you said?' He shook the doll, threw it around in the sandbox, hit it with a shovel. 'I'm going to make a prison for you with a big lock on the door', he said. 'You'll be sorry for all the mean things you did'.

He got the blocks and began to line the hole with the blocks, building the prison for the father doll. He worked quickly and efficiently. 'Please don't do this to me,' he cried out for the father doll. 'I'm sorry I ever hurt you. Please give me another chance.'

'I will punish you for everything you have ever done!' Dibs cried out. He put the father doll down in the sand and came over to me.

'I used to be afraid of Papa', he said. 'He used to be very mean to me.'

'You used to be afraid of him?' I said.

'He isn't mean to me anymore,' Dibs said. 'But I am going to punish him anyhow.'

Dibs continued to punish his 'father' until the boy doll rescued the father doll from his durance vile and the father doll 'said that he loved Dibs; and needed him'. This is a fine example of a child experiencing relief and gaining help through the medium of play with appropriate play-things and a caring care-ful adult at hand. But it also shows how that adult by real presence, present but not intrusive and with the trust of the child, was enabled to learn about him through both her clear observation and his deliberate communication to her.

Barbara Williams's play with Jackie also took place in a psychiatric setting, this time a child psychiatric unit to which the eight-year-old girl was admitted after a period as an out-patient. Barbara Williams (1978, p. 9) was a social worker working for a short time in the daily playgroup in the unit.

> Jackie would arrange chairs to represent a cot and take delight in being wrapped in blankets and then lying 'asleep', sucking her thumb. On waking she would fetch the plastic bottle with a nozzle which had been filled with water, sit on the knee of the adult and ask to be fed
> In another game, Jackie would be the mother of a baby doll, while the adult would be assigned to a more distant role such as shop-keeper. She would lavish care on the 'baby', dressing and undressing it, feeding and bathing it, but when she decided that the 'baby' had been naughty she would smack it vigorously, and this would be accompanied by harsh verbal chastisements.
> Even fairly brief observations of Jackie's play clearly illustrated her intense feelings and resentment towards her younger siblings which could never have been expressed in words.

As with Dibs it is likely that Jackie was gaining relief and help by the very process of playing fantasy games and in having an attentive adult present to use as required. And like Virginia Axline, Barbara Williams was alert for any message which the child might be trying to communicate in order to aid understanding of and planning for further help for the child. As Barbara Williams says, Jackie's feelings 'could never have been expressed in words'. Dibs could use words but without the play his ability for clear and penetrating articulation could never have been learnt about and freed.

Although the play with Jackie took place in a specialized residential setting I do not think there is anything in the description of the activities and interactions between Jackie and the caring adults which could not have occurred within the context of day-to-day social casework. The kinds of play could have been arranged in a social-work department or park for example and they could certainly be noticed within a foster home or residential home.

In these examples the three children were all very busy doing things and the helping adults were equally busy noticing and learning from them. But as much may be learned from children not-doing and perhaps Dibs even in the midst of his disturbed childhood knew something very important:

> He lay down full length. 'Want to take your shoes off, Dibs?' he asked himself. 'No', he answered. 'Well, what *do* you want to do, Dibs?' he asked. 'Make up your mind!' He rolled over and stuck his face down against the sand. 'I'm in no hurry,' he said. 'For now, I'll just *be*!' (Axline, 1971, p. 103).

'Just being' is what play is all about; what life is all about. And just being, quietly and without obvious activity, is not something which adults often allow in children especially if they are supposed to be achieving something together in some particular relationship. Even Dibs who at that moment knew just what he meant and what he wanted did not 'just be' for long. But I suggest that one of the main purposes of social workers communicating with children through play or any other medium is to learn what they really 'be' and that the other main purpose is to help those children to *be* what they *really* are.

Sharing activity and developing communication

Learning about social workers

However much a social worker thinks she knows about a child her observations and speculations will be of very little service to the child unless the child too has made observations and speculations – about his social worker. I suggest that accurate and useful assessments can be made only if the assessed child chooses to place enough trust in his assessors to reveal his true self. Without that trust it may be possible to recognize that much is being covered and withheld but it is surely not possible to describe what that 'much' is. And the task of helping the child to reach his true self can be achieved only if trust between child and helping adult exists. So that any communication between child and social worker is developed as much for the child to learn about the social worker as vice versa. As Noel Timms (1962, p. 52) says:

> Communication is established by allowing and helping the child to discover the kind of person the caseworker is.

This may seem like an obvious statement but in my experience and perception it is a fairly recent development for social caseworkers to be supposed to be 'discovered'.

I am not of course suggesting that social workers should impose and intrude their personal lives and problems onto their clients. It is it seems to me one thing to collapse in an armchair in a smooth-running foster home and be revived with tea, letting the foster mother know that you're having a hard day but then giving proper professional time and attention to her and the children. It would be quite another thing if the social worker collapsed in such a way as to prevent the foster mother from revealing that some problems had developed for fear of putting even greater burdens on this overburdened person. Or if she drank the tea and started to pour forth her own tale of woe.

The way in which social workers as well as children play is likely to be very revealing. Does she play wholeheartedly or sit on the park bench: if she sits on the park bench does that indicate age and unfitness, lack of interest in the child and the play or trust in the child that he will have a good race round and then come back rather than using this as a chance for absconding? If the game is competitive does the social worker rig it so that the child inevitably wins (thus protecting herself from losing if the child should *really* win or the difficulty of managing the child's distress if he should *really* lose) or does she make it a fair fight? If she loses is she upset (however well concealed) or cheerful? And so on.

Ella Zwerdling (1974, p. 7) suggests that

> Play can be used to build up the prestige of the social worker in the small client's eyes. If you can make interesting things, draw pictures and so forth, you'll get some respect.

I don't think the social worker has actually to be *good* at such activities. Children are critics not of adult ideas of excellence but of genuine interest and endeavour. However 'bad' the picture it will surely be appreciated if it has been drawn with good intention *for* the child. However 'good' the picture, it is of little use if it is given without love.

Let down your hair

One thing which playing will rapidly reveal to the child is the importance the social worker attaches to her dignity. Play and conventional dignity do not really go together (although the ability really to play reveals dignity of the soul, a rather more precious attribute). John Holt (1970) spent a hectic morning in charge of two children aged three and a half and two. When they strayed out of sight against his instructions

> I had to fetch them back, protesting and wailing. They were furious. They told me that I was bad and they were going to tell their mommy on me. I told them to go ahead. Patrick then said that his mommy would spank me 'like this'. I pretended to cry. This is an absolutely foolproof game to play with children; they all love it (pp. 19–20).

Dr Winnicott (1978) initiated his relationship with the Piggle (a two-year-old girl) less painfully but with no less willingness to sacrifice adult dignity to the needs of the child. He wanted to see the Piggle on her own but she was too shy!

> I therefore got the mother in with her and told her not to help at all, and she sat back on the couch with the Piggle beside her. Already I had made friends with the teddy-bear who was sitting on the floor by the desk. . . . I said to the Piggle . . . 'Bring teddy over here, I want to show him the toys' (p. 9).

And they're away. Because they were willing to look foolish both John Holt and Dr Winnicott achieved the dignity of communication with their children.

John Willis too risked looking foolish when he began to try to develop a relationship with a young mentally handicapped boy also named John in a subnormality hospital. John, aged 10 (chronologically), was moving from the hospital into a children's home in his native city. The social worker needed really to get to know John in order both to aid assessment and planning and to assist John move from the hospital if this was eventually arranged. John Willis (1978) knew that play was a good way to start communication but how to play let alone communicate with a mentally handicapped child?

> The adventure playground was extremely useful here. John was a little apprehensive about the swing and would not commit himself too far. With time and a little patience he eventually allowed me to push him quite high and so developed a trust in me that I would not allow him to fall or hurt himself. I wanted this to be and seem to be a mutual trust. I allowed him to use my car keys to open the doors and to lock them; also to let him blow air into my tyres with a foot pump. This I feel was valuable as a number of children in John's class at school have a fascination for keys, he knows that I always keep them well away from them, but not from him. If we go on outings he will now leave his little purse and money in my keeping . . . . . . After some time playing together he became much more confident in himself and me (pp. 8–9).

Not only did the social worker achieve the mutual trust he sought but also mutual confidence. John Willis had not previously endeavoured to communicate with a mentally handicapped child for professional purposes and the warm positive response he gained from John gave him more confidence in 'himself and me' too.

I will finish this section with two further examples of social workers using play to help establish trust and communication.

Tim was an eight-year-old in hospital for cardiac surgery. His social worker 'suggested that we should form a club to meet, talk and play together'. Tim agreed and the club was formed.

> I hoped to achieve several purposes: to learn how the hospital experience was affecting Tim so I could help him master it, for now and the future; to be a patient, understanding person unconnected with his treatments and medicine, to whom he could talk about his daily ups and downs and thus help him to accept and benefit from his difficult medical regimen. The club would be a place where he could assert his independence, make decisions rather than simply obey them, talk about new things, have new experiences, be encouraged, within the hospital limitations, to exercise a boy's natural curiosity. Finally, I hoped our relationship would provide Tim with confidence to express his feelings and give him experience of a healthy male relationship (Richman, 1972, p. 42).

The word 'confidence' appears again. The playing, an opportunity for children whatever their circumstances and environment to be in control of their activity and of materials, is a means for children in threatening and uncontrollable circumstances to develop some confidence in both themselves and the adults around them. It is a chance for an activity whether of the mind or the body to be shared with an adult on equal terms. The child may make decisions, even win.

Joan Brown (1972) writes about work with children aged three and four living a children's home before eventual placement with foster parents. During this time they were brought regularly to the social worker's office to spend time with their natural parents:

> they were taken to the worker's own office where they were allowed to draw. This occupation was familiarly connected with the worker, who had originally introduced it when supervising the children at home to achieve some quiet. . . . During the parents' visit they called out frequently, 'Where are you, Miss Graham?' and occasionally came to make a personal check. When this routine had been thoroughly established over five or more visits, longer time was spent in the office after a visit and they were enticed into the general office where they were allowed to play with (and incidentally break) such interesting toys as the stapler and the punch (p. 28).

The playing is a means of the children establishing themselves and some sense of control. It is important that they were allowed to break that precious equipment without recrimination for their need of having something (in this case the acceptance of the office staff and social worker) that they could not lose by such harm must have been very great at a delicate time when they were in transit, in the children's home after removal from their natural parents, and eventually to lose that brief security by moving again. No wonder they wanted to be sure that the social worker was safely around. And no wonder that they formed some kind of relationship with the caseworker's office (Timms, 1962, p. 52) which became at this crucial time a place of safety.

Helping children in stressful situations

The final section of this chapter comprises examples of ways of playing with children in various specific situations involving stress, physical, mental and/or emotional. Not all the examples are of social workers playing but all the children and all their experiences might well be known to social workers and the playing might, indeed should, in the absence of the other professional players have been played by social workers.

Hospitals

In the literature known to me most of the comments on, suggestions for, rationale and examples of playing with children under stress are related to children in or attending hospitals. The needs of children in hospital for care and attention to more than their physical and medical needs has attracted attention for some years. For example, one of the aims of the National Association for the Welfare of Children in Hospital (NAWCH) set up in 1961 is to develop opportunities for the provision of play in hospital. The Ministry of

Health *Report on the Welfare of Children in Hospital* in 1958 (*The Platt Report*) gave official recognition to the notion of the importance of the child's whole welfare while in hospital and in 1976 the DHSS *Report of the Expert Group on Play in Hospital* recommended that 'hospitals should employ play workers to meet children's play needs... in each ward where there are children and during each children's out-patient session' (NAWCH, 1976, p. 2). While much has been done in recent years to introduce play-leaders, set up play schemes and in many ways acknowledge the vital role of play for the child in hospital there are still plenty of wards where children 'might well be lying in bed quietly awaiting their turn in the operating theatre' (Zwart, 1976, p. 10) (and the 1976 Report was accompanied by a circular saying that all the recommendations could not be implemented because of financial constraints!)

In contrast to the children mentioned above,

> A little boy in flaming red pyjamas does battle with an imaginary enemy. He sits astride a tiny tricycle several sizes too small for him. In a corner seven-year-old Terence sits painting... both boys are... due to have an operation this afternoon (Zwart, p. 10).

Hugh Jolly (1976, p. 6) a paediatrician writes that

> Play in hospital not only keeps [a child] happy but also makes tolerable the new and strange things that are happening to him. To achieve this, the play should be part of the normal ward activity both at the bedside and in the ward playroom.

One of the prime purposes of play in hospital is to help the child to feel as happy and un-stressed as possible in a time and place where pain and stress are prevalent and he is almost certainly separated for long periods from his family and friends and from familiar routine. Michael's mother wrote:

> I should like to thank you and your colleagues for helping Michael to overcome his fear of hospitals and making his short stay a happy one. Although the surgeons decided to postpone his operation until he is older I am sure his time in the ward has reassured him that hospitals have kind people in them who give them some fun, and he has actually volunteered to go back to hospital when the time comes; I hope he does not change his mind!
> He is thrilled to bits with his clay bowl he made with your help. I have varnished it for him and I am sure he will always associate it happily with his hospital stay. I am sure he has been helped a lot psychologically! (Harvey and Hales-Tooke, 1972, p. 99).

This letter suggests the existence for Michael of the perfect team which includes a mother who will understand exactly what is happening and will varnish the prized clay bowl. This team would probably operate well again when in the future Michael should re-enter the ward this time for the operation.

Just as play, including the creation of his bowl, helped Michael to manage and even enjoy his first hospital stay it would also be invaluable in helping him to prepare for his next admission and for the experience of anaesthesia, operation, discomfort and immobility. *Let's Make a Game of it* (Harding and Walker, 1972, p. 3) suggests a programme for preparation by a play specialist. A large teddy bear is essential equipment and is subjected to innumerable injections, stitching up and unstitching:

> We stitch teddy, the child removing the stitches with plastic tweezers; then he dresses the wound, just as his nurse does. The emphasis on the final procedure is that although it hurts a little after the operation, it is getting better all the time.

I write as one who would need a general anaesthetic to enter a hospital at all and while I think that the familiarizing activity of injecting poor old teddies is excellent I must on behalf of all such cowards as myself stress that teddy's suffering is in vain if the child is not, through the activity, enabled to express his fear. It seems to me that injecting teddy could be used as a way of controlling or even holding at bay the child's fear, as if the activity could be a substitute for the feeling, the toy a scape-teddy in the original sense, an animal bearing the burden of humans' sufferings and thereby removing the sufferings from their true owners. However many times the teddy's arm is attacked it will after all be *my* arm which hurts when it is *my* turn for the needle.

Returning teddy to the security of the toy cupboard, here are two examples of work with individual children by playleaders.

Five-year-old John spent two months in hospital for treatment of a brain tumour. His unmarried mother visited for two hours daily.

> [John] was very quiet and withdrawn on his own, yet when his mother arrived he would become hostile and aggressive, even physically violent towards her. When she left he would become momentarily upset and would then withdraw again. He became very distressed when going for his treatment, so much so that his mother, who had agreed to accompany him to the Radiotherapy Department, felt that she could no longer continue to take him down, and this job became the responsibility of a different member of the nursing staff each day (Lee, 1978, p. 28).

The playworker recognized both aspects of John's problem, that is, the interaction with his mother and the anxiety about attending the Radiotherapy Department. Her intervention brought about improvement in both:

> He remained withdrawn for a time, but gradually became more trusting and with her help would get over more quickly his upset when his mother left. The playworker was also able to help the relationship between mother and child. It was quite obvious that the mother did not understand John's aggressive behaviour, nor did she know how to cope with it, or how to play with John while she was visiting in the hospital. The playworker, therefore, began to show the mother how she could play with

the child and then she would withdraw from the situation so that the mother did not feel threatened.

The playworker was also able to take over the role of accompanying John to his daily treatment. She fabricated a story of a 'secret mission' and 'space travel' around it, which she repeated every day. She always took the same route to the treatment room, at the same time each day. Having relieved the tension and anxiety and established a repetitive routine it was not long before John stopped showing signs of disturbance both before and after his treatment, and in himself became more relaxed and progressed well (p. 28).

I am struck by the vivid contrast between John's road to Calvary along interminable corridors each day in the custody of a different caretaker who however kind, was merely fulfilling yet another task, and his exciting journeys into space where the unknown, while terrifying and even uncomfortably, would be tolerable, even desirable, in the company of a dependable fellow explorer. I am also struck by this question: in the absence of a playworker would a social worker have undertaken this kind of work or would John have been left to the ever-changing rota of nurses? And if a social worker had *not* undertaken the work would this have been to lack of thought and imagination, to shortage of time, to definition of roles and tasks within the hospital? And if shortage of time is the answer would the social worker have taken steps to ensure that time should be available for such essential work or to procure the appointment of a playworker? It is useful to repeat Judith Lee's last comment that John 'became more relaxed and progressed well'. The playing affected and helped the whole child; it was no optional extra, rather it was the spring which enabled the child to endure, accept and eventually benefit from medical treatment.

Like John, four-year-old Mark also had problems with his mother who

... found him unmanageable as he had temper tantrums when she tried to prevent him from doing dangerous things like crossing busy roads on his own (Harvey and Hales-Tooke, 1972, p. 103).

Mark was admitted to hospital with a skin disease which necessitated placement in the isolation ward where he was shaking with fright.

Because of his temper tantrums the junior nurses spent as little time as possible with him, but the playleader found he became deeply absorbed in his play and she could often maintain his interest during the nursing procedures.

Mark became more relaxed and the nurses appreciated the contribution which the playleader made to his care. ... With treatment his physical condition improved and this was reflected in his play.

The agonies of isolation may be considerably relieved through play.

Sometimes children have dressed up, mimed and acted to each other through the glass. They have made masks and hats, becoming in turn actors and audience. Puppet shows have been given by one child to entertain patients in five nearby cubicles, and this has led to other patients making puppets (p. 101).

Writers like Harvey and Hales-Tooke, and Emma Plank (1971) are generous with suggestions for activities but my nagging question remains; do social workers in hospital take play seriously? Do they regard playing as an essential part of their work? Do they ensure that play is available on the children's wards together with the milk and medication?

To conclude this section on children in hospital here are two examples of playing social work.

Harold Richman (1972, p. 41), to whom I referred earlier in this chapter, worked with eight-year-old Tim who

> . . . was afraid. As Tim's social worker, I was concerned with his fear, a fear that remained even beyond the immediate physical crisis. As his health slowly began to return, I tried to help this weakened boy wrestle with his fears and nightmares.

Tim and his social worker formed the 'Two Men Club' whose membership was strictly confined to themselves. At club meetings they shared stories and drawing and conversation, played games and visited various parts of the hospital:

> He responded eagerly to these new experiences, but in his creative play, his art work, and his relationship with me (except for constant complaints about injections) he was restrained and rejected any reference to his own thoughts or experiences. In our play with a doctor's kit, he refused to find anything wrong with the doll patient and would not give injections or medication (p. 43).

(Teddy was no doubt relieved for once!)

But eventually Tim was able to trust his social worker and to gain through contact relief from intolerable strain. (A strain which would be hard enough for a mature adult surrounded by love and security to tolerate, let alone a small boy). Tim revealed that he was terrified about the (recent) operation and in particular about 'the knife':

> When he was calmer I asked Tim to describe the knife. He drew hesitantly, a picture of a large curved knife with a sharp toothed edge (p. 46).

Playing together had led to this moment when the agonized child could confide this and other facts. Even in this moment play was of use. I have said nothing in this chapter about drawing for I shall discuss that activity in its own chapter but here is a vivid picture of the play of drawing being used to express something for which words are, to this child at this instant, inadequate, perhaps impossible.

Despite Tim's desperation the social worker did not succumb to any temptation to offer false reassurance, to 'play games':

> I could not reassure him that he would not have to undergo the knife again; instead I emphasized his great progress over the last three weeks. No words or gestures, however, could really soothe the starkness of his terror. I hoped that my presence and our mutual trust would lighten the burden of his fears (p. 47).

No scape-teddying here. Play was definitely a means of communication, to helping the child imagine his fears and situation but the adult was in no danger of confusing the playing with the true task of confronting and acknowledging and holding the child through his ordeal of body and mind.

Another eight-year-old, Sue, was admitted to hospital for repair surgery on her cleft lip and palate. The social worker saw her task as to

> help her to move to the use of more constructive defences than those of denial, escape, regression, and projection. In the beginning Sue alternately tries to escape from the painful situation or to fight it or project responsibility for it on her doctors, saying that they want to hurt her. As she becomes more secure with the worker, however, she is able temporarily to lay aside these defences and discuss the problem with the worker a little at a time. . . . . . She also gets great help by means of playing out an identification with the doctor who appears to her as an aggressor (Lloyd, 1965, p. 105).

The social worker used various forms of play to help Sue to get to know her.

> Sue begins to realize the worker is someone who understands what it is like to be lonely and who helps her to enjoy playing simple games and doing things within her capacity so that even in this strange place she can get some sense of achievement. She comes to understand that this person is a source of strength, a person who does not regard the frightening future as something that cannot be understood and faced. Moreover, apparently this person is going to be there constantly throughout all these new and alarming experiences (p. 107).

Like Harold Richman, this social worker was demonstrating that she could survive not only the frightening place but also the child's fear and that she would be a stable and continuous presence in the child's life throughout the ordeal.

After some time Sue and the worker shared some direct hospital-fantasy play which I will quote in full.
(This time the scape-teddy is a panda.)

> On my next visit with Sue I took a doctor's play kit. She examined the equipment and made careful preparation for an operation on a large panda which had acquired a slightly crooked nose. She announced, 'We will operate on her crooked nose'. The stethoscope was placed to the panda's heart, and Sue solemnly said, 'Her heart is fluttering'. I said the panda was scared of the operation, and she answered 'Yes, and she cries at

night', I said I was sorry that she felt so frightened and said I would like to help her so she wouldn't be afraid. We listened to the heart and I said it had stopped fluttering and was all right because Panda knew Sue would take good care of her. With much giggling she then ordered me to carry Panda to the bed and hold her. Sue then went to the other end of the room to play with one of the children. However she kept an eye on me and watched to see that I was taking good care of Panda. After a few minutes, I said Panda was feeling very good after the operation, and I asked if I could leave. Sue said, 'Yes, Panda is all right now'. I told Sue that she would be all right too, I knew that she was very upset about the operation, but I would be with her as much of the time as possible, and we would all take special care of her. Happily she was content to have me leave then (p. 110).

The play was simple but the purpose was complex. Sue was being enabled to express anxiety directly to the worker and to have it accepted and acknowledged; she was not being told not to be silly or to be brave. She was told that she would be looked after whatever happened and that although bad things might happen to her she would be alright in due course. She was also given the opportunity to handle possibly frightening objects, whether the objects themselves cause pain or whether like the stethoscope they were symbols of her oppressors, the doctors. By handling such objects she could become familiar with them as Tim was never able to handle and become familiar with the terrible knife. Fantasy and terror may be kept at bay even if only a little. Handling fear-full objects also gives an opportunity for the child to be master, to be the wielder of the knife, to feel control.

John and Mark, Tim and Sue were the lucky ones, helped by playleaders and social workers during their times of stress and terror, helped by play to manage the work of survival.

Between bases

If there is one time when a social worker is bound to be working directly with a child it is during moves into or within or out of care. The social worker may be the only person to know all concerned with the child and his move. I think of the social worker's activity and involvement at these times as being wave-shaped. If the social worker has been in regular touch with the child, perhaps in a children's home, the sea may have been fairly smooth, the social worker being familiar but not remarkable, a small wave among small everyday waves. If the move is made suddenly, in emergency, there is no preliminary sea. But in either kind of situation, when a move is planned or enforced the social worker begins to be increasingly important to the child. Visits increase and the child is encouraged to place more and more trust in the social worker who is responsible for his destiny. The social worker helps the child to loosen ties with his present carers, to form new ties with those who will, it is hoped, become his permanent family. The crest of the wave is reached when the move is imminent and occuring. Once the move is achieved the social worker's involvement decreases, the wave rolls on gently, ever present for the shore is called 'eighteenth birthday' and may be far away. The social worker's sea is smooth again with, perhaps ripples and peaks at occasional crises. The safe strong wave has carried the child.

Perhaps this sounds romantic. It is playing. Word playing. Finding a picture to express and illuminate a prosaic idea so that that idea may be easier to grasp or more attractive because the image is beautiful. Just as social workers play with children to help them grasp ideas which may be difficult or even· threatening. And there can be few things more difficult than being expected to move home, not with your own family but from somewhere you might have thought of as safe and yours (even if you possessed only a foot or two of wall space for your poster of today's idol), to someone else's territory, a house full already of a complete family with a spare bed.

I think the social worker has two tasks. One is to ensure that all members of the caring team cooperate to understand and help the child for the social worker herself will see the child for fairly short stretches of time. The residential workers, foster parents or natural parents from whom the child is moving will have most time with him and may need help to manage their own feelings (whether of mourning or relief) about his departure as well as offering help to the child. The other task is to work directly with the child using every possible means to communicate with him so that the child may acknowledge and express fear and anxiety, dislike and anger, pleasure and acceptance and may ask questions directly and indirectly and be sure that they will be heard, respected and answered.

Any kind of play can be useful but at times of move perhaps small doll play is particularly appropriate. The following quotation is from an account of work with an eight-year-old boy during intensive work within his second long-stay foster home (the Felhams), within the reception centre when that placement has broken down, and during placement in his third foster home. This extract is taken from the ninth interview when David has shown confusion about the first two placements and takes place in the reception centre.

I told David I was going to play with the dolls, and he could help me if he liked. I arranged a 'sick' Mummy doll on one bed, with a nurse doll. On the other bed, was a Mummy doll and a Daddy doll and a baby doll. And on the third, a Mummy and Daddy doll. I explained to David what all the dolls were, and put a baby doll by the side of the first sick Mummy doll. I said that the Mummy doll could not look after the baby doll because she was sick and the nurse was so busy; and that the Mummy doll wanted someone to look after the baby doll and give him lots of love, that she couldn't do. I told him how she had not known what to do, but then here was a Mummy and Daddy doll with a little baby boy to play with, and ... As I picked the baby doll up, David who had been watching and then had held his breath sharply, dashed across the room shouting, 'I know, I know, it's me'. He took the doll that was himself to the next bed, and asked who that was. I said it was Mr and Mrs Carter and Jackie. David looked at the third bed, and said that he thought that was Mummy and Daddy Felham. I said yes it was. He asked me to tell him more about the Carters. We played games with the dolls, how they sat round the table for tea, and how they stayed with Mummy Carter all day and did not go to school. David said that was because he was only little. After a while, David's play seemed to be standing still, I asked him what happened then, and he said he did not know; he was quiet and withdrawn. I told him to watch me, and I explained that Daddy Carter had died, so he was not there any more to give Mummy Carter pennies for the children. I said that Mummy Carter wanted David to be looked after properly and she could not do it without enough pennies, and so she had thought it better for David to live somewhere else. David looked across at the Felham dolls, and back again (Kastell, 1962, p. 288–289).

I include this long quotation because it is such a detailed and vivid picture of interaction between child and social worker. You can see David shyly watching the play begin, staying safely on the edge of the activity but thoroughly absorbed; then suddenly drawn in as he identifies with the baby doll; then withdrawn as the story reaches a point of anxiety and bewilderment. Meanwhile the social worker is totally sensitive to him. She never forces his attention, involvement or identification; always she waits for him, making offers and continuing the play and the explanations for him to use or reject as *he* wishes. The play and continuing conversation are sustained for a remarkably long time and David is eventually enabled to express his present anxiety about his future, to cry and to be cuddled.

This play with David was therapeutic for the little boy was helped and healed though the medium of the playing; David's social worker was engaged in an activity which is a proper, indeed essential, part of social work practice. The excellence of her work depended on her sensitivity, her commitment to David, her understanding of his history and his needs and her willingness to recognize her own role, responsibility and ability. During these weeks of crisis for David her wave was at its crest.

Separation and death

David's doll play centred around his confusion about and loss of natural and foster parents including the death of a foster father. These are subjects difficult to face with a child particularly if he does not directly initiate discussion. Playing, particularly in the company of a safe and interested but unobtrusive adult, may be sufficient in itself to enable a child to realize and deal with fears.

During the war one particular three-year-old boy suffered such anxiety when his father, an airman, was away that he 'became unmanageable'. He was offered treatment at the Tavistock Clinic where he

> played with figures which represented himself and his parents, and with a train and a lorry and a plane, and the model of a village. On this first visit to the playroom his play took the form of pretending that the father was a pilot on leave but was fetched to take the plane for one flight only and then he had to go home to his little boy (Bristol, 1945, p. 96).

This play was repeated over some time and the boy was able to tolerate the father doll being away for ever longer periods until eventually his play became 'freer and fuller and sturdier and reflected the normal interest of his age'.

Writing at the same time, Clare Winnicott (Britton 1945, p. 92) described the play of 'the most completely cut-off child imaginable'. He had been rescued from an air-raid shelter but both parents had been killed and he had been boarded out. The foster mother

> became fond of him, but did not try to force herself on him or get at him. She let him go his own pace. After about eighteen months when he was seven or eight he began to respond and recover. His first efforts at play were pathetic, and he would look sheepish and give up if anyone noticed him. . . . He would play with bricks, stopping always when anyone came in. Gradually the play became more complicated, and one day he actually built an air-raid shelter and played out his parents' death, suddenly asking, 'Does it hurt to get killed?'

It had taken eighteen months of careful, quiet waiting and availability by the foster mother for the little boy to feel safe enough to ask the question which haunted him and introduce the terrible subject.

The social worker herself may not be in a position to wait for and participate in the kinds of play mentioned in this section but she may need to help foster and residential workers and natural parents to be alert for and respond helpfully to such playing.

Playless children and aggression

Many children known to social workers may be unable to play and it is essential that such children should be recognized and helped. This is a huge subject and I will not attempt to discuss it here, not least because the social worker is unlikely to be in a position to be the prime player for these children. Her task is almost certainly to find play-helpers whether within child guidance or psychiatric units, day care or residential setting. However I will refer briefly to the importance of cooperating with ordinary day schools, for children spend so much time in school and teachers have so much skill and influence and yet are sometimes, if not often, overlooked as part of the group of carers. In her book *Children with Special Needs in the Infants' School* Lesley Webb (1969) gives vignettes of a number of small children with many difficulties including playlessness and she shows how teachers and social workers are bound together in order to effect any cure. Padraic for example was

> A very tense boy, alternating between extreme aggression and extreme anxiety. Third child of young parents, with two slightly older sisters who alternately fussed over and bullied him. Said by the Child Guidance Clinic to be of average intelligence, but very retarded in all language skills and number work, and seeming incapable of sustained effort in creative work or play of any kind (p. 66).

In school Padraic was enabled and encouraged to play and

> he was particularly soothed and helped to some persistence in activities by play with 'small world' toys such as farm animals, Noah's Ark set, a family of tiny dolls, etc. He could be heard muttering about their being 'killed', 'smacked', 'sent to prison' and so on as he played. It is not for the teacher to interpret such play to the child – only to provide opportunity for it and restrain the child from actual (as opposed to symbolic) destruction of the material. Padriac's therapist however, noted that his play with similar toys at the clinic became more purposeful and his conversation about it more significant after he had had opportunity to engage in it at school for several weeks. It was likely that he was able to 'carry over' his therapy between weekly sessions at the clinic in this activity at school (p. 67–8).

And for 'school' one can easily substitute 'children's home', 'foster home', 'home'.

Although an overstretched social worker, especially in a social services department, may not, as I suggested above, be in a position to bring play to a playless child herself, rather recognizing the need for help for the child and finding and making it available, it may be possible for individual social workers to undertake intensive play-work with particular children. Some social-work departments and agencies recognize the importance of such work. For example, Leicester Family Service Unit's philosophy and policy enabled their children's counsellor Michael Ingram to undertake between ten and fifteen hours work a week with a highly disturbed, unhappy and neglected nine-year-old boy. One of the first tasks was to help Jimmy play. In the course of the first fortnight's work Jimmy moved from no play at all, just rocking, through 'very bizarre' play with animals, furniture and dolls to an interest in 'playing with keys, knobs, buttons and any sort of mechanical controls' (1975, p. 42). Michael Ingram used this interest by rigging up 'a very elaborate electronic system' and showing Jimmy how to use a tape recorder and numerous other pieces of equipment. Quite soon he took Jimmy away for a week's holiday:

> After this holiday, he began to show me his aggression. He would play games in which he insulted me and I was supposed to chase him in some way. Then he started calling me 'Frankenstein' or 'Vampire' or 'Monster' and the punishments I was supposed to administer became increasingly

sadistic. I was to crush his head, bite his throat, flay him, torture him, and so on.... These games proved to be the most rewarding part of the treatment, for the playful discharge of aggressive fantasies loosened his tongue and we were able to have long conversations afterwards (p. 43).

Even more useful than Michael Ingram's description of Jimmy's behaviour is his comment on his own feelings:

I found . . . that these games caused me anxiety at times and I had to limit them to what I could easily tolerate, which was unfortunate, as he began to have a need to discharge in this way and if he did not play because I was tired, he went berserk at home and smashed things up (p. 43).

(The social worker used this problem to engage other members of the family in holding and controlling Jimmy, which proved very beneficial.) It is not very common to read such an honest account of work and feelings. In chapter 1 I referred to Robina Prestage's (1972) confession of her boredom and anger while Kim climbed and silently sat in his tree for week after week while in treatment at the Child Guidance Clinic at which she was a social worker but the reader is usually left to *assume* that the worker suffers from anxiety, exhaustion and so on and thus feel reassured or to infer that the super-worker achieves her aims with never a yawn or a shiver. Michael Ingram's point is very important indeed; intensive work of any kind takes a considerable toll of the worker who should, before she starts, accept that there will be a good deal of suffering for her. There will also be risk, certainly emotional and, if the work involves playing with a strongish youngster, possibly physical.

Michael Ingram's comment also raises the question of responsibility. Since his play with Jimmy had repercussions of a violent nature at home the social worker was responsible to the child's parents for the behaviour he had helped to stimulate. I am reminded of stories of a well intentioned group of play-stimulators who spent a glorious hour in a children's home helping everyone become ever so released and relaxed and lively. And then left leaving the staff to settle the children down. I was very conscious of the annoyance expressed by those residential staff when in another children's home I romped around with two little boys in care. The play had something to do with tigers who started off in the garden but gradually moved indoors to where we were. Like Jimmy, these two children needed to express a good deal of aggression and the play began to get quite rough, with one young female social worker fearing for her tights. One way or another we all had a good time and the boys got something out of their system and I did manage to control the play so that we were (reasonably) quiet together for a while before the end of my visit and and I was able to return them to the residential staff in a calm state.

Stimulating play in children whose play is either abnormally limited or non-existent is likely to release aggressive and excessively lively behaviour and social workers who undertake such activity must be aware of the dangers.

Who's in charge?

Children known to social workers are unlikely to be in charge of anything and social workers are very much occupied in sorting out who is in charge of this and that child. Which parent should have custody, should there be a care order, should this child be boarded out with these foster parents, should that child be placed for adoption with those applications? Another responsibility of the social worker is to enable the child to discover in what ways he can be responsible for himself, in charge of his own life. Four-year-old Sally demonstrated this need when in the first year of her visits to her father and stepmother she asked who was 'in charge' of various activities in their household; they told her about cooking and shoe cleaning and shopping and car maintenance, all easily attributable to one or the other adult. Then she asked 'Can I be in charge of the jelly?' What she meant was, I suppose, 'Can I have first go at the jelly every time . . . and the biggest helpings?' But her father heard also something like 'Can I have some control over *something* that happens to me since all you adults seem to want to move me around between you?' And also perhaps something about being prepared to share his household whenever she was in residence. So he said, 'Oh yes, what a good idea. But being 'in charge' of the jelly doesn't just mean eating it. It means that you make it (with help of course) and if you don't make it each week, it doesn't get made. And then you can serve it out at tea time'. Amazingly it worked and there were not for a time many jellyless weeks. The jelly-play helped the little girl in her working-out about her new way of life.

Here is another example of play as a help to children feeling in control in a stressful situation. Three little girls and I were confined in the incredible gloom of the girls' detention room of the Juvenile Court. We shouldn't have been there at all but there was *nowhere else* to wait for the hours before we should be called. We *could* have waited in the general public waiting area but the half dozen benches were all being sat on by the other waiters. So we obtained a concession and sat in this dusty, dreary dump. The girls were aged between four and twelve. We were there because their mother was applying for discharge of the care order. The history was extensive and complicated but the girls had not been in care long. With great anguish I was opposing the application. After much agonizing I was convinced that the children should stay in care. I knew the mother well and had tried over the past year or so to help her keep her family together. In the end we all failed and nothing had happened to alter her circumstances or ability to manage.

So there we all were. Three little girls wondering what on earth was going to happen to them both in the next hour or two and the future next after that. And a social worker in a bomb-burst of emotions; anxiety about the court appearance, ambivalence about the children because of my long work to keep them with their mother before the reluctant decision to bring them into care and apply for the then existing supervision order to be converted to a care order, ambivalence about the mother whom I would shortly be meeting in court as an 'enemy' when I had tried so hard to be her friend and who, whichever way the court decided, would continue to be my client and would be bound to be hostile. In addition I was uncomfortable and tired and I had to keep my charges occupied for as long as the court thought fit to keep us waiting.

I have set this scene at some length although I am sure it is all too familiar.

After some time we had exhausted the possibilities for fun with the ever-present pencils and paper. We had sung songs and said rhymes. I had anxiously tried to stop the youngest from running round. But why was I worried? Whatever could we do next? We *all* needed to be occupied.

Something sparked us off and there we were playing operations. I was mum sitting in the corner; I was powerless and unwanted while the all-powerful surgeon began to operate. The oldest girl was the surgeon, her sister the nurse and the little girl, the victim. We had our coats off and were really thoroughly absorbed. At last we had forgotten ourselves and our situation and the surgeon had raised her arm for an incision which would grace a human sacrifice and the door opened and the court usher came in. And of course we were wanted in a hurry.

The game was the idea of the children. Like Sally with the jelly, I doubt if they intended anything more than an acting out of a television programme or book, that is, they meant just what they said and did, a game. But I thought then and still think that the kind of game was significant; it was a game of power and action, impotent children wielding the power of life and death, an apparently powerful adult relegated to the sidelines. I needed that game too, for my feelings to be caught up in a drama different from the 'tru-life' drama of that court. For I was in no more control of the situation than the children. I could not control the court to provide a decent waiting area (a magistrate once sent an usher out to tell a social worker to keep a child quiet!); I could not control the length of waiting time; I could not foresee or control what would happen inside the court room. There another kind of game took place, the word game of courts throughout the world and familiar from a million court-room dramas.

It was a long time ago but that playing has stayed vivid in my mind. It was nothing in the lives of those children I suppose, only a few minutes of time and not likely to be remembered by them. But it was important for those moments and social workers and children should have the opportunity to make such moments more bearable, if possible to use them constructively. And if juvenile courts do not agree . . . ?

The care order was discharged.

PS: Play therapy

I do not believe that play therapists have a monopoly on therapeutic playing and I hope that everything I have said in this chapter will help to give confidence to any social worker who has thought that play is not part of her job. However it would be very wrong not to say strongly that play therapy is a highly developed and important contribution to the range of possibilities of help for distress.

I am struck by the basic principles of guidance for play therapists formulated by Virginia Axline (1947) and listed (below) by Martin Herbert (1975, pp. 423–4). It seems to me that everything in this list is of direct relevance to the playing social worker and as such forms an appropriate conclusion to this chapter.

1 The therapist must develop a warm, friendly relationship with the child.
2 He accepts the child exactly as he is.
3 He establishes a feeling of permissiveness in the relationship so that the child feels entirely free to express his feelings.
4 The therapist is alert to recognize the feelings expressed by the child and to reflect those feelings back to him in such a manner that he gains insight into his behaviour.
5 He maintains a deep respect for the child's ability to solve his own problems if given an opportunity to do so. The responsibility for making choices and for instituting change is the child's.
6 The clinician does not attempt to hurry therapy along. It is a gradual process.
7 He does not attempt to direct the child's actions or conversation in any manner. The child leads the way and the therapist follows.
8 The therapist establishes only those limitations to the child's behaviour that are necessary to anchor the therapy to the world of reality and to make the child aware of his responsibility in the relationship [and surely to protect him from physical harm!].

Chapter 4

Words About Words

'I can't get the words out' said a twelve-year-old boy to his social worker. 'Perhaps', said his social worker to me, 'it's *my* need for communication. I'm a very verbal and articulate person.'

Thirteen-year-old Maurice said to his child guidance clinic social worker

'How do you know what I feel, when I don't?' He imagined that I had a secret store of books where I looked up everything that I said (Richards, 1971, p. 7).

The social worker may well understand that 'The child cannot always express in words his inner feelings, even when he has a great need to do so' (Kastell, 1962, p. 228) but this understanding will not necessarily free her from the feeling that she can succeed in communicating with the child only if full verbalization is achieved.

Most social workers must be familiar with attempting to talk to an adolescent client, only to be met with long, uncomfortable silences, interspersed with the occasional 'don't know', accompanied by angry penetrating glances which say 'what's it got to do with you anyway?' Under such circumstances I have often been compelled to burble like an idiot to fill in uncomfortable silences, particularly if another adult is witness to my sorry failure to establish contact with the young person. Sometimes I have been ashamed to confirm for a child the view that an adult is someone who turns up now and again to ask dull or irrelevant questions such as 'How are you getting on at school these days?' (Williams, 1978, p. 15).

Barbara Williams is well aware that 'words alone as a means of communication are not enough' (p. 15). Perhaps the pinnacle of communication is illustrated by this story about Dr Winnicott.

He had stayed with a family in Denmark. The following year he was to make a return visit and the children of the family when told of this showed obvious delight. Questioned about this, they referred to him as 'the Englishman who spoke Danish'. Donald Winnicott spoke no Danish. But his exceptional facility for communicating with children, even when words were not involved, had led them to experience him as speaking their language (Thomas, 1977, p. 1).

Endeavour to achieve perfect verbal understanding may be misleading and may inhibit real communication; I once spent some days with some *educateurs spécialisés* in France. Since I spoke no French and my first contact, Mlle Jarny, spoke no English, I was accompanied by two French English-teachers who, however, knew nothing about social work in either country. For two hours Mlle Jarny and I spoke urgently to our interpreters and they consulted together and translated. Then I was invited to stay for lunch but they had to leave. Mlle Jarny and I assured them that we thought we could manage and with evident doubt of that they left. After that Mlle Jarny and her colleagues and I started to communicate. Left to ourselves we timidly tried out our smatterings of each other's language and found that we could understand best if we each spoke our own native tongue, particularly as I had taken my old school dictionary. But what most helped communication was not facility with the language of either France or England but our shared familiarity with the language of our professional preoccupation, working directly with children. Perhaps it was significant that of all names that of Dr Winnicott was spoken by all of us with respect and that he even provided us with a chance to enjoy the most universal use of the voice, laughter, as we shared a bi-lingual joke about transitional objects. I tell this story to illustrate the point that sometimes too much attention to the precise usage and meaning of words may obscure true meaning and prevent rather than enhance communication. Spontaneity, directness, shared interest and caring can transcend barriers of language where these are erected by nationality, intelligence, age or experience.

However difficult it may be and however many other means of communication are employed, social workers do have to use words and this chapter is a discussion of some aspects of verbal language in social work with children.

Words

Words are so useful and so dangerous. Because they are the usual currency of communication, if not always the prime means of transmitting messages almost always accompanying the other methods, it is easy to overlook their power, their ambiguity and the fact that verbal intercourse does not necessarily imply communication. It is also easy to attribute

> communication failure ... to the ambiguities and deficiencies of the medium used, language for example, as if language is constructed to mislead the people who use it. But words are instruments of expression to the perception, motivation and capacity of the people who use them (Day, 1972, p. 7).

Words are not little demons with blowpipes and poisoned darts, but instruments of thought and expression which can be used well or ill according to the user's percipience (Parry, 1968, p. 59).

In most of her professional contacts the social worker is likely to have greater mastery of spoken language than her clients and this is almost certain to be so if the clients are children. For one thing the social worker has had more years to practice using language in many different ways and for another the client (adult or child) is probably less confident than the social worker during their contacts and therefore more likely to be self-conscious about and inhibited in the choice and use of words.

> The interviewer is more skilled in the use of words than is the child, partly because he is an adult, but more particularly because they are his familiar tools. The responsibility for their proper use, and for understanding what the child means when they are used inappropriately, is the interviewer's (Rich, 1968, p. 41).

John Rich does not expand his point about an inappropriate use of words (I write below about individual use of words) nor does he explain what is their proper use but the essence of the sentence is that 'the responsibility . . . for understanding what the child means . . . is the interviewer's.'

In order to achieve this understanding the social worker needs to be aware of many things including her own use and understanding of and emotional investment in and reaction to words and her reaction to the use of words by other people in general as well as of this child in particular. For example, I once knew of someone who was extremely sensitive to split infinitives to the extent that a point made in a staff meeting might lose all force for her if the speaker had thus offended ; thus my acquaintance had an emotional reaction to a use of language which coloured her reaction to the content of the actual words and the intent of the speaker. It is well known that the 'wrong' accent can prejudice the reception of spoken material.

In an experiment different groups of students were given the same lecture by an actor who adopted a different accent for each presentation; the students rated the lecture according to its serious-ness and usefulness and general academic efficacy and the result of the experiment showed that this identical material was rated as better or worse according to the attitude of the students to the accent used by the actor, so that, for example, the delivery in so-called received pronunciation was regarded as more authoritative than that in certain regional accents.

Social workers must, like anyone else, be subject to such traps and prejudices. What social worker has not been seduced into assuming the presence of insight when a client can speak fluently with a good vocabulary, an 'educated' accent, and even familiarity with Freud? While poor verbalization may all too easily be taken to reflect inability to understand.

We pour forth and waste words because they are free, because perhaps we do not trust other forms of communication, perhaps we fear silence. The gifts of spoken language and of free speech are trampled and exploited in all manner of meaningless and dangerous and bitter ways. We rejoice when our children learn to speak and yet how quickly they learn too to contaminate their speech with the expression and communication of hating and hurting, greed and dissatisfaction. If words had to be paid for would they not be used with more care?

Words used between social workers and clients *are* paid for (even though social workers are not paid by the word or even by the interview). Only so many words can be spoken and received in an hour and *this* hour, *these* words may be crucial to *this* client *now*. How precious therefore are those words, how vital for the social worker to attend to and care about everything that is said, to *hear* everything and also to remember that

> It is not so much the words that are used in an interview of stress that will be of interest to the caseworker, but the feeling tone behind them. . . . Words are not absolute in their usage, and communication between individuals can be hampered by words as much as assisted by them (Kastell, 1962, p. 17).

Sound without sight

In our strange society one sense is often used exclusively. I sometimes wonder whether it is a function of civilization to separate the senses, for primitive man needed fully to employ all his senses all the time to survive (for example when hunting). Not only is twentieth-century western man expected to manage communication by sight alone (reading/writing) and sound alone (telephone/radio) but he is even well on the way to reproducing himself without physical contact between man and woman.

It is customary to regard people deprived of a sense as handicapped, for example, blind or deaf, and to expect them to have more difficulty in managing their interaction with the world than those with the use of all senses. And yet normal people are often artifically deprived of the use of all but one sense and expected with perfect ease to use this remaining sense to effect complete communication.

Social workers are particularly affected by this dual blessing and curse of modern technology. Reports, records and letters are written and read, and hours without number and spent on the telephone disussing with invisible and possibly never-met people the lives and destinies of not-present clients.

Yet what a difficult instrument the telephone is. Responses are expected quickly; there is no way to play for time except by talking feverishly while thinking of a way out from an awkward question; in face-to-face contact pauses can be achieved in any number of non-verbal ways but on the telephone the slightest silence is met with

'Are you still there?' 'Yes', you may say, 'I'm just thinking about it.'
But thinking costs as much as talking on the telephone and
expensive minutes must be spent on words not on thoughts. At least
words prove that the other person *is* 'still there', at least physically.
For the telephone is a great encourager of lies. You may hold the
receiver in one hand and a book or pen in the other while assuring
your interlocutor that she has your full attention. You may yawn or
grimace to yourself while promising that you are enormously
looking forward to meeting her soon. You may say that you are in
London when you are really in Leeds. All too often that desperate
plea 'Are you still there?' is met with the silence which shows that
indeed you have gone, cut off by the implacable mechanism of the
telephone system. Sometimes not knowing that the connection has
been severed you talk on, sometimes exasperated by the conversation you hang up. To be cut off in that way is in my experience
cruel in the extreme. At least in face-to-face contact if the other
person starts to leave before *you* have finished you can call to her, run
after her, even catch hold of her and there is a chance of renewing
negotiations. If the telephone is slammed against you, you must go
through that slow process of dialling the number; and perhaps your
call will not be answered. For many people talking via a machine and
without visual contact is very difficult and threatening and yet this
handicap is never expected of and rarely confessed by those such as
social workers who need to use the telephone in order to work
effectively. I believe that much poor communication and distrust
of one another is caused by discomfort and lack of ability in using
the telephone. Many people are unnaturally brusque or diffident or show less concern and sensitivity than they would face to
face.

I think social workers probably engage with children on the
telephone less than with adults not least because the problems of
telephone conversation are often exacerbated when between adult
and child. Although children usually love the telephone and wish to
speak to any caller their conversation is often far below the level of
their face-to-face discourse because unless they know the other
speaker very well indeed they have difficulty in putting together the
disembodied voice and the real person; (I suspect that for many
people this is never overcome).

I have spent some time on this discussion of the telephone because
not only do I think it is of importance to social workers in its own
right but also I see the points above as of equal relevance to
communication when all the senses are available. To concentrate the
discussion on working with children, whenever a social worker and
child meet together their contact is fundamentally as contrived and
artificial as a telephone conversation. The child may have all his
senses and his wits about him but he cannot be sure just which bits of
himself are required in this interaction. Like an unsure person on

the telephone he may have great difficulty in regulating the force and form of his utterances; something passionately felt may come out apathetically, something in which he is not greatly interested may sound amazingly definite. This because he is not sure of the medium of communication (that is, conversation on his own with an apparently interested adult) and has very little clue about the expectations and inner reactions of the other party to the communication (that is the social worker). Does a child ever ask his social worker 'Are you still there?' If he did, what answer would he get? Often, I am sure, the child puts down his mental receiver, maybe still offering verbal responses but no longer listening to a conversation which does not really seem to be of concern to him.

Do you understand?

How often does an adult say to a child 'Do you understand?' and how often dare that child say 'No'? I include a section on this common question because it seems to me that it is all but impossible to answer.

'Do you understand?' can be asked in relation to so many different kinds of question and subject. The only occasions on which one is really likely to say a straightforward 'No' are when being addressed in a foreign language. ' "Wspominam dnie – gdy ojciec gryzlz zalu paznokcie," ... Do you understand?' No, because I don't understand Polish; (this is actually a line from a poem, 'I remember the days – when father bit his nails in woe'). The foreign language need not necessarily be that of another country; talk to me about statistics or nuclear physics and I can still confidently say that I do *not* understand especially if you use the technical vocabulary of the subject.

To some questions one can give a straightforward 'Yes'. 'Do you understand how to make a cup of tea?' 'Yes'; I understand the question and I know how to perform the action of making tea (although even that question may be deceptively simple since I may not have understood that the questioner is interested in the finer points of Lapsang Souchong and Earl Grey and the philosophy of Eastern tea ceremonies).

Social workers are constantly met with far more complex 'Do you understand?' questions. 'I feel so depressed; do you understand?' The answer may be 'Yes' (I know how *I feel* when I describe myself as depressed and I know how *you behave* when you describe yourself as depressed). But it may also be 'No' (I don't understand exactly what *you* mean by depression and *I* don't know what feelings and experiences you may have which I either could not recognize or understand even if you did try to communicate them to me). Or, 'I hate my mother; do you understand?' 'Yes' (I think your mother is a cow and I'm not surprised you hate her). 'No' (I have never experienced such a feeling about either your mother or mine so I cannot understand what you mean). 'No' (I don't know what hating feels like to you; it may be different from my idea of hatred; do you mean that you don't like her much today or that you're on your way to kill her?).

The main problem about understanding is knowing that you *don't* understand. It is easy enough to acknowledge that I don't understand relativity or how a terrorist can kill a child but if I believe that I understand Christianity or how my husband feels today or what are the essential requirements in a foster home or what my social worker expects of me, how will I know that I *don't* understand? And if I say that I *do* understand, how will anyone *know* that I *don't*? It may be revealed in my words and actions; if I say that I understand how to make tea and then use cold water it will be plain that I don't understand. But if you tell me that I am a bad, wicked girl for jumping on the bed with my friends in the midst of a glorious romp and ask if I understand I am bound to say 'Yes' to avoid further censure and you may go away satisfied (especially if I say I'm sorry); but I'm sure *I* won't have understood and *you* won't know whether I have or not.

Often and often we say 'Yes, I understand' to avoid the embarrassment or disgrace of revealing that it is all too difficult; (an everyday example of this is when asking directions: after the third repetition of incomprehensible instructions one says 'Thank you' and drives away, no wiser but desperate to simulate comprehension because further elucidation will be too irritating or painful).

The particular relevance of all this to working with children is that I believe it is very often difficult for them to acknowledge lack of understanding even if they recognize it. Not that I think social workers bombard their child clients with 'Do you understand?' (or do they?). But this question must surely underlie a great deal of social worker – child interaction since so much of this is concerned with the endeavour to help children understand and manage their past, present and future. The social worker must all the time bear in mind that she does not understand what and how the child understands; nothing can be taken for granted and no question or piece of information is simple.

There's glory for you

'I don't know what you mean by "glory" ', Alice said. Humpty Dumpty smiled contemptuously. 'Of course you don't – till I tell you. I meant "there's a nice knock-down argument for you." '
'But "glory" doesn't mean "a nice knock-down argument",' Alice objected.
'When *I* use a word,' Humpty Dumpty said in rather a scornful tone, 'it means just what I choose it to mean – neither more nor less.'

'The question is,' said Alice, 'whether you *can* make words mean so many different things.'
'The question is,' said Humpty Dumpty, 'which is to be the master – that's all.' (Carroll, 1948, p. 116).

I am hardly the first writer to leap with joy on this glorious interchange between Humpty Dumpty and Alice; how beautifully Carroll sums up not only a philosophical dilemma but also a fact of verbal life; learning and using language is about one kind of mastery but there is also the mastery of imposing one's own meaning on a word and then imposing that meaning on other people's use of that word. Common English usage is full of words whose original meanings have been changed by the force of habit (for example sophisticated, prestigious, sublime). Far more common than such national 'misuses' of words are local, family and individual uses of words which to the general public mean one thing and to the initiated user, something else. Easy to think of are the myriad names for the lavatory (WC, toilet, ladies, gents, loo, little room, george, john, bathroom, powder room . . .) These are so straightforward and well known that it takes a minute to realize that the names are in fact euphemisms or individual names. Beginning a job in a new city, I was confused to be invited into the house when I was already indoors; 'house' meant the living room, while on a boating holiday the little girl used 'house' to mean the seat at the stern.

Very often children's attempts to master words lead to glory but inaccuracy and confusion and maybe to interesting individual usage. As a child my husband, hearing 'a long felt want' as 'a long felt mont' looked vainly for a lengthy cuddly article. As a Girl Guide at church parade I used to feel desperately embarrassed when in the Creed we all announced that 'He did not abhor the Virgin's womb'. I had no clue what 'abhor' meant but associated with 'womb' I thought it must be something which should really not be mentioned in front of the Scouts. Everyone must have memories of this kind. Yet children accept and do not like to ask about these words which seem to be calmly accepted as perfectly sensible by adults.

Often if a child does not know the usual word for a thing he will supply the deficiency with a coverall word for, example 'thingy', or use another word which sounds likely. In a group of four adolescent girls, Gillian

> . . . made a face whilst drinking coffee, and when I asked her why, she attempted to overcome her verbal limitations and replied, 'There's a stapler in between my sugars.' She had found a staple at the bottom of her coffee cup. I asked her what, if 'staple' was 'stapler', she called the stapling machine. 'A stabilizer' she replied (McConnell, 1979, pp. 25–6).

Marilyn McConnell's work with her group was characterized by her care never to put down a girl for verbal inability or mistakes; rather she accepted conversation on its own level and helped the girls to develop confidence in using words, partly by gently supplying the correct word by introducing it into a sentence herself without criticizing a misuse.

> K (to me, pointing at the ceiling). 'I broke the long thing at Christmas.'
> M. 'She means the light bulb.' (interupting).
> Me. 'Oh, you mean the fluorescent tube.' (elaborating) (p. 26).

Adults all too often play word games with children and then wonder why those children are inarticulate with them. A girl in school asked her headmaster if she might 'have a lay down on the couch'. In her local accent she said 'doon' and 'cooch'. 'On the what?' asked the adult. 'The bed?' 'The what?' 'The sofa?' 'The what?'. The girl was getting desperate. How many words did he want from her for a thing for lying down on; and what a lot of words she had been able to supply considering that she was feeling poorly and faced with the stressful situation of approaching her headmaster. She tried once more: 'The settee?'. She was dismissed for her 'lay doon' and the headmaster revealed (in his own local accent) that he had wanted her to say 'couch' like 'cowch'.

Much questioning of children (in school and out of it) is of the word-game variety too. Five-year-old Daniel told his mother after his first day at school, 'They had a Union Jack and they asked if anyone knew what it was. So I put my hand up. I thought *someone* had better tell them.' Poor Daniel. He still believed that adults asked children questions because they genuinely wanted to know the answers.

Just as a child may use any word in an individual and idiosyncratic way, any word may have for him a particular and unique significance.

> Walking along a lane with some children I knew well, I idly picked some of the flowers *I* knew as cow parsley; the oldest child stopped me with evidence of some distress because *he* called the flowers 'mother-die'; his mother's desertion years ago had resulted in the children's current residence in care and the boy was still grieving and bewildered; I knew and he knew I knew, though we seldom spoke of it; the flower name made an opportunity for him to refer to his feelings without either of us having to embark on lengthy conversation (Wardle, 1975, p. 431).

Understanding and respecting the personal and unique use of language can save a great many words; not understanding or despising it can lead to waste of words and impossibility of communication.

What's your name?

One of the most common ways of using words in unique and individual applications is in naming of people. A first name may be lengthened or shortened (John, Johnny, Jo), a surname altered into a nickname (Brown, Browny) or a completely new name attached

(Mouse, Thing). Use of a personal or nickname is usually limited to a group of friends and family or perhaps to only one other person (I refer *not* to nicknames used only behind someone's back). It can be a grave mistake to use a personal name without permission for child or adult will feel this to be an intrusion.

One's name expresses oneself and something about the image which one is hoping to project in any particular situation. Addressed by the wrong name one may be very disappointed. For example, in common with many people I am known by my second name; on official lists and documents I appear as Joan instead of Margaret. If therefore someone addresses me as 'Joan Crompton' I feel disorientated because I can be called that only by someone who knows not *me* but only my official name; and I would be called by this name only in some potentially uncomfortable setting such as a doctor's waiting room or hospital, where in any case I would be having a hard time keeping sense of self and confidence.

I am sometimes slightly affronted if someone addresses me just as Margaret if I have not given permission for that and certainly if I am not expected to address that person by first name also; the staff of various institutions are very prone to this practice, addressing patients and residents by first names but expecting to be known as Nurse or Doctor, Mrs or even Sir. A patient in a psychiatric unit was known for years by his first name (Fred) which had been learned by the staff from his file. But in the outside world he was known by his second name (Jo); since apparently no one took the trouble to ask what he would like to be known as he was doomed to be misnamed and thus, in a way, insulted.

Children are particularly likely to be misnamed or to have their private names used without permission by adults. It is absolutely vital for adults to discover and respect by what name any child wishes to be known or any other person in the variety of situations in which the child lives. Here is a beautiful picture of the problems raised for a misnamed child. The heroine is seven and this is her first day at school.

'Anna Grå' says the teacher, suddenly. And for Josephine everything stands still. You could hear a pin drop where she sits. Her heart flies up into her throat, but she can't move a muscle. Anna Grå – that's the name Josephine used to have – ages and ages ago; she doesn't like it and doesn't want to be called by it. She'd almost forgotten it! Instead she called herself Josephine Joandersson. And everyone calls her Josephine. Everyone! 'Anna Grå.' The teacher's voice is heard again. But Josephine just sits, as if turned to stone. Now it is doubly clear to her: this *can't* be her real teacher. The real one would have known that Anna Grå no longer exists. She'd have called out Josephine.
'Isn't Anna Grå here, either?' the imposter asks; and then Mama goes up to her and says quietly, but so that everyone can hear:
'Yes, of course she is.' And looking at Josephine she says, a little more loudly: 'Get up now, Josephine dear.' Then Josephine obeys and meets

teacher's eyes – pierces her with a look – while Mama explains that at home she is usually called Josephine. Josephine, she says, isn't used to being called Anna. That's why she didn't get up at once. The teacher laughs . . All the mothers laugh. But not the children. They stare at her. All of them.

'Oh, so it's like that, is it?' says the teacher. 'But here in school we must all be known by our proper names. Mustn't we, Anna, dear?'

Josephine looks at her without replying. And when teacher says she can sit down, she goes on standing. Because it is Anna Grå the teacher is addressing, not her.

'Sit down, Josephine, dear,' Mama's voice is heard saying: and instantly Josephine sits down (Gripe, 1974, pp. 12–13).

Josephine is betrayed by both mother and teacher because neither understands the importance to her whole self-image of her name. Worse than that, neither adult shows any sensitivity at all to the little girl's feelings in the terrifying world of the new schoolroom. Not only is she worried about going to school at all but also she is depersonalized, stripped of her way of finding dignity and significance and laughed at by the very person who should be offering help. And such experience is by no means uncommon for children in schools and hospitals and residential institutions and social-work contacts. 'Here in school', says the teacher, 'We must all be known by our proper names'. But who decides if a name is proper or not?

If the teacher is able to force Josephine to respond to the hated name Anna Grå she will prove that she is a person of enormous power, power so great that she can even change another person's name. Naming and power have been associated since man first used names. Loss of name means loss of identity and therefore of the power of being and knowing oneself to be *this* particular unique person. Giving one's name to another person gives them the potential for exercising some power over one. If you have my name you have, for example, the means to discover my telephone number and address and thus to be able to contact me by telephone, letter or visit. Depending on what information and permission I give you you can address me as Mrs Crompton or Margaret. If I am a child caught by you committing some offence with other children you can name me both on the spot and to other people. If with the other children I run away I am more likely to respond to 'Stop, Margaret' than to a generalized 'Stop'.

Naming is of the most universal, subtle and ancient importance. Social workers who hope to communicate with children must be aware of the many significances which may attach to the name or names of those children. It may be that the child wishes to be known by one particular name but is prevented either by the refusal of the powerful adults to use it or the inability of the child to let un-listening adults know. Or it may be equally important to the child to keep private his personal name, whether this is a nickname exclusive to friends or family or a name kept completely secret, precious to the child and not to be sought by anyone else.

'What's your name?' is probably one of the most frequently asked questions and the two or three words which constitute one's name are probably written down more times than any other words in one's life. And all without thought.

One last word about words and power, this time not about the use of personal names for people but of the power of naming an object or condition.

The extract speaks for itself.

> I heard of a child who played all day inseparably with a boy called Johnny, a West Indian boy. Johnny's mother went to work and Mandy's didn't, so Johnny had his meals with Mandy and went home at night. When Mandy and Johnny were five they started school. Mandy came home – without Johnny.
> 'Where's Johnny, then?' said her mother.
> A haughty shrug. Silence.
> 'Where is he?'
> Silence.
> 'Is he coming later?'
> Silence. The mother, perplexed, left her and went inside to get tea ready. Then –
> 'Tea's ready. Has Johnny come?'
> Silence.
> 'Isn't he having tea today?'
> Silence.
> 'What's the matter? Where *is* Johnny? Have you had a quarrel? What's happened?'
> 'Well,' said Mandy, tossing her head with what Blake called Experience. 'He never told me he was black!' (Berg, 1972, p. 36).

'Tell us what you think'

> 'It's the only thing to do' said Mama. Something hard and unhappy rose inside Anna.
> 'Is it all settled, then?' she asked. 'Don't you even want to know what we think?'
> 'Of course we do,' said Mama, 'but the way things are, we haven't much choice.'
> 'Tell us what you think,' said Papa (Kerr, 1974, p. 177–8).

The conversation is within a family of Jews. The decision is to leave Hitler's Germany. It is indeed 'the only thing to do' but Anna is right, the opinions of herself and her brother should be sought and attended to even if they cannot affect the action of the adults who are not only powerful *vis-a-vis* the children but also responsible for them.

The decisions on which social workers need to consult children will be less globally dramatic than that in which Anna was involved but they will be of no less importance to the individual children. However

> the adult world tends to ignore children unless they are causing trouble ... there is always a tendency for a child being interviewed by a stranger to jump to the conclusion that the only reason for the adult's interest is because the child has done something wrong. (I once heard the porter on a train trying to be friendly with a young child. He opened the conversation by saying, 'Are you a good boy?' Would he have approached the child's mother saying 'Are you a moral woman?') (Rich, 1968, p. 34).

I am reminded of the quotation from Barbara Williams (1978, p. 15)

> Sometimes I have been ashamed to confirm for a child that an adult is someone who turns up now and again to ask dull or irrelevant questions.

I think that when adults are reluctant to engage in conversation with children there are three main reasons. One is that the adult thinks there is some special language which must be employed in order that that strange creature, a child, may understand communication from this quite different creature, an adult; but (not surprisingly) the adult does not know this language and therefore, feeling tongue tied and inadequate, prefers not to risk failure. The second is that the adult does not trust the child and is therefore not interested in trying to communicate because the contribution of the child cannot have any effect or validity. And the third is that the adult is concerned only with his own interests and occupation and cannot be bothered to find out how the child converses. If these attitudes are present singly or in any combination the child will be aware and one of the main sources of cue will be in the language used by the adult. Thus 'Are you a good boy?' cannot achieve any response but a reluctant 'Yes' and an end to further contribution from the child and Barbara Williams's question 'How are you getting on at school these days?' may seem to the child to be inspectorial or intrusive but unlikely to be associated with real interest in the *real* life of the child at school (as opposed to his examination results or attendance record).

A delightful illustration of the difference between adult and child perception of the use of language and interaction ... is drawn from the description of Hugo's first day at school already quoted in chapter 1, p. 19. Seven-year-old Hugo has turned up to start school several days late. After making considerable entrance he is given his school books by the teacher who

> exhorts him to look after them and make paper covers.
> Interested, Hugo examines everything. He looks at the pictures and pronounces an opinion on them:
> 'Must be fine to be able to draw like that. Only thing is, it all becomes so flat, when it's drawn. Not like when you carve, that's something you can take hold of.'
> Several times the teacher opens her mouth. Then shuts it again. She looks

like a fish out of water. In the end, she has to interrupt Hugo to make herself heard at all. She realizes that Hugo doesn't understand, she says, but in school children have to sit still and be quiet. The teacher does the talking, and the children just answer when the teacher asks them a question.
Hugo listens attentively to this, but looks frankly astonished.
'Now that's odd,' he says.
'What's so odd about it?' the teacher asks.
'There's no sense in our answering, when we don't know anything. We're the ones who ought to ask the questions' (Gripe, 1962, p. 59).

The teacher is completely unable to converse with Hugo because his innocent and wholly un-cheeky comments and questions challenge her tightly held view of her relationship with and attitude towards both teaching and children. Hugo is suggesting that she should show some interest in him and his ideas and expertise (the carving); what an interesting conversation could have developed out of that. And he quite properly wonders why the system of teaching seems to be topsy-turvy. But this teacher can function only if her system and plan are operated.

In chapter 1 (p. 20) I followed this reference to Hugo and his teacher with a tale from an American school; I repeat this here because I think the juxtaposition makes a poignant and important impact. Hugo would, I am sure, have enjoyed school so much better with teacher John Holt (1970, p. 75) who:

 ... was talking about my class to a twelve-year-old friend. . . . I happened to say that some of the children in may class had been having a conversation. At this my friend looked puzzled. She said, 'You mean these kids were talking about this stuff in class?' . . . 'Yes . . . there are lots of times during the day when the kids can talk to each other, if they wish it, about whatever interests them most. Don't you ever have a time in class when you can talk to other people?' She was almost too astonished to answer.
 Of course I knew what she would answer even before I asked her. Bill Hull once said to me, 'Who needs the most practice talking in school? Who gets the most?' Exactly. The children need it, the teacher gets it.

John Holt's own choice of words in this extract is very interesting. He refers to the girl as his 'friend' and his report of their conversation suggests that indeed adult and child here did interact in a totally equal and 'Adult' manner. But I do not think it is very common for adults to develop true friendships with children (as opposed to friendly relationships deriving from some blood relationship or professional contact). By this I mean that a friendship must have elements of equality and reciprocation; if I accept hospitality at my friend's house I must be prepared to invite her to mine and vice versa. If I expect my friend to accept help from me I must be able to accept her assistance. If my friend and I disappoint each other in some way we must be able to discuss the difficulty without recrimination and with a view to repairing and strengthening our friendship on equal terms. But many adults who think that they have a true friendship with a child would not subscribe to or enact these principles, needing rather to maintain their distance and essential dominance. I suggest that social workers are rarely in a position to be the friends of the children on their caseloads in the full manner which I describe here but that these principles of friendship should underlie the essential professional nature, context and content of this particular kind of contact (that is structured, purposeful, inevitably ending when the need for the relationship ends and with clear roles for both parties to the relationship; if social worker and child continue to know each other after the end of their necessary professional contact, this should be redefined as a true friendship in terms of my comments above).

'Of course I knew what she would answer even before I asked her' is a very interesting statement. In the context of the story and its point, there is no problem about John Holt's claim to foreknowledge. But some points of relevance to social workers arise from it. Even though John Holt thought that he knew what the girl would say he still asked her; and this meant giving her the chance to say what she really thought. In this example we would all expect that the girl would have said a simple factual 'No' but there are plenty of occasions when the adult thinks that he knows what the child's answer will be and in consequence does not bother to ask the question. Or if the question is asked the adult is so concerned with what he expects to hear that he does not listen to what is actually being said.

To comment briefly on the final sentences in the extract I am sure that social worker could be substituted for teacher.

I believe that teachers and social workers have a great deal to learn from and give to each other and this not least in the whole exciting area of language and its use by children and adults. In an exquisitely clear and honest article Hilary Minns (1976, p. 4), an infant-school teacher, quotes from and discusses some tape recordings of conversations between herself and five-year-old John, who was having difficulty in adjusting to life at school.

> I thought it might help the teacher's group to get a clearer picture of John if I talked to him and taped the conversation. : . . . When we sat down I had no idea what we would talk about or how the conversation would develop – in fact although I didn't realize it at the time, I had created an artificial situation where the purpose was outside the talk itself. After all, normally when one talks, there is either a specific task to be performed, or the talk acts as the cement of a relationship. But here, the talk was different: it was something I wanted to capture and detach from John, and show to other people. So John didn't matter to me, really. The content of the talk was unimportant as long as John conveyed some information about himself – his use of language and his personality –

which I could relate to the rest of the group. In fact it was a contrived situation which made any spontaneous talk impossible. I realized afterwards that the conversation was little more than an interview situation, where John was patiently answering my laborious questions.

The last sentence is I think a sad but all too true summary of interviewing; how dreadful that conversation should have to be seen as distinct from (rather than part of) interviewing.

It is tempting to reproduce the whole of this article with its transcripts of snatches of the conversation between not only the teacher and John but also John and his friend Keith where

The tense atmosphere that I think we had both felt during the interrogation is nowhere to be found in this relaxed and informal setting where the children seem to be completely at ease and are able, through spontaneous talk, to share an experience which is real to them both [feeding guinea pigs]. They are using the talk for their own purposes – it isn't itself the focus of the encounter as it was in the first tape [referred to above]. John even seems to be *enjoying* talking... an aspect of the conversation which never emerged when he was answering my questions (pp. 5–6).

I am sure that many social workers are familiar with the apparent sadness and frustration experienced by Hilary Minns in observing the difference between the lively intense conversation of children together '*enjoying talking*' and the reluctant minimal answers to the adult's well meaning questions.

From this experience Hilary Minns concludes that

I think we must try to listen to children a great deal more and question them a great deal less. We must be less concerned with the information we are trying to extract from them – more often for our own benefit than for theirs – and concentrate more on what they want to learn. We must encourage them to ask us questions and deliberately set up situations for them where they can talk to each other – with or without a tape recorder – but without the presence of a teacher. And, perhaps most important of all, we must be wary of drawing hasty conclusions about a child's failures with language when our information is inadequate; by learning to listen to children and to value what they say at all times, we will be in a much better position to understand the way they talk (p. 8).

Apart from those vital exhortations to listen and to value I think the most important point in that paragraph for social workers is that about being wary of drawing hasty conclusions. On the basis of her own abortive attempts to converse with John the teacher could have made

... a series of decisions about John – that he 'didn't have any language', that 'no one could get through to him' or whatever. And if I had, I would have planned a whole curriculum on that basis... (p. 5).

The truth about John's verbal interactive capabilities was learned only because the teacher was sensitive to his behaviour with both herself and his friend; she respected him enough to look at her own contribution to their failure to communicate instead of taking the easy way and deciding that the child was not communicating while the adult was providing every opportunity for communication. And she trusted him and his friend to be behaving in a way that was normal showing John in his true colours, as his real self, she did not say, 'Ah, of course they're just playing, just being children, what really counts is how he behaves in class or with me'; she said, in effect, 'That is what John is really like, that is what his speech is when he is not constrained; what can *I* do to change.'

The next step from really listening and attending to what a child says and from believing that his views have as much validity as those of any adult is to involve the child fully in discussion of what is to happen between himself and the social worker. Under the heading 'Use of the Child as Consultant', Donald Keat (1974, pp. 87–8) says:

The author has found it useful to discuss the child's views of the solution to his problem. An example follows:

Counsellor: What would you change in order to help with your problem?

Child: I don't know, that's a hard decision. I might change myself so I could get rid of three or four of my problems. I might change myself so I was perfect. Then my mother wouldn't have any reason to yell at me.

Counsellor: Three or four of your problems. Would you tell me some more about the things you would change?

Child: Well, well, I would never say anything at all bad or do anything at all bad. Then my mother wouldn't have anybody to . . . . anything to yell at me about. I'd be better at sports. Do things like that – be, have more friends. Things like that.

In two brief statements, this ten-year-old boy delineated his problems and some possible solutions. The core of his difficulty was a destructive mother-son relationship. His solution was to be good, perhaps too good, in order to meet expectations. This situation required concurrent counselling of mother and son. His second main reason for referral was difficulty getting along with peers. His solution was to be better at sports and to have more friends. This outlook, of course, required some cognitive restructuring regarding the importance of sports and some actual education about the kinds of behaviour that lead to friendships.

At first glance I think the boy's comments seem very sweeping. But at second glance it seems to me that he is partly articulating what is the main aim of every client (of every social worker?) – to be perfect – with more simplicity and honesty than most adults would express. And he is providing one concrete aim, to be better at sports, showing that he is ready, even keen, to undertake work both physical and emotional to solve his problems and improve his life. I cannot help hoping that the counsellor did not dissuade the boy from being better at sports since whatever the counsellor's view of the importance of sports, surely the strength of the boy in identifying an area of his life which he could improve himself and in suggesting that he would work at it was worth far more than any objective view of what kinds of behaviour lead to friendships. In fact, was the counsellor *really* using the Child as Consultant or do his later comments suggest that he was doing no more than engage the boy into his (the counsellor's) own plan for therapy?

An interview situation

Social workers and children are often together in an 'interview situation' whether the setting is social-work department or child's own home, coffee bar or hostel and whether the participants are sitting side by side (or even face to face) or walking along a country lane. An interview is, in my definition, any contact between two or more people where at least one is in the position of client (that is, seeker and/or receiver of service) and at least one is in the position of helper (that is offerer and/or provider of service). The contact becomes an interview when at least one party regards it as having a purpose connected with the underlying reason for the contact (for example, a child in residential care is visited by his social worker *because* he is in care so that is the underlying reason; the social worker hopes to help the child discover why he rejects his mother who wishes to visit him and if possible to enable a relationship to develop between mother and son; contacts are therefore purposeful). I do not see interviews as characterized by deep and long discussion and in working with children the "point" (as seen by the social worker) may never actually be referred to, for a number of contacts may be required in order that social worker and child may meet and begin to trust each other.

I shall in this section use the word 'interview' but stress that I am employing the definition given above.

The essential components of interviewing children are exactly the same as with adults. The social worker is responsible to ensure that her client understands why she is offering or imposing contact at all and what is the purpose for any particular contact. Clarification will probably be a repetitive and developing process; it is never enough to assume that because an explanation has been given at the beginning of the contact the client will continue to remember the substance of that explanation or to accept its relevance to whatever happens later in the contact. The child needs the opportunity to ask questions and to be offered explanations time and again as he relates, in this context, the presence, behaviour and demands of the social worker to his own life and perception of his environment. Clarification includes talking

> in detail about the event which led to her [the social worker's] coming,
> why the child's own parents cannot keep him any longer, where they are,

and when he can expect to see them again. These simple explanations must be given straight away even to very young children and even if they appear not to be listening or understanding. In subsequent interviews these explanations may have to be repeated over and over again together with any new facts about himself and his feelings which the child may contribute to the conversation (Winnicott, 1966, p. 142).

It is sometimes very difficult to decide how much information about his background to give a child and it is very tempting to withhold if the adult considers that some fact might be painful and distressing to the child. But I believe that children have the right to receive and to be trusted and helped to manage their own life histories and circumstances; and painful matters will be far less devastating and easier to manage if they are introduced and discussed by a sensitive and caring social worker than if they are learned in some casual and shocking manner in the playground or from some document. Clare Winnicott (1977, p. 10) suggests

> that the imparting of painful and damaging information could be a long job, and that first much hard work has to be done to build up the child's confidence and trust in the social worker through . . . shared experiences. As these shared experiences are talked over and become part of the child's remembered history, it is likely that sooner or later questions about the past will be raised, tentatively at first, and then bit by bit details will be filled in as the child becomes strong enough for the next part of the story. If the first question can be answered briefly and factually without anything added or commented on that is not implied in the question, the process of finding out the truth is likely to progress at the child's pace.

Recognizing and going at the child's own pace is vital. The child's own pace is likely to be rather different from that of the social worker, with a large caseload and tight schedules, and of the department, with pressures for action of some kind. But nothing positive can be achieved for and with a child who feels rushed or bullied or ignored. Children always indicate when they have had enough just as they indicate when they are involved. As Clare Winnicott says, they may 'appear not to be listening or understanding' but an aware adult can sense that the child with his nose deep in a comic is really listening very hard at this moment while at another moment a wriggle or a question about something on a completely different subject will show that the child now needs a change and continuance with the conversation will lead to nothing but boredom and disengagement.

Which leads me into what may seem like a sidetrack but is I think an important but often overlooked point in working with children. Boredom. In chapter 1 I discussed the boredom of the adult but how often do social workers take into account the boredom of the children? For example, two adults were discussing the welfare and handling of a child who was present during a conversation in which there was a great deal of disagreement. The child was sitting close to one of the adults, cuddling up and clearly involved in the discussion although he was apparently reading a comic and did not make any active contribution (although he was invited to do so in a manner which would have permitted him to question and comment if he had so wished). Later one of the adults asked the child, with whom there was a very good rapport

A 'How did you feel about that?' [typical open social-work question].
C 'I don't know'. [typical reply to impossible question].
A 'Shall I ask you some things you might have felt and you can say if any of them are right?'
C 'Yes'. [no pressure here, the child was interested to see what the answer might be himself].
A 'Did you feel pleased?' [deliberately choosing unlikely emotion].
C 'No'.
A 'Did you feel worried?'
C 'No'.
A 'Did you feel bored?'
C 'Yes' [with a smile; that is right, how funny].
A 'Did you think, "I wish they'd stop all this and let me get my tea"?' [a follow up question to the boredom, partly to let the child know that this feeling was perfectly understandable and acceptable].
C 'Yes.' [more smiling].
A 'What else might you have felt? I can't think of anything.' ['A' genuinely couldn't think of any other feelings at this point but it proved to be a useful question since the child now felt free enough to produce ideas].
C 'Did I *enjoy* it.'
A 'Oh yes – *did* you enjoy it?'
C 'No'. [general amusement but the child had been able to use the word game to give some more information: he had not enjoyed the experience].

I vouch for the authenticity of the conversation and the feelings of the adult as it was myself. As I could see the visual cues of the child's behaviour and as I do know him well I can feel sure that his claim to boredom as the predominating emotion during the long discussion was honest; there would have been no recrimination if he had expressed worry and indeed he was able to say that he had not enjoyed it. But he *was* bored; not disturbed or anxious or upset or guilty. And I do think that those strong emotions are often wrongly and too freely attributed to children who are then expected to manifest the behaviour which accompanies them; and nothing more provokes a kind of behaviour than expectation. I have bored a great many children in my social working life by my insistence they should conform to my agenda and I know the signs!

In the conversation quoted above the adult was trying to help the child express any feelings he might have about the activity and behaviour of some adults which directly affected him and this is another of the prime components of social-work interviewing. It is often more convenient *not* to know what a client thinks about what is happening to or planned for him, particularly if there is the slightest chance that he might not like it. Clare Winnicott (1966, pp. 142–3) refers to

> a thirteen-year-old boy whose mother had died when he was three and who had lived ever since in a foster home where the father was also a lodger. One day when he was twelve and a half the father went away with no explanation to the boy and then after some weeks reappeared with a wife, having settled down to live in another town. In the meantime the boy had been received into the care of the local authority but remained in the same foster home. The father then wanted the boy to go and live with him in the new house, and everyone concerned felt this to be the best plan – except the boy, who said to the child-care worker, 'If you make me go and see my father I'll be ill'. When the day came for him to go and visit his father, who hoped to be able to persuade him to stay, the boy was in fact ill. What was urgently needed in this case was for everyone to stop trying to manage the external situation and for the worker to apply the casework technique of helping the boy to put into words his feelings about his father. . . . . Verbalizations . . . do not immediately solve problems but they are the first step towards the possibility of a solution.

A next step from verbalization is discussion, for simply to state that one feels and thinks this or that cannot be helpful on its own. Encouraging a child to put his feelings into words may be hard enough for a social worker who is busy but she has then to be prepared to respond to and help with those feelings and for this a considerable amount of time may be needed, for such commitments cannot be fulfilled in one meeting. Louise DeCosta (1976, p. 13) writes of work with bereaved adolescents who were in urgent need of help and who

> were described to us variously as 'sad, withdrawn, having poor appetite, upsetting the rest of the family with uncontrollable behaviour, moping a lot, talking about leaving school and feeling as if everything is too much'. Although referring agents presented a fairly typical picture of three troubled adolescent girls we sensed the referrers were themselves quite anxious and responded by offering individual appointments within a week.
> During the first ten minutes of our initial meeting, each of the girls said their fathers had died during the past year and added they were 'just like dad'. They voiced feelings of personal helplessness, a lack of self-respect, and continuing depression. It seemed to us that in fact these adolescents 'set the agenda' for the limited work together. They themselves introduced father's death but, remarkably, none of the referrers mentioned it.

A small group was set up and many aspects of the girls' lives with and feelings about their fathers (including *how each girl saw herself before and since father's death*) were discussed.

> The final session included a review of what in our work was experienced as helpful and the girls were offered the possibility of returning to the clinic at some time in the future. . . .

The girls later told us this was the first time they had 'really talked' about the loss of father and what it meant to them (p. 14).

There is a great deal of interest in these extracts (indeed in the whole article) but I will emphasize two points. One is that the referrers (who are not identified) 'were themselves quite anxious' about the girls and, I infer, about themselves in this context but (or should that be 'and'?) did not refer to the bereavements when referring the girls. These workers had, it seems, been inhibited by the problem which the girls presented to themselves from properly attending to or helping the girls, to the point where they could or did not acknowledge the key area of the girls' distress.

The other point is that the girls were not only regarded with respect and care within this agency so that they were given very quick individual appointments and then offered the opportunity to talk about themselves in a well thought out group but also they were involved in 'a review of what . . . was experienced as helpful', they were actually asked what they thought about what the worker and her agency had offered them. Moreover they were not dismissed once the official treatment was thought by the agency to be completed but were 'offered the possibility of returning to the clinic at some time in the future'.

There is of course no point in encouraging another person to talk or to offer an opportunity for discussion if one is not prepared to listen; *really* to listen, to hear and attend to and consider every word. A friend recently told me that she intended to lose a large amount of weight by a certain date. I expressed interest but did not enquire whether or not that date had any significance; I *assumed* that it was chosen simply to help her discipline herself on her diet. Later her boy friend asked if she had told me that they had decided to get married – on that date. My friend *had* been trying to tell me but I had not recognized the cue. I could forgive myself for that poor listening since that was not the only chance for my friends to give the information but I did feel annoyed with myself for not having noticed that I had not given a wholly satisfactory response to the first information about slimming. And how often this kind of cue is missed in social-work contacts because the social worker is not really listening and is content, as I was here, with her own assumption about the significance of a comment.

However I do not think that even social workers can hear and respond appropriately to every significant comment and cue all the time and if that were the standard to be attained I imagine most of us would give up in despair. Sometimes one doesn't really *hear* what has been said (or may have been meant) until long after the actual conversation; then strikes the ray of recognition and the painful self-questioning begins, 'why didn't I realize what he meant?', and one works out those perfect scripts; first the one that might have been and then the one that will be read together at the next contact. I believe that the ability to hear after the event may be even more important than responding immediately during an interview, provided that it is linked with the ability to go back and offer the opportunity for a further discussion. Which doesn't mean imposing one's own and exciting discovery on the startled child but does imply finding a way to go back and to give the child the opportunity to return to that point if he so wishes. As a social worker I often used to feel distressed and guilty if I realized that I had not heard properly the first time and it was not easy to go back to a client, child or adult, to try and gain another chance. But I now think that it may often be an advantage to both client and social worker to work in this way for the client too may have heard things in a new way after the contact; further, the social worker during the interview may have responded intuitively to many spoken and unspoken cues and quite properly have ignored those points which later seem to vital; to have responded at the time might well have been to break into some other important piece of interaction. Also it must, I think, be very beneficial to the relationship between social worker and client if the social worker is able to say 'I'm sorry, I didn't really realize what you were saying last week when . . .' or 'I was thinking about what you said and I suddenly thought . . .' I suppose I am writing about basic social casework practice and yet I feel that, particularly in work with children, there is still the possibility of reluctance to 'go back'.

Sometimes not-listening occurs because adults have not recognized that verbal communication is being offered and sought. For example Emma, resident in a ward of a mental-subnormality hospital,

> was lying quietly on a mattress, watching the end of the room where she occasionally saw a nurse walk past, or a volunteer pushing one of the more able children up and down in a wheelchair.
> Two visitors arrived to see . . . another of the children. . . . Emma looked up at the visitors as they passed her on the mat and said 'ah-ah-ah-ah', but they did not notice her. . . .
> Emma's apparently meaningless babblings and threshings about ceased to be meaningless when there was time to notice her vocalizations and movements in the context of what was taking place in the immediate environment. She made the 'ah-ah' noise when the visitors arrived and straightaway began her slow kicking movements towards them. Her behaviour may be likened to that of any young child who is pleased to see visitors and wants to see what they have brought. A non-handicapped child in that situation may have said a clear 'hello' and run up to the visitors. (Oswin, 1978, pp. 112–13).

This picture of Emma is dramatic because Emma's language is so obviously different from that of a non-handicapped child and because, like the visitors, many adults including social workers would ignore what seemed to be meaningless babblings. But I suggest that the communications of more articulate children using recognizable language are also passed by, mistaken also for meaningless babblings. Both children and adolescents are likely to be unable and/or unwilling to engage in conversations comprising more than a few exchanges and social workers need to listen both within those exchanges and between them in order both to catch everything which is said and to be ready for the next moment at which conversation as opposed to chat becomes possible.

Clare Winnicott (1977, p. 10) requires

> Social workers . . . to train themselves to listen with a third ear, only thus will they catch and understand the real purpose of communication and be in a position to respond appropriately and help the child to a new understanding of himself and his anxieties;

but I think that the two ears we have already would be quite sufficient if we really used them for really listening.

Listening is needed not only for the comments and statements of children but also for their questions. This is not the place to list and discuss different kinds of questions and possible responses; I wish only to emphasize that the questions people ask often indicate a great deal about their hopes and anxieties and preoccupations and that a question framed in one way may well mask a more important but more difficult or dangerous question.

It is the social worker's job not only to listen meticulously but also to provide opportunities for children to listen without necessarily offering any response. Although it is vital that children should never feel that they are being talked about behind their backs it is sometimes very useful if concerned adults talk to each other over their heads. If the conversation is purposeful and the adults are engaging in it deliberately and are aware of possible effects on the particular child, much relief and benefit may be gained, especially if the child is free to join in at will. A child in a sulk or a tantrum may be unable to engage in discussion of his feelings and behaviour because he is at that moment too much involved in feeling and behaving. But if the adults who care for and about him station themselves within easy listening distance and discuss him in a benign way he may become interested and relieved and subsequently relax. For example, Jill was in a very bad temper and could not be reached directly. She was tense and stood far away from her parents angrily moving things around on the kitchen table. Her parents were not at all sure what to do and by chance began to talk to each other about her, in her presence:

> 'It's not like Jill to be like this.'
> 'Do you think there's something worrying her?'
> 'I don't know, she just suddenly got cross.'
> 'Could it be anything to do with going to school? She gets terribly tired sometimes.'
> 'She doesn't seem tired today.'

'She might be worried about something. I suppose it must be quite difficult to start at school and make new friends and everything.'

Towards the end of this Jill crept down from the table and approached her parents. By the end she was holding her mother's hand. Her parents had hit on the ideal way to help her; they had not imposed discussion on her but had by their conversation shown her that they were interested in discovering why she was behaving badly (rather than punishing her for it) and that they eventually identified the cause (without seeming to be frighteningly omniscient!).

Joan Smith and Audrey Harker of Newcastle Family Service Unit discovered a number of uses for this kind of overhead conversation in the course of transporting children by car between home and Unit. They would deliberately talk together about matters of importance and the children, free to join in or not, would listen intently. One of their realizations was that these children rarely heard adults conversing (as opposed to arguing or complaining). On one occasion a little girl who was 'too old' and had too much to do at home, regressed during play in the Unit group (see chapter 9 on FSU Groups) and didn't come out of it by the end of the session. The workers carried her to the car and then talked about her and her home life until she was ready to 'come back'. On other occasions the technique was used to give children comments on themselves, for example 'Isn't Jo speaking much more clearly now?' encouraged Jo to improve his speech because he could hear that the adults approved but did not have to endure direct reference to and discussion of his speaking which he might at that time have found difficult to handle. Once they had discovered this method of verbal communication by accident, Joan Smith and Audrey Harker regarded it as a 'definite technique' and now use it in a planned way. For example they decided to tackle the problem of the children's somewhat dirty condition by engaging together in a discussion on cleanliness in general during one of the car rides. The children became interested and spontaneously joined in.

Sometimes an adult on his own may choose to avoid eye contact with a child, perhaps to allow him the freest possible choice about whether or not to respond directly to whatever is being said. The adult may talk to the child perhaps in the form of a monologue. In the children's novel *The Trouble with Donovan Croft* the foster mother talked to Donovan, her foster son who has become mute through shock and distress; in an attempt to reach him Mrs Chapman tried to speak of some important topics but kept her back to him while she washed up so that he could hear but need not respond. However when she turned round after a few minutes

> to her surprise he wasn't there any more, and from way up the hall she heard the slow, heavy closing of the front door. She sighed. It didn't always pay to have your back to someone when you had something personal to say (Ashley, 1974, p. 99).

But perhaps it did pay because Donovan might well have listened well to as much of Mrs Chapman's talking as he could manage at that time and then quietly retreated when he was ready. If she had caught and pinioned him with her eyes he might have rejected everything, interested only in how he would eventually be able to escape.

In this long section I have suggested so... of the characteristics of social work interviewing with particular reference to working with children but I must stress that this has in no way set out to be a thorough discussion of interviewing; this chapter is about the use and importance of words and this section has been primarily about some ways of employing and enjoying them in what may be generally defined as 'an interview situation'.

To conclude the section here are two examples of workers, both within hospitals, putting into practice some of the principles discussed above.

Patty

Three-year-old Patty had spent 'More than half her life . . . in hospitals because of a chronic, infantile skin condition with urological complications' (Jacobs, 1972, p. 14). She was 'a "holy terror" on the ward'. The social worker 'felt that the child should be directly included' in the treatment plan and

> started out by seeing Patty daily. . . . Perhaps twenty interviews were spent in sitting by her bed, my expressing interest in her, in what she was doing, in what was happening to her—and getting almost no response. I explained my presence to Patty by telling her that I was a lady who came to see the children in the hospital to talk to them. I liked her and wanted to be her friend. Gradually I put out feelers – indicated that I knew she didn't feel well, was sad. I talked to her about some of the things that went on in the hospital – the injections, special trays, being away from home. Finally Patty began to respond, to talk about neutral subjects, and a friendship between us gradually developed. As she began to trust me she showed more interest in the people and things around her (p. 16).

Patty began to ask questions, primarily 'Is my mummy coming?' and this was repeated time and again even though a frequent visiting pattern was established.

With regard to her medical treatment

> Patty initially denied negative feelings . . ., but I scrupulously attempted to prepare her for new procedures and to verbalize appropriate feelings for her (p. 16).

The patience, care and sensitivity of the social worker were rewarded for Patty responded and as she

> slowly became able to express herself more appropriately her hospital adjustment improved remarkably. There were still tantrums and exp-

losions, but these were far less frequent and the little girl began to be able to have relationships with other people (p. 16–17).

Tina Jacobs's work with Patty did not end here but these extracts are sufficient to illustrate how loving, gentle work could achieve real communication with and relief for even so young and anxious a child as Patty. I don't suppose that those first twenty interviews were long but even so the social worker had to make and honour a considerable commitment of time and interest to maintain those repeated expressions of caring with almost no response. She was scrupulous in explaining who she was and why she was there, not once but many times and when Patty eventually began to express her anxiety verbally and to ask questions about her mother's visits the social worker again accepted and responded to repetition. Tina Jacobs was able to listen to Patty, to wait for her and to respond warmly and appropriately whenever Patty gave a lead. And so Patty was enabled 'to express herself more appropriately' and 'to be able to have relationships with other people'.

Ruthie

Ruthie, aged four, faced amputation of her left leg from the knee and the toes of her right foot. The social worker was asked by the paediatric staff

> to take over the preparation of the child for the operation and to help the parents accept the tragic necessity, so that they too could help the child (Plank and Horwood, 1961, p. 406)

and she worked in close liaison with one of the doctors from whose comments the following extracts are taken.

This excellent account gives many details of communication between adults and child but here I select a few examples of verbal exchanges.

> After I had known her for about ten days, I stayed with her while the dressing was being changed. . . . . . The doctors, forgetting her presence, frequently alluded to the forthcoming operation, e.g. 'We can save the knee'; 'It's no good here'. . . .
> In view of the fact that the child had already heard so much from the doctors, which undoubtedly contributed to any fantasies that she had formed about her legs, we [the social worker and the doctor] felt it would be wise to start to broach the reality of the plans for her now. Therefore, that day I went to her room before the playroom opened and said, 'I know how sick you have been, Ruthie. Everything is almost well now except for one leg. The doctors will have to do something to help you walk again.' To elucidate further, I added, 'You know when you touch your leg you don't feel anything?' She immediately changed the subject: 'If you touch my TV set, it will break.' No further mention was made of this the rest of the day by her or myself (p. 409).

Work with Ruthie continued, largely through play until

> The day before the operation, Ruthie was completely unable to concentrate, moving from play with the doll house to the tinker toys, to the playing cards, etc; in less than ten minutes. I therefore decided to start to prepare her for the details of the surgery. I took her into a side room alone and began by saying, 'I know that your parents and the doctors have told you about having an operation tomorrow.' She replied, 'No, they didn't.' I then gave the standard preparation regarding the trip to the operating room and the anaesthetic, and explained what would happen while she was asleep. Then we both went to get the prosthesis doll for the first time. I explained and showed her that one leg was black and sick and that the doll was not able to walk. She wanted to hold the doll herself and hold the black leg on. Then I showed her how the doctor would take part of the black leg off, so that later they could help her to walk with the artificial leg. At this point she said, 'I don't want to walk'. I said, 'I can understand that you would feel that way now, but how nice it will be when you don't have to stay in a wheel chair and can walk and play like other girls'.
> She then asked, 'She'll have another leg?' I said, 'No, she will not grow one, but she will have a leg she and her mommy can put on just like the artificial leg that was on the doll. It is hard, but it looks like a real leg, and she will be able to learn to walk on it again'. The Ruthie, pointing to the doll's black leg, said, 'Throw it away, it's no good'. (This was repeated twice) (p. 411).

Some time after the operation Ruthie became very angry. As Carla Horwood was away, Emma Plank, the social worker, was called in and the talk

> became a turning point in the child's behaviour.
> Mrs Plank commiserated with her that she must be very hungry and wondered whether they could not get some food from the kitchen. [Ruthie had refused to eat.] The student nurse . . . brought toast and milk, but this did not satisfy Ruthie either, and she continued furiously to insist on getting her own breakfast tray, which of course was not available. After a while, Mrs Plank said that she was not going to stay any longer because Ruthie did not really want her to help, and she had many other things to do. However, if Ruthie would eat her toast now, Mrs Plank would gladly wait for her and then take her to the playroom. At this point, Ruthie sat up in bed and screamed: 'You are not here to give orders, I am here to give orders,' to which Mrs Plank replied, 'No, you don't give orders and I am not here to give orders either. I am here to help you and other children.' Ruthie looked surprised and relieved, ate her toast, and was willing to come to the playroom (p. 413).

From this point until her discharge, Ruthie became generally happier and more relaxed.

Both Emma Plank and Carla Horwood were working under considerable difficulties not least being the emotions of the other staff concerned with Ruthie, for anxiety sometimes provoked lack of sympathy for their work. Also they felt that they were 'feeling our way. This was such an unusual case that we could not draw on previous experience' (p. 422). However this might have been an advantage, causing them to be even more alert than usual to the particular needs, reactions and ways of communicating of the particular child in her particular setting and situation. The danger of previous experience and, perhaps, of unquestioning support from colleagues may be that what worked before is expected to work now. Here the workers had to be completely aware of everything they said and did.

They were, as is so often the experience in social work, precipitated into facing with Ruthie the reality of the plans for her by the unthinking behaviour of another adult, in this case the doctor who forgot that children (indeed patients at all) do not lose the powers of hearing and understanding just because they *are* children and patients. Carla Horwood met the challenge with courage and sensitivity. Twice in the article she mentions making sure that she saw Ruthie privately, at one point going to her room before the playroom opened. Adults do not always respect the child's need for privacy, especially I suspect in such residential institutions as hospitals and children's homes. Here Ruthie was to be given or at least prepared for terrible news and she needed to be protected from observation by other people, children or adults. Later when Carla Horwood visited her before the operation, she took her into a side room alone. Privacy also seems to have been important during the interaction with Emma Plank for it was essential that Ruthie should be able to find release from her anger without losing face, an achievement almost impossible if others are watching.

In the first contact reported above, the doctor was very careful not to overload Ruthie. She stopped talking about the operation as soon as Ruthie changed the subject and did not force return to the discussion. It occurs to me that Ruthie's comment 'If you touch my TV set, it will break' might be seen as a reference to herself and possible fears that if her leg should be touched it might break but this is the kind of speculation which it may be more useful to keep in mind than to respond to – at least on the spot. I referred above to hearing cues after the event but not necessarily needing to offer overt response to them. For Ruthie it was clearly enough that her workers attended and listened to her so well that, even if that *had* been an important cue, she might feel confident that there would be other chances. Carla Horwood had after all been visiting her for ten days and had in this particular visit demonstrated her willingness to refer to the sick leg, which must have been causing Ruthie anxiety.

The other point I want to emphasize from these extracts is central to the interaction between Ruthie and the social worker. Here Emma Plank recognized the child's need to sort out something about control. The anger which Ruthie displayed seems to be associated with the way in which adults controlled everything that happened to her culminating in messing up her mealtimes (in order to administer anaesthesia). Emma Plank indicated to Ruthie that she, the child, was in control of whether or not she used the social worker since if she did not want her to help the social worker would go away. This released Ruthie's outburst about orders, to which the social worker could respond simply and directly that orders were not concerned in this contact; helping was. Ruthie did not seem to need to discuss her feelings about control; it was sufficient that an adult had tolerated her anger and met her with a straight response which demonstrated that, although this adult understood what the child felt and considered it to be of importance, she would not take any old buck. Ruthie was thus it seems released from tension and anxiety about both her general situation and treatment and also perhaps about possible punishment for her recent bad behaviour (not, I must add, that I think her behaviour was bad; it was surely a sign of health that she could dare to let off steam in this dangerous place where they could, after, all cut bits of you off!).

These accounts of work with young children demonstrate very well how much communication is possible, using words as a prime method, when the helping adults care about, understand and trust the children enough to offer *real* contact, to listen, to be honest, to be alert to the children's feelings, words and pace, to be patient, consistent and direct and not to fear.

Dear social worker....

The use of words for communication is not of course confined to face-to-face (or telephone-to-telephone) speech. As many words are written and read as are spoken. In the chapter on Books and Bibliotherapy (chapter 5) I develop my thoughts on the written word in the form of books and poems but here I refer briefly to the epistolary art.

Social workers are all too familiar with the pains of letter writing, the difficulty of having to imagine how the reader will receive and react to this statement or question when the social worker is not present to say, 'No, I didn't mean quite that' or, 'Do you understand'. A great deal of trouble can be caused by an ambiguously worded or misinterpreted letter.

There is not room here for a whole essay on letters but I hope that one or two points will provide stimulus for further thought.

A letter can be used as a means of control or even a weapon. In a striking article, remarkable for its humour and honesty as well as its subject, Peter Jewell (1978, p. 14) wrote about his work with Max, who had been known to him for years. Max, now 21, had written a letter:

It can be helpful when the client speaks out. For me the most helpful response is often one which stops me in my tracks and causes me to take a

completely fresh look at a situation from every angle. What Max had to say in his lengthy letter was a very effective stopper in the tracks:
'I would say this here and now, that since September 1976 you have done more damage than good to me: you have always thought yourself wiser and more superior than me; for seven years you and the Undertons have steered my life and have (so you have believed) had complete control of me. I really can't see the sense or value in maintaining our client relationship any longer for it is really like an old record, it is scratched and worn out, as unwholesome as a loaf of mouldy old bread . . .'

Peter Jewell had been Max's social worker through out his life in a children's home and various foster homes. He knew him well:

Letters have been Max's most powerful weapon for a number of years now. Writing has a special significance for him. Unlike the spoken word, the written one has a substance and realness and does not pass instantly into history beyond tangible recall.

The social worker knew how to receive the correspondence; he was not complacent about the verbal attacks, he didn't dismiss Max as a nuisance or paranoid; he was courageous and loving enough to face

soul searching to sort out how many of my responses were appropriate to Max's needs and how much they were a reaction to my own need to be in control.

Eventually he was ready to reply:

Dear Max,
Thank you for letting me know how you are feeling at present. I can appreciate how frustrating it must be to have me always on your neck when things seem not to be working out.
Briefly, I am willing to terminate our relationship when it seems appropriate to do so. I don't think it is appropriate for it to be done in a fit of bad temper, nor when there is unfinished business to be done.
See you Thursday around mid-day (p. 16).

On Thursday Peter Jewell called:

He knew I was coming and did not have to be at home if he wished to avoid me. The door opened and from the darkness of the hallway, came Max's voice: 'Please come in'.

The exchange of letters was a vital part of the interaction and relationship between social worker and boy (for although Max was now 21, Peter Jewell said that this procedure had been maintained for some years). Max used letter writing as a way of feeling in control and he was certainly successful in reaching his social worker and in ensuring that his thoughts and feelings were fully considered; Peter Jewell did not just file the letter in some vast in-tray; he absorbed and considered and thought about it until he was ready to compile a careful answer. And he never said, 'Don't be silly'. He indicated that he understood and cared but would not be browbeaten and could not be destroyed or lost by bad temper. And by putting this in writing he offered Max an important evidence of his good faith and commitment.

Very often the fact rather than the content of a letter is of prime importance. There is still to me something miraculous about the whole process of letter writing and receiving. How thrilling it is to have letters from foreign countries; pieces of paper in envelopes can travel so easily and cheaply where people are constrained by money and passports and time. How reassuring to receive a note that tells you that you are remembered and thought about. How worrying if a looked-for letter does not arrive.

For children under some kind of stress written communication may be of considerable significance. For example, I was recently caring for a small child during his mother's temporary absence. The mother did not write to or telephone her son and in consequence he had no guarantee that she had not completely disappeared. For a few weeks after her return he was anxious and clinging and could not tolerate absence from her. Even a post card would have helped him to believe what everyone kept telling him, that she was well and would soon return to him. Similarly, the grandfather of a little girl (he lived with her family), was admitted to hospital in the middle of the night so that when she awoke in the morning he had simply disappeared. During the first days of his illness no one thought to talk with the little girl about him; all that seemed to be communicated to her was bustle and anxiety and disruption to normal family life. Grandfather had gone and no one had time to notice her signs of distress. Eventually her grandfather recovered enough to send a picture postcard and written message to her via her mother. Although she couldn't read the message she could understand that this tangible object (with a picture of a cat not unlike her own) had come from grandpa who was therefore thinking about her and able to communicate with her. (Fortunately she was soon able to visit him in hospital and prove that he really was still in existence.)

In my work with the Beck family (referred to in chapter 3) I strove to maintain communication between the members of the family when they were separated. When the oldest child was admitted to residential school I helped the other children to write to him. I soon found that the parents too wanted write letters and was ashamed that I had overlooked this.

During her work with eight-year-old Sue in hospital awaiting surgery, Katherine Lloyd (1965, pp. 105–6) took note that the little girl

> wanted to write home. I had brought some picture postcards. If she wanted to write and would like me to help her, I would write for her. She brightened when I said this. This was the first time she smiled at me. She began musing about as to what the various family members were doing. She asked me to write the first card to her mother to see if her work was finished. I asked why she asked this, and she replied it was because her

mother had promised she could visit when her work was done. This anxiety about visiting was not expressed in the card to her father, but rather a feeling of friendly interest in what he was doing.

Like Patty (p. 110), Sue was preoccupied with the visiting or not-visiting of her parents, especially her mother, and writing the cards enabled her both to enquire, if in a slightly indirect way, whether or not she would be visited and to initiate some form of communication with them. The card writing also provided the social worker with an opportunity to demonstrate to the child that she was thinking about her and aware of her needs and interests to the. extent that she actually acquired the cards and would help to write them. From this the shared activity gave both Sue and her social worker the chance to talk about matters which might have been far more difficult if only face-to-face conversation had been available.

Letters (like books) provide the opportunity to say what you wish without the danger of interruption or disruption. Of course letters (like books) need not be read but sometimes the act of writing (both letters and books!) may be as important and useful to the writer as the response of the reader. For many people writing is like talking; they imagine their prospective reader and talk directly to them on paper. Max's letters to Peter Jewell were like this.

They also provide the opportunity to control and delay response. Peter Jewell didn't hurry to throw together an answer to Max; he waited until he could give proper attention to the letter. Had Max said all he wanted to say face to face, the social worker would have been forced to make some immediate response. The letter which Peter Jewell eventually sent was very careful and, in particular, it gave Max the chance to control what happened to him in so far that he could refuse the suggested visit. I don't think I ever wrote to a child to make an appointment to see him; I telephoned foster parents or residential staff or just arrived; the child *had* to receive me if I cared to call but the adults could, usually, say 'No, sorry, not convenient on that day'.

Last word

Up to this point in this chapter I have written approximately 14,000 words about words and I have hardly touched the surface. My intention has been to offer thoughts and ideas not, as I said above, to write a chapter about interviewing. Words are part of interviewing, interviewing is part of social work. Words are gifts to be cherished and used for good; and if they are used as weapons, social workers must catch and hold them and turn them again into vehicles of caring communication.

Chapter 5

Of Books and Bibliotherapy*

Stories for all

There are only two ways of communicating with words; questions and stories. Answers to questions are stories. 'How are you?' 'Not too bad thank you,' is a tiny story, a hint given by the respondent to the questioner who will probably now ask 'Oh, what's the trouble?' leading into the full story perhaps.

All those short statements of everyday life are stories ('I'm dying for a drink', 'I love you', 'I feel terrible') or pictures ('it's raining', 'you're filthy').

We are telling and listening to stories all the time. Sometimes they are deliberate narrations about William the Conqueror and the First World War, about Coronation Street and Anna Karenina, black holes and nuclear fission. Listen to any news programme and you will hear a string of stories. These stories are presented as accounts of current events true and factual but they are very often to say the least inaccurate and frequently futurological; for example who *will* win the election, Grand National, Miss World Contest, Crufts, this or that strike. So really 'the news' is often a collection of fairy stories, fantasies based on real life. Speculation is far more interesting than the actual event; can you remember who won Miss World or the Grand National (or even the election) this year? Do you care? After all we care about Cinderella only *until* she wins the contest and becomes a princess.

Many other everyday stories are probably not thought of as deliberate narrations but have all the action and excitement and emotion of the most carefully constructed thriller or love story. These are the never ending tales of what I did at school/work today, how my wife is treating me, how United did in the match this afternoon, how the onions are coming on. It is only by listening to and being able to tell these stories that we can communicate.

Then there are professional stories. 'Now all can be revealed' about some pop star or royal personage, total exposure by a

* Parts of this chapter are based on ideas published in my article (1979), Bibliotherapy in Social Work with Children.

journalist and photographer. The pop stars and royals are really ordinary people in unusual situations but it's nice to think that they are different – and, often, worse. Social workers write professional stories too in the form of reports and records and notes on review sheets. (The clients too are 'ordinary people in unusual situations' but perhaps it is reassuring to think of them as different – and worse?) Writing about people helps to define them and to make their lives in some ways firm, crystallized; as surely as Cinderella lost her glass slipper, Cindy is a precocious promiscuous little nuisance who needs firm control. Except that Cinderella's 'glass' slipper was possibly a mistranslation from the eighteen-century French word for 'fur', and maybe Cindy's story too has been distorted by being written down. Supervision sessions and case conferences are forums for people to tell stories about other books and about their own feelings.

I think most social workers love stories and *that* love is part of what attracts them to social work. Perhaps they suffer from insatiable curiosity like the Elephant's Child. Not even the greatest novelist can capture the complexity of personality and life which social workers meet, learn and record every day. All novels have endings but the stories which social workers hear and tell are endless – and end-less.

There is no doubt at all that all children love stories; bedtime stories, rhymes, jokes, comics, everything. (Irritatingly, they often most like those stories which adults consider to be unsuitable, crude and boring.)

If both social workers and children like stories it seems to be good sense for them to indulge this when they are trying to communicate and this chapter is a discussion of ways of using stories in social work with children. Following this introduction there is a brief comment on bibliotherapy but I do not offer this chapter as a critique of that topic. Bibliotherapy is a large subject in itself and my ideas about stories and books, social workers and children include some things also found in the literature of bibliotherapy but do not follow all the bibliotherapeutic arguments. In this chapter I shall at certain points support and extend my ideas by reference to a tiny fraction of the American literature of bibliotherapy.

Bibliotherapy

There is in America an ever-growing literature of bibliotherapy not only of fiction, non-fiction and 'quasi'-fiction produced with a specifically therapeutic intention but also of books and articles which discuss the history and uses of bibliotherapy, whether it is an art or a science, who is qualified to select the books and apply the therapy; there are also a number of annotated guides to potentially thera-peutic books. Books are employed as agents of therapy in work with people grappling with a wide range of problems, in particular with psychiatric and emotional disturbances and much of the literature is concerned with the application of bibliotherapy by medical staff and counsellors together with librarians.

Definitions of bibliotherapy abound. 'Therapy' should imply the intent to change and heal or at least to offer help in coping with a difficult situation:

> everyone can be helped through reading. One might not necessarily be faced with a problem, one might not be in therapy, and one might not be directed to the reading material. . . . bibliotherapy is a process in which every literate person participates at one time or another. Bibliotherapy is seen as the self-examination and insights that are gained from reading, no matter what the source. The source can be fiction or non-fiction; the reading can be directed (in settings ranging from reading guidance to formal therapy), self-directed, or accidental. The reader might begin reading when actively looking for insights or the insights might come unexpectedly. In any case, the insight is utilized to create a richer and healthier life (Bernstein, 1977, p. 21).

Joanne Bernstein's definition is broad but is to my mind the most useful in a discussion of the therapeutic employment of books by social workers with children under stress. In this discussion I shall suggest a number of ways in which books and stories may be used as tools and vehicles of communication but, as with any other form of activity in which social worker and child engage for some purpose beyond that of the activity itself, it is essential that that activity is regarded as of value *in itself* and is not *merely* a vehicle. Further if the activity is not itself regarded by both social worker and child as enjoyable there will be little chance of any useful and therapeutic consequence.

Who chooses?

As Joanne Bernstein implies, any book may be a source of help and insight. A person who enjoys reading will probably be drawn to the right book at the right time, whether what is sought is escape and relaxation, encounter with beautiful language or the challenge of new ideas and vicariously experienced emotional turmoils. Few people gain much from an unwillingly read book (unless to glean facts for essay writing and examination passing).

The notion of encouraging a child to read a particular book for the purpose of anything other than study or enjoyment is very problematic particularly if the book is to be read privately by the child rather than read aloud by the adult. It is very unlikely that a specially produced problem-centred book would be selected by a child in a stressful situation. After all, 'Adults are not expected to buy books called *Mrs Sue Jones – alcoholic's wife*' (Aiken cited in Tucker, 1975, p. 249).

If a social worker considers that a particular book would be of use there are several ways in which she may introduce it to the child. She may offer it directly to the child explaining, for example, that she has read it herself, that something about it put her in mind of the child and his life and that she wonders if the child would like to read it and see what *he* thinks. (Or she could ask if the child thinks the book might be of any use to *other* children.) If the child says 'No, thank you' the social worker will have to decide whether to suggest that he keeps the book for a while anyway or to take it away, recognizing that the whole idea or perhaps only the particular book or the timing are wrong.

The social worker may suggest to other adults concerned with the child that they should introduce a book directly in the same kind of way. Or she may suggest that it should be made available but not directly offered to the child:

> The suggestion of the book by its presence in a collection, rather than by its presentation, gives children the central role. The book is not forced upon children with the implication 'It's good for you' (Bernstein, 1977, p. 31–2).

I believe that every children's home, social-work department, hospital, foster home – everywhere where children are, particularly if they are in some actually or potentially stressful situation, should contain a good library of children's books; *any* books; fantasies, funny stories, fairy stories, books about adventure and 'real life', books with explicit therapeutic intent and books for passing the time.

One problem about the selection of a book for a child relates to the quality of the book. Should social workers confine themselves to books which are unexceptionably 'good' in both content and production? 'Sound morals should never excuse shoddy production, at least from any commercial publisher' (Tucker, 1975, p. 248).

This is certainly true if a book is produced with some therapeutic or educational aim. However Nicholas Tucker follows this statement with a quotation from Elaine Moss, who wrote about her adopted daughter's affection for a book called *Peppermint*: 'Heaven knows how *Peppermint* got into our house – a visiting aunt must have given it . . . instead of a packet of jelly babies.'

Peppermint is a little lost cat who is found and loved and Elaine Moss realizes that her daughter is identifying with him

> not just for the duration of the story, but at a deep, warm, comforting and enduring level. The artistically worthless book – hack-written and poorly illustrated – may, if its emotional content is sound, hold a message of supreme significance for a particular child.

And a group of members of NAWCH (the National Association for the Welfare of Children in Hospital) reported that of all the books about children in hospitals, the children known to them were attracted more by *Zozo Goes to Hospital* (Rey, 1967) a lively, funny story about a monkey, than by the beautifully thought out and produced and rather earnest accounts of well-behaved children undergoing hospital treatment. *Zozo* is primarily an amusing children's story; any educational or therapeutic effect is a bonus and perhaps a result of this.

However child and book are introduced to each other, the social worker is responsible at least to be aware of any possible impact the book may have. With children of any age she must be familiar with the book and ready to answer any question or to respect silence but be ready for any future discussions or repercussions.

The impact of any particular book on any particular child is impossible to predict and the social worker must be ready to recognize any anxieties which arise from what might appear to be straightforward and innocuous material. An eleven-year-old boy read *The Hunchback of Notre Dame* and asked if *he* might grow a hump. A five-year-old girl was given a book about children in a children's home whose intention was to show that life was for them as ordinary and routine as that in a normal household; but the donor of the book felt sudden anxiety at the sentence 'We are here because our own mums and dads can't look after us' which could perhaps inspire the question 'Might *my* mum and dad not look after *me*?' (Crompton, 1978a, p. 13).

It may be that an incident or even a single sentence in a book gives rise to some question which can lead to discussion of the child's particular background or anxieties. The boy's question about a hump might have reflected a deep anxiety about physical handicap. A child in care might respond to 'We are here because our own mums and dads can't look after us' with 'Why can't my mum and dad look after me?'. But such questions can only be asked if some sensitive and caring adult is on hand to hear and to respond. The answer to 'Could *I* grow a hump?' is not 'No, of course not'.

The real world

> Reading . . . gives children greater insight into themselves and helps them grow in appreciation of other people, in understanding the world they live in and the forces which operate to make people think, feel and behave as they do (Frank, 1977).

Whatever secondary objectives are proposed, the prime objective of using a book as a means of communication in social work is always to encourage and enable development of the individual child's understanding of himself in relation to the world he lives in and thus to enhance his ability to take responsibility for and manage himself and his life. (In other words the prime objective of any method of communication within social work is identical with that of the social work itself.)

Not all adults believe that children should be encouraged to develop such insight and understanding:

Sheltering the child from the real world is a foible of many parents who feel that at a 'magic age' the child will automatically switch from innocence to maturity (Weinstein, 1978).

The magic age is never defined and children whose parents hold this belief are likely never to attain it. Such cotton-wool protection may bre_d anxiety impossible to express to such parents.

> There is such a widespread refusal to let children know that the source of much that goes wrong in life is due to our very own natures – the propensity of all men to act aggressively, asocially, selfishly, out of anger and anxiety. Instead, we want our children to believe that, inherently, all men are good. But children know that *they* are not always good; and often, even when they are, they would prefer not to be (Bettelheim, 1978, p. 7).

Conflict between the child's sense of his 'wrong' thoughts, wishes and actions and the apparent world view of his parents may lead to great suffering and even the belief that the child is himself distorted. It is essential to distinguish between the anxiety which may result from exposure to 'real life' (an anxiety which is an essential element of growth to maturity and which can be managed and experienced as positive if adults have the courage to recognize and discuss it) and the anxiety born of avoidance and deception, the pretence that children live in some candy world, that their feelings are less strong than those of adults, their experiences less intense, that they cannot manage 'real life'. This anxiety is the anxiety of confusion and self-doubt, militating against the acceptance of responsibility and the development of confidence and very often incurable.

It must often be tempting for social workers to believe that because a child is already in some stressful situation he should not be expected to manage more exposure to 'reality'. Timing and occasion are, of course, of vital importance but I think that opportunities for helping children to learn about and manage their own realities are often lost because social workers and those who have the day-to-day care of children share

> the prevalent parental belief . . . that a child must be diverted from what troubles him most: his formless, nameless anxieties, and his chaotic, angry, and even violent fantasies. Many parents believe that only conscious reality or pleasant and wish-fulfilling images should be presented to the child – that he should be exposed to the sunny side of things. But such one-sided fare nourishes the mind only in a one-sided way, and real life is not all sunny (Bettelheim, 1978, p. 7)

Joan Cass (1967, pp. 85–6), writing about residential workers, offers another aspect of the same view:

> We need to keep *feeling* alive in children, particularly perhaps the child in care, because there is always the temptation here to jolly children along and give them insufficient time to experience loss and grief. We sometimes feel that the unhappy children are a reproach to ourselves and what we are trying to do to make life full and interesting for them yet

mourning for loss or rejection, is something children need to experience fully.

Stories can help children to share in the universal emotions of mankind, not only the pleasures and delights of life but also the sorrow, sufferings, despairs, and mistakes mankind has undergone and endured. (emphasis added)

Life is, as I have suggested above, a constant succession of stories and the uses of both narrating and listening to them are many and various. Certainly fantasies and fairy tales, adventures of the body and the imagination have for all races and all ages (both of the individual and the world) enormous significance. Bettelheim (1978, pp. 6–7) suggests one important use of fantasizing and tale hearing for children:

In order to master the psychological problems of growing up . . . a child needs to understand what is going on within his conscious self so that he can also cope with that which goes on in his unconscious. He can achieve this understanding and with it the ability to cope, not through rational comprehension of the nature and content of his unconscious, but by becoming familiar with it through spinning out daydreams – ruminating, rearranging and fantasizing about suitable story elements in response to unconscious pressures. By doing this, the child fits unconscious content into conscious fantasies, which enable him to deal with that content. It is here that fairy tales have unequalled value, because they offer new dimensions to the child's imagination which would be impossible for him to discover as truly on his own. Even more important the form and structure of fairy tales suggest images to the child by which he can structure his daydreams and with them give better direction to his life.

Some of the content of this long quotation may be controversial but the points I wish to draw from it are that children naturally and constantly make stories themselves, spin out daydreams, and that contact with stories made by other people serves to stimulate and extend their own use of imagination and consequent ability to comprehend the world.

An important aspect of learning about the world and developing insight is discovering how one appears to other people and what is one's own place in the world. To complete this section here is an account of how the use of story telling helped a child to learn something about this and thus to modify her behaviour.

Ellen, a seven-year-old girl, . . . was an extremely difficult problem in her elementary school class because she stole money from everyone. She took things both from the teachers and from the other children; nothing of value was safe in the class. Besides stealing, she had temper tantrums, ran out of the room when frustrated, and demanded excessive attention and affection from her teachers (Glasser, 1975, p. 202).

Everything possible was tried but nothing had any effect and the teacher and her consultants were ready to give up:

Finally someone suggested that perhaps the teacher could get the child's attention and confidence and get her to stop stealing by telling the whole class a story about a little girl who stole. Giving the little girl the same name, Ellen, as the child who stole, the teacher would say that Ellen was unhappy, that Ellen was always upsetting the teacher and the class, and that everyone would love Ellen much more if she would stop stealing. Ellen listened very attentively.

Shortly after the story was told, she reduced her stealing and improved her other behaviour. The child felt enough involved so that ceasing to act irresponsibly became worthwhile to her. The teacher was advised to repeat the story with various current embellishments until the child realized that she could get more attention and affection from the teacher by not stealing. In about six weeks the stealing stopped. During the rest of the semester Ellen's behaviour and school work showed steady improvement so that it was not necessary for the teacher to tell the story any more for her; she did, however, use the same technique successfully with other children who presented problems (pp. 203–4).

It is perhaps important to stress that this approach was successful for Ellen and some other particular children as used by a particular teacher in her own way. This teacher might not have been able to use it successfully for all children and some teachers might not be able to use it at all. No means of communication is universal; the essential factor is always the relationship and interaction between the individuals who are endeavouring to communicate.

Identification?

The child can find emotional release as he identifies with a character with the same or similar problems (Schultheis, 1977).
In reading, identification takes place when the readers see themselves as aligned with characters, groups, settings, or ideas presented in the material (Bernstein, 1977, p. 25).

The 'bibliotherapeutic' writers of my acquaintance use the word *identification* very freely and I think inaccurately. Identification with a character in a book surely implies that the reader (child or adult) perceives in that character and his behaviour and experiences an almost exact replica of himself as he believes himself to be. Although it is perfectly possible for this to occur I think it is far more usual for a reader to *recognize* in characters of both fact and fiction elements of and similarities to his own person and life while maintaining full realization of the essential differences between the characters and himself. *Recognition* is therefore a more accurate and useful concept than identification. This is in no way quibbling for it is vital that understanding of the probable or actual experience of the child is not inhibited by use of a misleading label.

One of the most important benefits of recognition is release from isolation. It may be very hard for a child to bear the belief that he is the only person ever to experience this or that suffering and the recognition of his own predicament, experience and/or feelings within a story may be very reassuring. Reading about a character not dissimilar to himself who experiences, endures and even overcomes problems may help to give hope to a child (provided that the character is not too perfect – comparison of himself with an over-successful character could lead to despair, something of which the social worker would need to be very aware). It may also help a child to realize that he is normal and ordinary even if there are about his life elements which are not, as far as he knows, common to all children (for example physical handicap or having only one parent). It is very easy to believe oneself to be at least odd and, not uncommonly, abnormal, unnatural or even a 'monster' and such feelings are encouraged by isolation, the inability to learn that what makes the individual unique is his particular combination of the common problems and experiences of life. Losing a parent causes no less grief, undergoing an operation no less anxiety, if the child knows that his experience is also known to millions of children; it is still *his* parent, *his* operation; but it will almost surely be helpful to him to learn that other people of no more power and maturity than himself have thus suffered and have survived.

Try life on for size

One of the greatest benefits of reading is the opportunity offered to explore experiences and adventures of the mind, body and emotions without danger.

Reading 'can help children "try life on for size" without being immediately faced with the problems themselves' (Chadbourne, 1977). The most basic problem of life (other than survival) is that of good and evil and social workers share with all other adults concerned with the care of children responsibility for ensuring that each child develops a sense of morality. Reading is for many people the best way to meet questions about moral conflict demonstrated and discussed in contexts other than the reader's own immediate environment. It seems to me that the great popularity of *The Lord of the Rings* (Tolkien, 1954/5) derives partly from the absence for people in their twenties of exposure to the massive conflicts of recent history, for example the Second World War, the development of the atom and hydrogen bombs and the Vietnam War. If my thesis is correct the freedom from fear of domination or destruction by some real force leaves a gap which is for many filled by grappling with representations of the good/evil conflict through fantasy (including space fiction). Children's books are frequently concerned with problems of morality; notable in the 1970s has been for example *Watership Down* (Adams, 1973) whose theme, set in an adventure story with appealing rabbits as characters, is that there are definitely right and wrong ways of living and that those in the right deserve to prosper. The book, a huge best-seller, was eventually filmed as a full-length cartoon. Was its appeal entirely in the rabbits and their exodus or was it also in the presentation of clear values and the prescription for right? Moreover was it bought by children or by their parents?

Issues relating to morality and 'proper' behaviour underlie many if not all the matters on which social workers may need to communicate with children: for example, facing death or an operation involves the child in expectation from those around him of 'right' and 'wrong' behaviour, (expectations which may vary from adult to adult; a nurse might perhaps expect a child to behave 'well', to be good and quiet, while a social worker might consider 'right' or appropriate behaviour to include manifestations of anger and anxiety). A child under supervision because of delinquent behaviour is certainly involved in discussions regarding his concept of morality with his social worker; by this I do not suggest that the word is ever used or even necessarily thought of but the very notion of delinquency suggests that certain behaviour offends some generally accepted definition of right behaviour and therefore of morality and thus the social worker of necessity represents that morality and is responsible to help the child develop an acceptable concept.

In no way am I suggesting that social workers should hand out 'good books' to their children. But I do think that they should be aware of what the children do read and should, if and when they deem it to be appropriate, encourage discussion of that reading; for example, discovery that a girl reads comics about teenage love and pop stars could in certain circumstances lead to useful discussion about her view of life and her own future.

Also there may, I think, be occasions when a book may be introduced by the social worker and deliberately used as the basis for discussion. An example of this within the context of trying on for size might be during work with prospective foster families. It is nearly impossible really to imagine any potential future event or experience. 'How do you think you would feel if . . . ?' is really an impossible question and people keen to be accepted for anything are almost bound to answer, in effect, 'Oh, it'll be alright'. The children of prospective foster parents are particularly vulnerable for it must be almost completely impossible for them to imagine what it would be like to share their home, their parents, perhaps their toys, bedrooms and friends with another child. At least the adults have some idea what it is like to share their home with children but even in a large family the advent of another child is potentially a disturbing event. If books can help exploration it might be helpful for the children in prospective foster families to read about the kinds of feelings and experiences of others in their prospective position. I doubt if true-life accounts would be of much value (although they probably are to the adults) but there are available a number of childrens' novels set within foster homes and including as part of the central theme the relationship between the foster parents' own children and the foster children. For example in *The Trouble with Donovan Croft* (Ashley, 1974), Keith's extremely nice parents consent to foster Donovan but omit to consult their own son. He manages his feelings well but suffers a good many strong and hostile emotions towards Donovan, whose problems cause Keith much suffering at school and distress and anxiety at home before the boys eventually reach a real friendship. Keith is about ten and shares his home with only one foster brother (albeit one with enough problems for fifteen). Despite his negative feelings Keith is able to show great understanding of Donovan and is at times the only person who can offer him help. A book like this could offer a potential Keith the opportunity to explore feelings about sharing with and being possibly the most important and helpful person to the foster child, within the setting of an enjoyable and dramatic story. Other references can be found via the various bibliographies available (some of which are listed at the end of this chapter) or by consulting children's librarians but I will here mention one other whose focus on the teenage daughter of foster parents may be unusual and of especial use to social workers. *Last Straw* (Dickinson, 1976) is a first person account of the trials and tribulations, affections and hopes of a girl whose foster siblings range in age from a small baby to another teenager. Rivalries abound and a good deal of work has to be done by everyone. (Unfortunately in neither of these books do the social workers come off very well.)

Although I have concentrated in this section on two particular areas, morality and potential experience, the range of topics for exploration through books is infinite and the social worker may be surprised at the books she finds herself reading, introducing and discussing. For example, an eleven-year-old boy

> looked at a sex education book with the therapist commenting about such topics as masturbation. The function here was to provide an educative service in an area with which the parents found difficulty in dealing (Keat, 1972, p. 458).

It's like this

Social workers may find it useful to offer children books which describe places and experiences which they are about to encounter. This is, I suppose, another version of exploration. There are easily available a number of special books intended for children in ordinary circumstances to learn either about such everyday crises as going to the doctor and hospital, starting school and enduring the advent of a new sibling or the death of a loved relative or animal, or about the unusual circumstances of some children who may be, for example, handicapped (mentally or physically).

Going to hospital seems to be the most popular and *apparently* easiest event to tackle in a book. There is an abundance of pictures of nurses and X-ray machines and children in bed with thermometers. To my mind the trouble is that the children are all being so good and unruffled. It may be very helpful for a child about to enter hospital to see pictures of wards and equipment so that the real thing will not be shocking but I think it would be even more helpful if he could learn that other children feel nervous and unhappy and frightened. Gemma's friend Olly has to go into hospital and Olly, unlike the children in some of the other hospital books, 'felt very unhappy and cried' when his mother left and he isn't at all keen on injections.

'I don't want that', said Olly.
'Don't worry', said the lady doctor, 'it's only like a little insect bite'.
'Well, I don't like insect bites', answered Olly crossly.
(Gydal and Danielsson, 1973 pp. 10, 13).

Fellow-patient Roy

got up and dressed himself. But instead of putting on his shoes, he suddenly threw them out of the window.
'Oh nurse, look what he's done', yelled Sandra.
'Tell-tale', shouted Roy. 'I'm not afraid of anyone. And when I came to hospital I was so ill and the ambulance went so fast that everyone had to stand still in the street, or they would have been run over. And I didn't cry'.
'He did too', said Sandra. 'He cried and cried. I was here. . . . He made an awful fuss' (pp. 18–19).

It is essential to remember that anxiety may be raised by such books. A child who was due to enter hospital might be worried by Roy's behaviour, wondering if he would meet any Roys himself or what had caused Roy to act so aggressively. But such a book could help to give form to otherwise possibly vague anxieties and thus provide material for the child to make tangible his worries and for the adult to offer discussion and preparation and, where appropriate, reassurance.

Such familiarization books might well be of use to children in preparation for boarding out or entering a children's home. For young people about to leave care or enter a hostel or flat for the first time I suggest a clear account of the rights of young adults at various ages together with information about, for example, banking and payment of bills.

Together

My theme throughout this chapter, indeed throughout the whole book, is that whatever activities are engaged in by social worker and child together the fundamental aim is always to enhance communication between the participants. Reading is for most people usually a private activity. Even if you read in a noisy or crowded environment you can create silence and privacy in your head in order to enter the world of the book and receive its pictures and messages.

In order for books to be used as aids to communication within social work that privacy must, as in education, be at least partly lost. Opportunity must be offered for the child to share with the caring adult any anxieties or thoughts which lead him to wish for discussion. As with any other communication, such discussion may not be of long duration or intensity and the social worker will, as always, need to be constantly aware of possible leads and references from the child (although an adolescent individual or group might enthusiastically respond to being asked to read and discuss a particular book or teen-comic).

Reading together

With a younger child communication about and arising from a book may coincide with the actual reading of the book since the adult may read aloud, probably cuddling the child on her knee while she does so. Thus both the content of the book itself and the activity of reading may be beneficial to the child and to the development of trust and relationship between child and adult. Use of a book in such a way is illustrated by the following account of interaction between a little girl and her stepmother. At the time when, as a four-year-old, Sally was getting used to the separation of her parents and her visits to her father in his new life, her stepmother came across *When Gemma's Parents got Divorced* (Gydal and Danielsson, 1976). This was added to her pile of books in her father's house (somewhat prominently) where she quickly spotted it and asked for it to be read. Gemma's story was told several times by either her father or her stepmother with the little girl curled up safely on the reader's knee. Gemma's experience was not unlike her own since the book tells how her parents are unhappy together and eventually decide to part. Gemma and her brother do not accept this easily or happily:

> 'We must all stay here – all of us', she sobbed.
> 'You and me and Mummy and John. Nobody must move'.
> 'There now, little darling', said Dad, 'everything is going to be all right'.
> 'But how will it be all right? You are yelling and quarrelling all the time', said Gemma, as she cuddled close in his arms.
> 'Yes, I know', said Dad, 'and that's why Mummy and I are talking about separating'. He looked very sad.
> 'I won't separate', murmured Gemma (p. 19).

Sometimes Sally asked questions about Gemma, sometimes about herself, sometimes she said nothing. Sometimes she looked at the book on her own. The book on its own would have been of little use to her even if she could have read it. As a focus for attention on her own anxieties and problem it was invaluable. A large part of its use was also to let her see that she was not the only little girl in the world to suffer the separation of her parents and the setting up of a new establishment by one of them.

Another book of use to this family was *Stepmother* (Mahy, 1974). Sally and her stepmother had during the three years of their acquaintance had a number of discussions about their particular relationship. Sally lived with her mother but frequently stayed with her father at weekends and for longer periods during holidays. She called her stepmother by her first name but occasionally slipped into 'Mummy'; this led to discussion about what 'mummies do'. She had never been very happy if the word 'stepmother' was used. As with *Gemma*, *Stepmother* was left around and Sally was soon attracted by the bright book. She read it straight through on her own and then told her stepmother that she liked it. It was difficult not to try to wring too much out of it with her; the whole idea was to have a casual and easy way of talking about the subject.

Princess Jenny knows that stepmothers are supposed to be full of wickedness, always changing princesses into frogs or worms or even making them do the housework and sit in the ashes (p. 9). Princess Jenny's stepmother turns out to be really smashing. The book helped in a number of ways. Sally's stepmother was able to say that she tried not to be wicked and Sally said that she wasn't (as she didn't have a book of spells). It also gave them a game of their own as they revelled in being Stepmother and Stepdaughter (which they considered to be rather special as not everyone can be either one or the other). They talked about all kinds of possible step-relationships and Sally remembered a friend who had a stepfather.

These books helped a young child in a long-term potentially stressful situation to learn about some of the universal aspects of her predicament. They provided an attractive and enjoyable opportunity for Sally and her stepmother (and at times her father) to explore stories about other children who, while not identical to Sally in personality or experience, did have enough in common with her to help her recognize that her position and possible feelings were not unique. It was essential that Sally was given control over the use of the books so that they were never forced on her. Sometimes she would ask for one of them to be read to her, sometimes she would quietly ponder over one on her own. In either event the adults tried to be aware that she might be indicating the wish further to explore some question concerning her own life and relationships and their aim was to offer but not impose opportunity for this. Sally was also able to control the ending of reading or discussion.

Although this example is of the use of books within a family there is no reason why a social worker should not work in a similar way either directly herself or by suggesting the idea to those with immediate care of the child. The two vital elements which contributed to the success of the book-use were that the adults were not afraid of whatever questions the child might ask and were prepared to answer and discuss clearly and honestly, and that much of the reading took place in a cuddle so that whatever anxieties the little girl might express, even if she might seem to be rejecting towards her father and stepmother, she could feel affection and security through their arms and laps.

Together to the library

Another way of sharing books with children under stress is demonstrated by a social worker who was given the always tricky task of getting to know some children whose family life was strained and not happy but sustainable. She took the older children to the local library once and finding it a success, made it a regular outing. The children had few if any books at home and this was a unique chance for them to discover and indulge a liking for reading. The social worker could be approached to enjoy books with them or ignored while the children looked at books in the safe knowledge that she was there with them but not insisting on conversation. But essentially she enjoyed the activity which she shared with the children so that her pleasure and relaxation were communicated to them and helped them to develop trust in her.

Reading aloud

Joan Cass (1967, pp. 87–8) suggests another use of sharing books and in particular of reading aloud:

> Children in care tend to be retarded in speech. Many of them have had a bad start for they have not had loving and thoughtful parents who talked, played, showed them picture books and told them stories when they were small, so House-parents may have a good deal to do in this respect.
> One of the qualities looked for in a book is the language the writer uses. Is it well written with a rich and stimulating vocabulary without being either verbose or over-repetitive?
> Sometimes a story is so boring to read aloud, its plot and characterization so meagre and trite, its language so ordinary, it is difficult for the adult to raise any enthusiasm about it. Although one does not want to refuse children's requests it is often quite easy to suggest they read these stories for themselves, as we have got something quite exciting we think they will enjoy and which we will read to them, and in the long run the better book is much more interesting.

It is, I believe, one of the duties of the social worker to help the child manage to the best of his *true* ability (and not just the often undervaluing assessment of, for example, schools and other establishments) his life in both the immediate environment (for example hospital ward, community home) and the world in which he will eventually be an adult. If the child is deficient in some aspect of socialization the social worker must endeavour to ensure that remedial help is offered. As Joan Cass suggests, many children known to social workers (whether in residential care or under some form of supervision) have poor mastery of speech and these children should be helped to gain confidence. Language can be very frightening; if an adult uses a long word what child will dare to ask what it means? Reading aloud can help to enrich vocabulary particularly if the reading adult ensures that the experience is pleasant and not threatening.

Joan Cass is right to reject stories that are boring to the adult if *only* the boredom would be communicated. But she is also right to suggest that the child's own choice of literature should not be denigrated. Sometimes it might, as with Sally, be important to read yet again a book chosen by the child because that choice might indicate that the reading would fulfil some need additional to the hearing of the story itself. And it is vital not to let any child feel that his choice of reading is in some way sub-standard or inferior. Some comics *may* be rubbish but if the child is at least reading something, that is something to work on. If a child feels that his choice is put down he may find it very difficult to listen to the approved choice of the adult. Perhaps the adult might sometimes accede to the child's request to read aloud literature which she considers to be poor and boring and then offer a reading from the book of *her* choice.

Tale telling and self-expression

So far I have written only about stories in commercially published books except in the account of the teacher's work with Ellen (Glasser, 1975). As in that work, social workers may have many opportunities to use spontaneous oral tale telling with children. Children love stories which are made entirely, uniquely and immediately for themselves. An anxious child may be helped and soothed by an exciting fantasy story into which he can escape for a while from the worry about what will happen in court or at the end of this long journey to a children's home.

Another way of reducing anxiety may be to tell a story about a child whose experience is very similar to that of this particular child. The real child can choose to express interest and recognition or not as he pleases. Jo was a 'bewildered little boy, . . . far from home.'

> I told him a story about a little boy whose home and recent experiences were similar to his own. Jo was huddled under some coats in the back of the car, refusing conversation and the silence having become prolonged and rather boring for both of us and perhaps rather stressful for him, I began to talk. When I had narrated all the events of Jo's past 24 hours, I said, 'And then he went home. I don't know what happened then.' Jo sat up brightly, 'I think he went to bed.' I had been careful not to use Jo's

name for the hero of the story and not to insist on any overt response (Wardle, 1975, p. 431).

In his work with eight-year-old Tim after severe heart surgery, Harold Richman (1972, pp. 47–8) also gave the child the chance to communicate through contributing to a tailor-made story:

> Tim was reluctant even to talk about going home, so I began the following story. At certain points I stopped and asked him to take over.
> *Worker*: Once upon a time there was a frog. His name was Fog the Frog. And Fog the Frog lived in a bog. And Fog the Frog who lived in a bog liked to sit in the mud, and he croaked in the mud. . . . And one day the people from the hospital saw Fog the Frog in the bog and they said: 'We think we should take Fog the Frog out of the bog and bring him to the hospital.' So they asked Fog the Frog whether he would leave the bog and come with them. He said–
> *Tim*: 'Yes.'
> *Worker*: So they took Fog the Frog out of the bog and brought him to the hospital–
> *Tim*: and the hospital took science research on him. . . . .
> *Worker*: and he sat in his little glass house on the seventh floor in the animal room. . . . . And he thought about where he was, and this is what he thought.
> *Tim*: He didn't like it in the animal room very much–
> *Worker*: and the little mouse who was his next-door neighbour said to the frog, 'Why don't you like it at the hospital here in the animal room?' And the frog said–
> *Tim*: I don't have any water.'
> *Worker*: Fog . . . belongs in the bog. But he stayed here for a while, and finally . . . he just decided that it was time to go back to the bog, but he didn't know if he wanted to go back to the bog or stay at the hospital. And he thought and thought and he decided–
> *Tim*: to stay at the hospital with his friend the little mouse.

Here the social worker invented an amusing animal character whose experience was in some way similar to that of Tim and he offered the frightened boy the chance to play through words and fantasy with the ideas which so worried him and to declare his preference for remaining in the hospital. Months later Fog reappeared enabling Tim to translate the worker's

> . . . glug, glug, glug, which in frog language means–
> *Tim*: thank you and all the people at the hospital for helping me.
> *Worker*: And the people at the hospital said they never had a nicer frog than Fog . . . (p. 51).

The confidence which had developed between social worker and child would have allowed these things to be said without the expedient of Fog but, at this point, the resurrection of the intermediary animal suggested a reference to the amount of progress, physical and emotional, made by Tim since the first Fog story. Use of frog language was a useful device for allowing Tim total freedom of 'translation'.

Expressing himself through the medium of a story may not necessarily be in the context of a conversation between child and adult but the story must still be shared with a caring adult if the child is to achieve his aim. Willy, for example, gave the staff at Shotton Hall the following picture of himself:

> I am a very dull sixpence. At the moment I am at the bottom of the sea, under an anchor which had been under a ship when the ship blew up, and now I'm very lonely. How I wish I was still the shiny sixpence I was when I was in the bank (Lenhoff, 1970, p. 42).

Willy then described his progress from his happy state when 'I had plenty of mates and I really enjoyed myself' to his present terrible position 'under an old broken anchor'. His message was read and understood by those for whom it was intended.

Poems too may be used by children to communicate with helping adults. In her account of work with Visha (a ten-year-old girl suffering together with her mother from unmanageable 'bereaved feelings of loss, anger, despair and disbelief' two and a half months after the death of her father) Elizabeth Tuters (1974, p. 228), senior social worker in a child psychiatric unit, writes that at the end of a session

> Mrs Hill handed us a poem Visha had written for us to read outside. It was about 'Jimmy' a most friendly spider who lived behind their TV set, who took very good care of himself and was no trouble at all but, the poem stated, if Jimmy were to be lost and never to return, then all the family would 'grieve' for him.
> We took this poem as a directive from Visha and her mother. We felt this indicated they were both wanting to grapple with feelings of loss and grief. We felt that by giving us the poem they were helping us to focus on this indeed painful area – a pain not only felt by the family but by the full team; for any loss by death stirs up in all of us our own painful memories which then makes our avoidance of these areas in our work with families seem natural and understandable.

Visha did not in fact appear to accept the worker's interpretation of her message and it is not clear from this account whether or not the interpretation was accurate. However it is an interesting description of an attempt by a child to communicate with her social worker and of that social worker with her colleagues to understand and build on that communication.

Making books together

A number of adults concerned with the care of children in stressful situations are exploring the possibilities of making books with the children. An early and, I believe, influential account of such book-making is given in *A Story for Mary*:

> During the first few weeks in foster care it was evident that Mary did not know why she was in the foster home. She could not discuss her feelings with the worker, but she revealed fantasies that her mother would buy a house and a car and then take all her children home to live together in a family (Eikenberry, 1972, p. 34).

The social worker took Mary out and in the children's book section of a store Mary

> asked the social worker to buy her a book. The social worker responded by offering her an alternative – that he and Mary write their own book (p. 35).

Mary was fully involved in selecting and helping to shop for materials. The social worker was to write the story and Mary to 'find pictures that would illustrate the story'.

> The story was typed on large sheets of paper, with a paragraph or two on each page, allowing much room for pictures. The process of putting the book together provided many opportunities to read all or selected parts of the story. Mary determined to a large extent which parts needed to be re-read and discussed. As a result, she talked about parts of her life that she had been unable to discuss earlier with the worker (p. 35).

ABAFA* is encouraging the creation of life story books and gives examples and suggestions in the Training Aids *Working with Children who are Joining New Families* (1977) and *Planning for Children in Long-Term Care* (1976). An eight-year-old writes:

> When I was born my mummy found it very hard to look after me.
> She loved me very much but she was poorly and she did not have much money. She had no house and she did not love my daddy so they did not live together. Because of these things my mummy felt she could not look after me properly. She asked the social workers to look after me instead. . . .
> Mr Turner, my first social worker, carried me to my first foster home. I was seven months old and already had red hair (ABAFA, 1977, p. 49).

There are pictures of 'MY MUM', heartrendingly pretty, 'My mum was slim and dark', and of 'Mr Turner carrying a carrycot'.
Our Happy Family is

> an album made by a family with eight children who came to them by birth, adoption and fostering. It tells the story of how the family was built up. An accompanying book tells the stories of the children before they joined the family (p. 48).

This album is illustrated with photographs.

Books such as these are long term projects and require a great deal of commitment on the part of both adult and child but there may also be considerable value in what might be called short stories. The following examples were written by children in hospital.

* Association of British Adoption and Fostering Agencies

We moved, so I'm gonna go to the playground that I don't know very good, but I'm gonna go anyway. I'm gonna go to the top of the hill and roll all the way down and break my neck, and then I'll be back in the hospital with my breaked neck' (Plank, 1971, p. 58).

Tom is a haemophiliac and not likely ever to indulge that fantasy.

Self-expression through writing helps children retain or regain their self-image and give us insight into their thoughts and feelings (p. 62).

Ten-year-old Diane writes about herself:

I get mad if I see chocolate cake or something like that because that's my favorite, chocolate cake and fudge. I can't eat it because I have sugar diabetes. So, it makes me mad because if I would eat it I'd wind up in hospital. I'd be in the hospital if I would eat it because sugar goes against my insulin. . . .
When I'm in a coma. I lay and whine all the time, my mouth is dry, and when I drink something, I throw it back up. Then I lay down and go to sleep. When I wake up, I'm in the hospital.
Those shots. They ain't very pleasant but I take them (p. 61).

One great advantage of creating a book with a particular child is that the ending does not have to be either conventionally happy or disconcertingly inconclusive or even sad as in commercially produced books. It may be very reassuring for the ending to reflect the child's own present position and to suggest the possibility of future happiness even if this is not attainable in the way which the child at this time most desires. I have on several occasions asked students on both field and residential social-work courses to make books for children in some particular stressful situation and the problem is always that without reference to and contribution by a real child, the books always have a clear and happy ending. For example *Moses the Mouse* is the sad tale of survival while Moses's mum goes off to seek his deserting dad. Moses was left with a foster-mouse:

Mum said 'Moses, I'm going away to look for Dad.'
'Oh good,' said Moses, 'can I come?'
'No; I'm sorry but you can't' Mum replied.
'But I know someone who will look after you till I come back.'
Moses was upset: he didn't want to stay behind, alone in a strange place. Moses sulked angrily.
'Come on,' said Mum. She packed the bags and took Moses right across town. They stopped at a big house. 'Here we are,' she said. 'And here's the person who will look after you. Call her Aunty.' Moses sat silently. 'Hello Moses' said Aunty. She had a big booming voice, 'Now say goodbye to your Mum. I'll go and make some tea.' (Amende, 1974).

Moses was more and more miserable but eventually he began to play; a pirate, a cowboy, a train driver and a fireman. This exciting, controlling play helped him to survive. At last Mum and Dad came home and we hope that they all lived happily ever after. But in real life often father does not come home and a book made by a social worker and child together might have to end with Moses getting used to life in the foster home or getting used to life with Mum alone.

Another advantage of making a book directly with a child is that the book itself is a tangible object which may be left with the child between the worker's visits, possibly with some enjoyable task for the child to perform and certainly acting as a symbol of the worker's intention to return. In *Jackie Goes to Hospital* the student author indicated that the social worker was working with

> a six-year-old girl who lives with her middle-aged foster parents. Osteomyelitis necessitates admission to hospital for possible surgery. Jackie is visited in hospital by a social worker she has known for some years. Together they make a book, talking about what Jackie indicates the worker should write and draw. The blank pages are for Jackie's drawings, completed while the book is being made, during and shortly after the period of hospitalization (Brown, 1974).

The author in fact wrote the book entirely on her own but it is impossible not to imagine 'Jackie' and her social worker compiling it together and it is quite frustrating not to see what 'Jackie' would have drawn on those blank pages, some completely free and some labelled tantalizingly 'Nurse', 'Fisher Ward' and 'Jackie with Auntie and Uncle'.

Compiling a book with a child is in no way an easy operation and any social worker undertaking such an activity must think very carefully about the context of her work and in particular about the timing for the child. It may be that the making of a life story book may prove to be an enormous asset in helping the child understand his own position in relation to foster family or children's home but it may also be that such a book is not for this child the most useful medium of communication or that this is for some reason the wrong time to embark on one. It is sometimes tempting for the adult to invest too much in the book itself and in the apparent benefit to be gained by the shared activity and it is always vital to remember that the child must retain a sense of control, that it is *his* book, that the communication is being offered for *his* benefit. One social worker expressed bewilderment that the children with whom she was creating life story books with photographs and drawings often seemed to be uninterested. Sometimes, she said, when she wanted them to remember and write about themselves chronologically, they would skip from, say, the age of three to their present ages. The social worker thought that the children were not responding to her plan and indeed, if rigid adherence to her concept of their perception of their own lives was her plan, they were not. But these children were perhaps responding excellently to a more sensible and beneficial plan, for were they not linking memories of past events and selves with their present lives and concepts of themselves? And should not this have underlain the social worker's aim in introducing the activity? It is very easy for the adult to forget whose book it is.

Sally's father and stepmother learned something about this too. During the first year of Sally's visits to them they thought a scrapbook would be a good idea. She could make her own story putting in pictures of her parents and the two houses where she is at home and that, they thought, might help with the sorting out process. They gave her a large scrapbook and introduced the idea. She was thrilled and flew to the glue. The scrapbook was full of pictures – of flowers and robins and funny animals all cut from old Christmas and birthday cards. Sally loved the scrapbook but it was hard for the adults to realize that it *was* hers not theirs and that she did not want or perhaps need to use it in their way. Sally's book had a use beyond that of providing enjoyable activity. It was something over which she had control. She could choose what if anything to put in and where to put it. Glue could be spread all over the pages or kept neatly to the picture and no one minded. The adults could be asked to help or not as she wished and they could certainly be asked to admire.

Making books with and for children is one thing but children may vary in their reactions once the creation is complete. The children in *Our Happy Family*

> like to refer to their book and see themselves as part of the family. It also answers in a clear and attractive way many of the questions asked by people meeting this family for the first time (ABAFA, 1977, p. 48).

Mary and her social worker spent two months of weekly contacts on her book.

> [Mary] was then ready to take the book home and give it to the foster mother for safekeeping. Mary chose to store the book on top of the refrigerator in the kitchen, where it was beyond the reach of the other children in the home. . . .
> Mary's attitude toward the book was one of quiet respect (Eikenberry 1972, p. 38).

However Kay Donley (1975, p. 28) has some warnings:

> What about the social worker's own possessiveness? I think I should warn you about this, particularly if you use the technique of running around buying ice-cream cones to avoid talking directly to a child. A colleague worked very hard with a scrapbook with a little girl and discovered one day, to her absolute dismay, that the child had discarded the scrapbook. As far as the child was concerned, she had finished with the thing and just tossed it away. When the worker discovered this she was so cross she almost cried: they had worked so hard and so constantly on this thing for many months that the worker felt disappointed, as if the child had somehow betrayed her, as she later explained. And she really had to do some hard thinking in order to accept that the child had a right to deal with the scrapbook as she wished. It was obvious to us as colleagues that the child no longer had an enormous investment in her past and, therefore, understandably had disposed of the thing rather casually. So I warn you – do not get too attached to the scrapbook.

As usual, there are at least two ways of looking at everything and I will set against Kay Donley's sensible comments the suggestion that it may sometimes be appropriate for the adult to rescue and preserve a, or the, book for possible use and value when the child is older. The decision about this will depend, as ever, on the particular child in his particular circumstances but it is, I think, a decision which must be considered in the light of Wynford Jones's (1970, p. 23) comment that

> Most childrens' books don't survive the pretty rough handling they often get. Sometimes a special book needs to be rescued and put away for a child, sometimes it might be a present from parents . . . A well loved book can be a great comfort when a child is ill in bed, and in later years a reminder of people and places.

My final comment on the benefits of personal book making is that the actual production of the book is likely to provide a sense of considerable achievement (for both child and adult). The finished book, however objectively beautiful or otherwise, is evidence for a child (who is very probably not receiving a great deal of praise at school) that he can actually produce a satisfying and enjoyable and useful book.

End piece

In this review of some of the ways in which books and stories may be of use to social workers in their endeavours to communicate with children I do not pretend fully to have covered the subject; I have only suggested some of the methods, benefits and pitfalls. Neither have I provided an exhaustive critique of bibliotherapy; some of the ideas contained above derive from or are reflected in the literature of bibliotherapy but this chapter is essentially a collection of my own ideas relating especially to field social workers in any agency concerned with working with children.

Some bibliographies

Many Children's and Schools Library Services will, I am advised, be glad to compile lists of books on specific topics on request. One such list which is available at the time of writing is:

Belfast Education and Library Board: *Trouble Shared*: A list of books dealing with the everyday fears and problems of young children.

Some other bibliographies of potentially bibliotherapeutic books are:

Cornwall Education Committee, Schools Library Service: A selection of novels for young adults about *Personal Relationships and Growing Up* etc.

Good, M. Stories about some Family Problems in *The School Librarian*, September 1978.

National Council for One Parent Families. One Parent Families, a Guide to

Books for Children and Young Adults (comp. by Trembath, D). *Information*, August 1978, No. 22.

Oldham Children's Library Service (compiled by Stott, P. and Mélia, R.) *Teenager 3*.

Another form of such bibliography is the annotated guide, of which these three books are good examples: (All publishers given in these are American but many of the books have British publishers also).

Baskin, B. H. and Harris, K. H. *Notes from a Different Drummer* (on handicap). R. R. Bowker & Co., 1977.

Bernstein, J. *Books to Help Children Cope with Separation and Loss*. R. R. Bowker & Co., 1977.

Gillis, R. J. *Children's Books for Times of Stress*. Indiana University Press, 1978

Chapter 6

Notes on Notes*

And it came to pass when the evil spirit from God was upon Saul that David took a harp and played with his hand: so Saul was refreshed and was well and the evil spirit departed from him (1 Samuel 16.23).

Music as a means of therapy has been used since man first differentiated 'music' from his other sounds. While references may be hard to find in ancient literature the story of Saul and David suggests that the use of music in such a way must have been common and esteemed.

Yet in the twentieth century AD music is probably the most neglected of the many forms of communication available to 'professional communicators', and it seems to be almost completely overlooked by social workers. For example *The ABCs of Casework with Children*, a book devoted to different methods and means of communicating with children under stress, refers to no musical instruments at all except 'noisemakers' and one piano and, rather in passing, advises social workers to learn current hit songs (Zwerdling, 1974, p. 7).

One area where music is increasingly widely used as a means of both communication and of therapy is with subnormal and mentally ill people. The British Society for Music Therapy is one body working hard to develop such use and the publications of this Society, while relating directly to therapy in specialized situations, may be found to have considerable relevance to social workers interested in developing the use of music within the context of social casework. It is important at this point to stress that although reference will be made throughout this chapter to the above mentioned Society, in no way do I intend to suggest that social workers should try to become music therapists or that the use of music which I advocate within the context of social casework should be as therapy. The task of the social worker is to develop means and opportunities for communication between herself and her client.

* This chapter is a revised and expanded version of an article which appeared in *Social Work Service*, October 1978 under the title, Harp-Assisted Casework: Music as an Aid to Communication with Children.

A quotation from Juliette Alvin (1971a, p. 39), founder and 'keynote' of the Society, may clarify the link between music as therapy and as communication. In an account of work with psychotic children and adults she writes:

> the main aim of music therapy had been to create different kinds of perceptual and psychological communication depending on the patients' needs and condition: communication with sound, with music heard or played, with oneself, with the therapist and with others. In the process, different kinds of awareness developed, awareness of sound, of self, of music, of movement, of the therapist, which helped the psychotic patient to come into contact with reality and to relate.

Social workers are always seeking ways in which to help their clients to come into contact with reality and relate and much may be learned from the ideas and experience of music therapists to help with work with children who although not 'psychotic' do have problems in communication and especially perhaps with the use of words.

The aim of this chapter is to discuss some of the ways in which music may be employed to aid communication between social workers and their child clients.

Problems and inhibitions

It seems important to consider some of the possible inhibitors to the development of the social worker as musician. In other words, what does come between the plain man and music?

Perhaps the prime problem is that any musical utterance involves an immediate and direct revelation of the self. Music is itself about, and an expression of, emotion and to perform music at once links the performer with that emotion. Of course this may often be a matter of acting, expressing for example love or grief which is certainly not at that moment being felt by the performer. But the attentive audience may recognize whether or not the expression is feigned, based on superficial 'performing' or some real understanding of the emotions within the performer.

Use of the naked voice is probably the most revealing form of musical activity. Most people use their voices most of the time without embarrassment for talking. But what happens when someone is asked to recite a poem (still a form of speaking) or to sing? There is likely to be a considerable difference in response according to whether the speaker or singer is alone – particularly in the bath where everyone sings like Sutherland or Sinatra – in a choir, a confident soloist or with a known and affectionate child. Is it trite to suggest that speech may be a protection but singing is for most people an exposure?

Another inhibitor to the use of music as a means of communication may be the contemporary availability of perfect performances on record. Everyone knows exactly how everything should sound so why expose imperfection when a record of perfection may so easily be played? Attempts to play or sing are so often preceded by 'I'm not much good, out of practice . . .' and so on. This leads to the notion that music and the mastery of instruments, including the voice, are about performance and observable ability rather than enjoyment, communication and self-expression.

The last inhibitor in this list is particularly relevant to social workers. Musical instruments tend to be bulky and expensive. Any number of pencils, pads, toys and books may be stowed in the car but the musical instruments available to most people are predominantly stationary. Musical instruments are also noisy and therefore difficult to use in overcrowded offices.

The easiest musical activity

> The main and easiest musical activity in a residential Home is naturally through singing, since everyone possesses a voice. (Alvin, 1967, p. 69).

So if it is impossible for the social worker to use a musical instrument to aid communication she has no excuse to shun music altogether; she can sing or hum or la la. Everyone possesses a voice and it doesn't have to be a good voice any more than only excellent artists can use drawing in communicating with children. It is the willingness to open the mouth and use that voice in some vaguely recognizably musical manner which matters.

Singing is, with percussion, the earliest and easiest method of music making. Very young children spontaneously sing. John Holt (1970, pp. 15–16) writes about sixteen-month-old Lisa and some other small friends:

> Lisa, walked round and round . . . singing, more or less her own version of 'Ring-around-a-rosie'. As she sang it, she began to change it, until before long it had become an entirely different song. Much of what she says, sings and does, is like this; it starts out as one thing, and gradually turns into another. A musician might call it variation on a theme.
>
> Many other little children I have known love to tell endless stories and sing endless songs. Sometimes the song is about what they did or would like to do. A mother told me her four-year-old boy, whose seven-year-old sister was in school, began one day, alone in his room, to chant a song about 'I wish I had a sister, who didn't have to go to school, and would do everything I say . . .' Often the song is nonsensical, words and nonsense syllables; sometimes sense and nonsense are mixed.

By really paying attention to his private chanting the little boy's mother was able to learn something important about his feelings and wishes. Social workers may not often be in a position to overhear such messages but they are in contact with people who do, for example parents, residential workers and nurses.

The association of words and music may offer clues to the development of contact with poorly communicating children. Clara

Claiborne Park (1972, p. 150) found that a song provided some key to the memory of her young autistic daughter. In an endeavour to unlock Elly's memories of home during a long stay abroad she drew a picture of the family house. Elly remained impassive until 'I drew the record-player' at which

> Tense and excited, she began to jump up and down, her signal for approval and delight. She... put her finger on the crude circle that represented the turntable and moved it round. Then she began to sing... the song 'Instead Of' from The Three-Penny Opera.
> It was almost a year since Elly had heard that music. She had been obsessed with it; for two months and more she had asked for the record every day.... We had left the record behind in America, and there it remained and the music with it, dissolved, extinguished, part of the irrevocable past. But it was not wholly irrecoverable. We had recaptured a minute of it. We could find more.

This leads to an even more important and significant sharing of memory indicated by the combination of drawing and singing:

> it was the rocking chair that excited her, and again it was music that let me know she shared my memory, for as I drew she began to sing the melody of 'Rockabye Baby', which she had first learned as I rocked her, so many times, in that very chair in her old room at home (p. 151).

One of the most deeply personal word – music links is with an individual's own name (which probably accounts for the popularity of such tunes as 'Laura' and 'Nichola'). Just as children enjoy stories which either reflect their own lives and adventures or have as hero a child with the same name, some children find excitement in hearing their own name associated with music. Paul Nordoff and Clive Robbins (1971, pp. 20–21) write of the way in which a severely handicapped ten-year-old Danish girl Pernilla was helped to communicate through the association of her name with a well known children's tune – not a popular song but one of those melodies which, like 'Chopsticks' seems to be known instinctively to every child.

Pernilla 'had no speech, her tongue was large and she had very limited control over it; she made three or four recognizable sounds'.

The tune was played and when Pernilla's name was sung to it 'she smiled and made sounds of pleasure'.

Eventually 'she was both aroused and amused and half-sang back with some intention'.

Pernilla continued to try to sing and even

made many efforts with her awkward tongue to say an 'L'. Her speech therapist observed this session and wheeled her back to the classroom. He reported that she tried over and over again to say her name. He was struck by the intensity of her drive to communicate verbally. 'We had a conversation', he said.

Nordoff and Robbins consider that

> The singing of a child's name is important in both individual and group therapy. A child's name carries his or her sense of self; it is the special symbol of identity. It can be a joyful or consoling experience for a handicapped child to hear his or her name set to music and sung.

It could be similarly 'consoling' for a child en route to some care establishment or court or in hospital at those times when sense of identity may be so vulnerable and when confirmation of identity by reference to that precious possession the name might be very reassuring.

Exploring an instrument

Although a musical instrument is an object, separate from the player, it may in some ways be as much part of the musician as the voice:

> If we consider that all musical instruments are a prolongation of the human body, it is obvious that the performer does identify in some way with his instrument. Even a young child if given a totally free choice will instinctively choose the instrument which appeals most to his personality and will be his own means of self-expression (Alvin, 1967, p. 96).

Irrespective of the music which is produced by the interaction of child and instrument, a child may gain a very great deal from simply being in contact with an instrument and perhaps, as Juliette Alvin suggests, identifying in some way with it. Juliette Alvin (1971b, p. 8) herself writes about such contacts, for example six-year-old Jeremy and a cello. Jeremy

> seems to understand a few simple words but cannot speak. He makes inarticulate sounds, very soft and almost inaudible. He is withdrawn and seems to be afraid. Noise frightens him particularly . . . there is no communication or any way to get hold of him.

For some time Jeremy was passive but seemed to enjoy listening to the cello and the instrument itself became a means of more direct contact between the adult and child:

> His relationship with the cello was characteristic. I let him open the case and help me take out the instrument. This he did with great care. I taught him to say 'Good morning, cello' and he tried to do this. Little by little I made him speak louder and louder to the cello, of which he was not afraid. . . .
> He touched its head and followed its contours. He also liked touching the

strings and he learnt to use his thumb or fingers to make them vibrate. . . . At the end of the sessions he helped to put the cello back in its case and said goodbye to it (p. 9).

This brief extract illustrates a number of ways in which the musical instrument itself may be of help to adults seeking to communicate with children.

First, it may be an object of curiosity and interest, something to attract the attention and be explored. Withdrawn Jeremy liked to touch the cello and experience it sensuously. John Holt (1970, p. 49) took his cello to school:

> I take it to a classroom, and give the children a turn at 'playing' it. Except for the timid ones, who make a few half-hearted passes with the bow and then quit, almost all little children attack the cello in the same way. They are really doing three things at once: they are making the machine go; they are enjoying the luxury of making sounds; and they are making scientific experiments. They start off by working the bow vigorously back and forth across one of the strings. They keep this up for a long time. Just the feel and sound of it are exciting. Then they begin to vary their bowing a bit, trying different rhythms. After a while, they begin to move the bow so that it touches more than one string, or they move to another string. But . . . the first few times they do this, they do not seem to be doing it in the spirit of an experiment, to find out what will happen. They do it for the sake of doing it.

Here the children were behaving in basically the same way as Jeremy, discovering and experiencing as many aspects of the instrument as they could find and, essentially, enjoying the instrument and the experience in their *own* way, *not* in some limited method prescribed by an adult. I am sure that many children part company with musical instruments almost before they have met them because adults believe that instruments should be played, that is to say that some rules should be learned and obeyed and some complex and rigid language mastered and interpreted. The rules and the language may well be learned and mastered but the learning and mastery will surely be most effective if they derive from exploration and excitement.

With particular reference to social workers and their endeavours to communicate with children, withdrawn or otherwise, a musical instrument with its many areas of interest (tactile, auditory, manipulative) is almost bound to be attractive and to provide a subject for conversation.

The musical instrument may also be a safe object for approach and sharing. Jeremy was 'not afraid' of the cello and his contact with the instrument led him into contact with the adult. Many other instruments were used to help this contact, for example: 'We shared the piano keyboard . . . sitting side by side and improvising or exploring from one end to the other' (Alvin, 1971b, p. 11). (This activity developed not only the communication between adult and child but also Jeremy's motor control and coordination.) The piano with its long keyboard is probably the ideal instrument for sharing. Not only are the noises produced and the experience of playing the notes shared but also the players sit side by side, or even, if the child is small, with the child on the adult's knee and thus physical contact of an intimate but non-threatening kind may be established. Four-year-old Ann, blind and exhibiting much disturbed behaviour, was offered intensive therapeutic visiting by a nursery school director who had experience in both teaching blind children and psycho-analytic therapy (however, her work with Ann based primarily on play is, I think, all within the compass of a social worker). The piano in Ann's home was a very useful aid to communication and as with Jeremy and the cello had considerable physical significance:

> gradually her hands moved along with mine as she played the piano. . . . Her inhibition about touching was compounded by the actual fact that her fingers were weak and inept. However, both her willingness to touch and her physical strength improved to the extent that by Christmas . . . she responded to encouragement to press hard enough to sound a note on the piano and kept time with a one-finger accompaniment to whatever I was playing. Ann could anticipate and hold the rhythm and also select notes which were in harmony with the songs I played (Omwake and Solnit, 1961, p. 363).

The third way in which the picture of Jeremy and the cello suggests the use of a musical instrument (as opposed to the music itself) as an aid to communication is as an encouragement to speech. Jeremy who, before he met the cello could not speak and made inarticulate sounds, is emboldened to say 'good morning' and 'goodbye' to the cello. The same method was introduced by Juliette Alvin to the mother of Simon, an autistic boy. Anne Lovell (1978, p. 60) bought for her son chime bars and provided

> several pieces of highly coloured cloth in which Simon might wrap his chime bars separately. For he had to be taught to cherish his musical instrument, to treat each note, in fact, as if it were a person. From the first, he was put in charge of the unwrapping and re-wrapping of each chime bar at the beginning and end of each session. What is more, he had to learn to greet each one individually, as he brought it out, by name, and to say goodbye to it as he put it away. He needed very little persuasion to do this, and before long 'Hello, A' or 'Hello, C' became a matter of expected routine. Shortly after this, he began to greet actual people, too.

A musical instrument with its body and voice and the ability to move (in the hands of an operator of course) in so many different ways is, I suggest, the nearest thing to another human being (except perhaps an animal) that a child can have contact with; so that gaining the courage to speak to an instrument is really quite a short step from addressing a person. Social workers may not often themselves undertake the kind of intensive work with a non-communicating child that has been demonstrated in the examples of Juliette Alvin, Eveline Omwake and Anne Lovell (although these ideas might encourage attempts to make contact with children in, for example, subnormality hospitals). However, they are involved with the families of non-communicating children and, as with all the ideas in this book, their prime work may be in introducing new ideas about communication to those caring for the child and supporting them in their endeavours to communicate.

A channel of communication

What they need first and foremost and above all things, is warm human contact and a means of communication. Music can help to make this contact, and music can be a channel of communication. So I try to make music a shared experience (Barclay, 1960, p. 11).

Priscilla Barclay is writing about her work with mentally handicapped children but I think that her comment can be applied to any children in a stressful or deprived situation and is relevant to those social workers who endeavour to help them.

One way of sharing the experience of music suggested by Priscilla Barclay is through movement by which 'I do not mean simply displacing oneself in space. There is a much more fundamental and more conscious joy than that in movement' (p. 12).

Juliette Alvin (1969, p. 32) writes about Andrew, a severely subnormal boy, that

He became more aware of everything related to the therapists, namely of her cello to be listend to and touched, and to dancing with her. Further work should include a one-to-one musical relationship with her, especially with regard to dancing. These movements to music might lead him to become aware of the group.

A social worker trying to make and develop contact with a child may find many opportunities to move to music, in other words to dance, once she becomes aware of this as a means of communication. Social workers are after all well aware of the importance of non-verbal cues and it is surely a short step from observing and interpreting body language to communicating with the whole body. The easiest way for a social worker to find the opportunity to dance with her young clients may be to join them in a disco; it is certainly worth remembering how much teenagers and indeed younger children enjoy disco dancing with its energetic use of the whole body and its response to the sound, rhythm and vibration of the music.

Not every social worker will feel young or uninhibited enough to go disco dancing but there are other ways of joining children in dance, for example spontaneously jigging around a bit to a record or singing and playing with children the old dance games (The Farmer's in his Den, In and Out the Dusty Bluebells . . .). The whole body need not necessarily be used. Hand jive used to be popular, feet may tap, heads may be nodded. The dancing use of júst one part of the body may be of great significance in the development of the child's ability to communicate at all or with the individual social worker. For example:

> Brian, a ten-year-old autistic and epileptic boy, had no speech and showed no volition towards anything or anybody. He usually kept immobile and withdrawn. During four months he did not react to any musical sound or music, whatever its pitch, speed or intensity. He was not deaf, but sounds simply did not seem to penetrate. One day I played to him on a small instrument consisting of a little box and imitating the song of a nightingale. The effect on the boy was unbelievable. He suddenly came to life, his face became lively, his eyes bright, and all his posture changed. He then answered the bird by making shrill rapid sounds quite expressive. He sustained a whole dialogue with the bird. The movements he made with his head, his neck attentive to the sounds resembled those of a bird. He also reacted with ritual unconscious movements, tapping rapidly on a table with his finger tips. . . .
> He often smiled and became active during the whole of his sessions. We have found a means of communication on which a development may be possible (Alvin, 1971a, pp. 35–6).

Helping a child to relax is one of the first necessities when trying to develop communication; a tense child will communicate only tension. Brian came to life in response to the nightingale box and part of his behaviour seems to have depended on relaxation; instead of being immobile and withdrawn he often smiled. Six-year-old Jeremy also found music an aid to relaxation.

> He sat on a low comfortable chair with a cushion under his head and I invited him to sleep. . . . I always played something very short, prolonging it when I saw that he was calm and attentive. At such times he was passive . . . but he smiled often and seemed happy (Alvin, 1971b, p. 9).

Music may be used to reduce tension and enhance relaxation anywhere. For example, a social worker may sing in the car, demonstrating that conversation is not essential for communication, that silence may be broken by noises which are benign and undemanding, that the child may or may not join in. Waiting for a child with no pressure on him to respond is always vital and singing or humming may provide an ideal means for waiting without a tension provoking and too long silence. It may also provide the opportunity for the child to indicate just when he is ready to make some contact, by noise if not yet words. Some background noise may be reassuring to a child used to the usual non-stop accompaniments to life, 'music' on television, radio and in shops and discos.

Earlier in this chapter I suggested that music might be exposing and potentially dangerous and conversation and speech protecting but in some circumstance music may be the less threatening medium:

In one situation involving a nonverbal child who stuttered, the worker sought a way to help the child express himself verbally and hit on the technique of many sessions of singing loudly at the piano. Later, the child was able to talk more in interviews (Zwerdling, 1974, p. 7).

Barbara Williams (1978, p. 16) wrote about her work with Karen 'a hostile, suspicious thirteen-year-old, the middle child of a family of three who had been rejected by her mother'. The social worker believes that

> Shared experiences can provide a safe, neutral area which can unite social worker and child, and become a non-threatening form of communication. These experiences can be referred to and talked over and relived in retrospect, enabling an individual language to evolve between worker and child and laying the basis for direct communication.

It was not easy to discover the basis for direct communication with Karen.

> For weeks my visits to her at her residential school were met with anger and hostility, and my efforts to get close to her met with rejection. She said that I asked too many questions and maintained that I had caused friction within her family. I resisted the temptation to visit less often, which would merely have confirmed Karen's low self-image and her feeling that she could not be liked, but *instead of attempting to talk, sat quietly* in the room used by the children to play records. Eventually, Karen was able to join me, and for many weeks we listened to music together, never talking about her or her family. *At times it was difficult for me to curb my own impatience and the feeling that I was wasting my time*, but eventually in the safety of the music room, Karen was able to express some of her feelings about her mother and her anxiety about the future. It had taken some time for me to realize that to establish communication with Karen, the language of facts alone was totally inadequate (p. 16). (emphasis added)

For Karen and her social worker music was a means to the end of sharing the experience of relaxation, peace and eventual communication. The music helped the social worker to *wait* for the child and the child to feel safe enough to confide in the patient, caring adult. But the content of the music itself seems to have been not important (except in so far as it was enjoyed by the child). Any particular piece of music may, however, have some special importance for a child (as for anyone else) and may well stimulate some memory or response not anticipated. Ten-year-old Martin in a residential special school listened to a record of the *Sinfonia Antarctica* by Vaughan Williams in company with other children and the Warden of the school:

> He became very relaxed as he lay curled up in an armchair with his eyes closed, and he did not appear to be awake when, at the end, he was carried upstairs and placed in his bed.
> The next day, Martin came up to me: 'Skipper' he said, 'that music we had last night – made me think of my Dad – and I dreamt about him all night, too –' Then, he sobbed, and said: 'I shall be eighteen before I see my Dad again – before my Dad comes out of prison – '

> [The music] gave him release, which enabled him to talk more freely to me ... about his Dad in prison, and about his unhappy and frightening feelings – and about his resentful feelings, too (Knight, 1960, p. 5).

The cathartic effect of music may be manifested in violent ways.

> An inarticulate young boy, very disturbed and withdrawn, was listening with others to a 'cradle song'. Each of the children was rocking for play an imaginary baby in his arms. I saw the boy suddenly seize the baby, wring its, neck violently and throw it on the floor. Then he looked round to make sure that no one had seen him. This revealing outburst relieved him better than any word. He was, in any case, unable to speak (Alvin, 1967, p. 92).

This is also another example of the combination of music and movement, in this instance mime, drama at its most intense and real. Music is also here combined with play and, in the next illustration, with drawing, where once again the expression of strong emotion is enabled.

> When an older child asked me to play a crocodile, he showed me what he meant by drawing on a paper a symbolic figure: four sharp angles in a row, like cruel teeth. The impact of my improvized evocative music brought him tremendous release. He 'lived' the crocodile throughout, becoming more and more tense, and then calmed down and was perfectly satisfied at the end, back to peaceful reality (Alvin, p. 93).

One of the most important points here is the return to peaceful reality. It would not, I think, be too difficult for even a non-musical social worker to improvize crocodile teeth but those teeth would have to be pulled or at least blunted, the crocodile would have to become, within the music, a benign beast, eventually perhaps sleeping in the sun. It is always important to seek a peaceful ending with and for a child even though it is likely that the crocodile will awaken, that tension and aggression will have to be released and enacted time after time in the future; but it cannot be right to leave a child in a state of tension and excitement for the sake either of the child himself or of those adults who have to cope with the emotion after the social worker has gone home.

In the above illustrations the children were responding to music played by other people either 'live' or on records but the child himself may use a musical instrument to express feeling either at or to another person, maybe a social worker, or entirely for his own relief, satisfaction, enjoyment or whatever. In 'Hippopotamus or Cow' I wrote about Fred, who apparently expressed feeling about the recent deaths of two close relatives by playing spontaneous and extremely dramatic and expressive music on the piano, on his own in the room but knowing that I was within easy earshot (Wardle, 1975, p. 431). The role of the adult at such times, whether as friend or parent or social worker, is to be aware that the child *may* be expressing something and to be ready then or at some later time to respond verbally.

A thirteen-year-old boy on leave from his residential special school used to call with his younger brothers. He would never speak but would sit at the piano and thunder out aggression (against, I think, the world). His headmaster said that he was not interested in music at the school although there was a well equipped music room; but the instruments were in good condition and such thundering would not, it seemed, be encouraged; the music room was for 'music'. His twelve-year-old brother also enjoyed the piano but in a quite different way for he would express the gentleness of his nature by long flowing lyrical creations. This boy always liked to have a book of music on the stand and although he could not read it he would from time to time turn the page and then continue to play.

Four-year-old blind Ann

> used the play at the piano to reveal the vague ideas and feelings which confused and often frightened her. With her voice and posture, and with a display of energy she attacked the piano, and in this way communicated her feelings of helplessness, anger, excitement, and dependency which she had been unable to express in a way that could be dealt with. Through such piano play, strange as it was, she found her first medium for communication associated with pleasure, mastery, and excitement (Omwake and Solnit, 1961, p. 364).

Pleasure, mastery and excitement may be rather rare experiences for many of the children who become the clients of social workers. Music may provide as well as means of self-expression and communication, a way to the discovery of some ability and satisfaction for the child. Mastery of a song or a simple instrument may well give a great boost to self-confidence. Many of the children known to social workers live in worlds of inability, failure and rejection and they have no control over anything, least of all their own lives and destinies. Control over a musical instrument or voice, production of lively, expressive sounds and the approval of other people could make a real difference to the self-esteem of the child. Indeed a child might even find enough ability and interest to learn how to play the instrument properly.

All together now

The main theme of this chapter has been the use of music as a shared activity and experience in attempts to develop communication with children and perhaps some of the illustrations have been rather sober. In this section I will redress that slightly by referring to some examples of music as a source of fun and sheer enjoyment, for these elements are vital in any communication developed with a view to aiding, help and healing.

> Music, apart from its therapeutic value, has the power to draw patients, staff and visitors into a group. In one hospital ward where the teacher

plays a guitar, what begins as a group activity for children, invariably attracts a large number of patients, nurses, orderlies, porters and medical staff who join in the fun (Harvey and Hales-Tooke, 1972, p. 99).

The atmosphere in a ward where such a thing can happen must surely be therapeutic in itself. I imagine that the children must gain greatly from contact with adults who are relaxed and human.

Simon Lovell's mother organized a band to help him enjoy music and use it as a means to further communication with other people:

> I invited every child I could lay hands on to join our 'band' Now ... Joanna [his sister] ... could join in, to her great excitement; and somewhat to her surprise our Dutch *au pair* found herself part of it. The din was unbelievable as they all joined in round the piano, with me at the keyboard belting out the tune in a way that would have startled my mother, who had only rarely succeeded in persuading me to practise. And here was Simon in the middle of it all, clashing his cymbals perfectly on the beat, loving every moment, and sharing his enjoyment with other children (Lovell, 1978, p. 61).

Once again the musicians were by no means expert but they were willing and the result was a happy, shared activity and no doubt some interesting noises. Social workers have need of every activity they can think of to aid communication with children and, whether or not under the heading *Intermediate Treatment*, they may find themselves working with groups. What better than a band! After the publication of 'Harp-Assisted Casework' a social worker telephoned me to say that he was going to form his intermediate treatment group into a comb-and-paper band. Music is so wide and rich and varied a medium; anything can be used to make melody, accompaniment and rhythm.

To conclude this chapter here is a lively account of some shared music, children and an adult having fun together, developing through that fun and shared activity trust and interest in one another, not inhibited by dignity and lack of expertise; but there are within the account one or two sad thoughts and questions which might exercise the mind of an interested social worker:

> The other day, I brought to school an old army bugle that I had bought second-hand for eight dollars. When the first-grade and kindergarten children went out to recess, I took the bugle out. I gave it a tentative blast or two (I can't play it), and about 20 children crowded around me, clamouring for a turn. I lined them up and off we went. Quite a number of them knew, from having watched me, what to do with their lips. Others put the whole mouthpiece in their mouths, like a lollipop, before realizing that that wouldn't work. Then they tried it the right way. Some I had to show, pursing my lips and blowing though them, what had to be done. Nine out of ten children were able to get a good sound – that is, a strong sound – out of the bugle. Some could make as much noise on it as I could. They got tremendous pleasure from it – particularly Martin. I could hardly get it away from him. A few, sad, defeated little children would

come up, give a weak puff through the instrument, and hand it back to me
with a resigned expression. Why did these few give up so easily?
After about four days of this, one of the teachers came out – from her
coffee break – and said to please stop playing the bugle, it made her too
nervous. So that was the end of that. But it was interesting to see, if only
for a short while, how energetically and confidently most of these little
children tackled the problem of getting a sound out of a difficult
instrument (Holt, 1970, p. 48).

Postlude

During the limbo time when the book was finished and en route
between editor and printer I received from the library a book which
I had ordered months before, and despaired of. And in that last
minute after which nothing can be added, I have slipped in this
paragraph to introduce *Give Your Child Music* by Jill Phillips (1979).
The front jacket flap says that the author 'addresses herself to
parents, playgroup leaders, instrumental teachers – and to anyone
else concerned with children from the earliest years to secondary
school age. A parent does not need to be a musician to discover the
possibilities of music together with a child, and non-specialists will
find that they can do far more to open up musical experience for a
child than they ever realized.'

The book is full of ideas, common sense, photographs, pictures by
children and, of course, music.

> Music is a gift to mankind. It is there to be enjoyed. If it is given in good
> time, with sympathy and understanding, who knows what may result?
> (p. 162).

Chapter 7

Talking Pictures

Frontispiece

> Children who find it difficult to communicate through words will often open up when provided with paint, clay, collages or three-dimensional materials. However, feelings of anger, frustration and anxiety are not always apparent to the casual observer who admires the finished product. It is not until you sit down with the child and invite him to share his thoughts about his work that you can begin to understand (Green, 1974, p. 21).

This quotation encapsulates the theme of this chapter which is a discussion of how the graphic and plastic arts may be employed in the development of communication between child and social worker.

Listen to the Children speaking ... through their Work
(Jameson, 1974, p. 1)

The exhortation to 'listen' appears in the introduction to a booklet intended primarily as a companion to an exhibition of children's art work but how appropriate it is to social workers. Of all the verbal people in this over-verbal society social workers are, I suspect, among the most highly word-dependent for communication. Kenneth Jameson suggests that pictures can, indeed must, be listened to and Jill Green in the opening quotation in this chapter considers that for some children under stress creative art activities may be an essential substitute for speech; they may 'help children in hospital to express their feelings in a natural and unthreatening way' (Green, 1974, p. 21).

Very occasionally drawing may be a complete substitute for speech. In 1977 the story of Nadia was told in a book (Selfe) and an article (Bugler). Nadia is an autistic girl whose astonishing art work apparently replaced her total lack of verbal language. As she gradually learnt to use language her drawing regressed and more or less stopped.

Nadia was surrounded by specialist teachers and therapists but social workers too sometimes have to try to communicate with completely non-verbal children. And many children are at times unable or unwilling to communicate verbally with adults. Social workers do not need to be expert artists or therapists to use and understand communication through art work. For example, six-year-old Julie

> showed some autistic features. In particular, she remained largely aloof and isolated from other children in the [Psychiatric] Unit, and found their chatter and the usual sounds of children playing unbearable, and would isolate herself further by covering her ears with her hands saying 'too noisy, too noisy'. . . she seemed locked inside herself and it was difficult to gain insight into her own feelings about herself and her life experience. Her play gave no clues. She rarely interacted with other children and seemed unable to let herself go in imaginative play, even of a solitary nature, preferring just to sit or wander around the room if left alone (Williams, 1978, p. 12).

The writer is a social worker seconded at that time to a specialist child-care course and undertaking a fieldwork placement in the play group at the Child Psychiatric Unit:

> On one occasion I was able to gain a small insight into the important factor in her home life, through drawing. When she refused to draw for me herself, I began to draw a house. She showed a glimmer of interest and I attempted to involve her by asking her who lived in the house. She instructed me to draw a mother at one window and a father at another, but of greatest importance for her, was 'Goldie'. Goldie she said, must be drawn outside the house, and repeated this several times. I guessed at Goldie's identity and drew a dog, at which Julie told me that the drawing was too small and was not satisfied until Goldie occupied a large part of the paper. Julie's affection for her pet proved a small opening for communication on other occasions, with a child who was otherwise distant and withdrawn (p. 13).

The social worker needed to be both sensitive and alert in order to recognize and encourage the 'glimmer of interest'. How easy it would have been to lose interest in Julie particularly when 'she refused to draw for me herself' and it might have been equally easy to over-organize the drawing, to put in the mother and father instead of giving the child the opportunity to influence and contribute to the drawing even though she did not wish to draw herself. And thus the drawing achieved at least two good effects; it elicited some information useful in the development of understanding of Julie and it provided a small opening for communication on other occasions.

Barbara Williams was, in common with many other social workers, shy about her encounter with art:

> The subject of children's drawings and their interpretation is extremely wide and accurate interpretation demands specific skill. Nevertheless . . . the content of drawing or the repetition of a particular theme in drawings can give valuable insight into what a child considers to be the most important in life. For social workers, interpretation to the child and discussion of the drawing will not be appropriate on most occasions, but I

think that the greatest value lies in learning about the child through a shared experience (p. 13).

I agree that interpretation of art (as of any apparent communication) demands not only skill but also caution. Very deep and detailed analysis of a picture is, I think, certainly an occupation for a specialist working within a very special context. But however highly trained and confident the specialist, surely interpretation must always be governed by the belief that the child *may* be trying to express and/or communicate something and that expression and/or communication *may* be this or that feeling about this or that experience or thought. Only the child himself can say, 'this *is* an expression of this'. And is not the social worker in exactly this position all the time with regard to any medium of communication? Surely she must always be alert to the possibility that the child *may* be saying something and must seek for *possible* significance.

Colour

Meaning may be communicated in many ways, not only through the subject of the picture, and social workers shown children's paintings may see so much without truly seeing. Jean Sloss (1978, pp. 14–15), a play therapist, writes about the painting of some 'maladjusted children':

> Three-quarters of one wall space is the painting area. The children prefer painting onto paper fixed to the wall rather than on easels. Floor space is saved and less paint spilt. Painting helps children to express their fantasies and fears about things they cannot put into words and talk about.
> One little boy of six who was very anxious and full of fears, had never dared to put brush to paper. Once he had begun to feel secure in the playroom, he did a masterly painting of great simplicity, reflecting his own anxious state. He covered a large piece of paper with black paint, with a ghostly green figure wandering over the dark surface. He told me it was a dark room, with a boy who was lost inside, which just described himself. I have found that anxious, frightened children tend to use the dark colours with little form or movement, and that aggressive children go for reds and purples which depict fires or catastrophes of one kind or another. The immature children paint square houses time after time and their people are either stick figures or have arms and legs growing out of their heads. After a period of time in the playroom, it is interesting to see their paintings change, with bright colours gradually taking over, and faces painted with smiles.

Jean Sloss's undogmatic choice of words is attractive and important: '*I have found that* anxious, frightened children *tend to use*'. The writer is indicating that she has not merely applied theory to the children; she has really looked at and listened to what they are doing, she is aware of who the children are and cares to know what they may be trying to say. And she attends carefully to every aspect of their paintings.

Communication by colour is also important in the paintings of Frank a severly withdrawn seven-year-old who

> drew lively active pictures of animals fighting, and as he drew . . . gave them names of both family members and class-mates at school. Feelings of hostility were expressed both in the representations of killings and also in the angry obliteration of figures by heavy scribbling. His own moods were accurately reflected in his choice of colours: black when he was depressed and red when things seemed more hopeful (Rutter, 1975, p. 308).

It is interesting to compare Frank's use of colour with that of Jean Sloss's children. Like the 'anxious, frightened children' he uses black, a dark colour when he is depressed; his use of red, thought to indicate hope by Michael Rutter, might well mirror the 'reds and purples' of the 'aggressive children' since Frank's sense of hope must have depended largely on the positive, active stirring of life in him with the aggression necessary for him to break out of his blackness. His lively aggressive animals contrast with the 'little form or movement' of the drawings of the 'anxious, frightened' children. The point which leaps out in black and red and all the colours of the rainbow is surely that however much his use of colour and subject may resemble that of any other child, the intention of and combination by each child is unique and can be understood only in relation to that particular child. (I am deliberately not referring to any general source on the interpretation of painting because my theme is, as ever, that the caring adult can learn about and communicate with the individual only by attending to the individual first.)

Paintings are not the only vehicles for expression and communication by colour. Mr Beck showed that he and his family had become undepressed by covering every stick and surface of furniture with paint. During the long period of greyness in every aspect of life·the Beck's house too had been grey; scabby, plasterless walls, dirty concrete floor, scuffed, decrepit furniture. When the intolerable difficulties of existence began to become manageable Mr Beck put lively wallpaper straight onto the brick and painted tables and chairs and cupboards and doors yellow and bright green (when the family was eventually rehoused the colours changed to purple and deep red).

Space

Besides subject and colour it is important to notice the positioning of people and objects in a picture because sometimes this too may be telling a story. A dramatic and moving example of this is illustrated in Dr Winnicott's (1971, p. 317) account of his work with eight year-old Ruth. She

> had been especially loved and had even been a little spoiled, and then she changed, and now she was stealing. The parents felt very guilty about this because (as they said) they had seen themselves bringing about this change. They could not avoid it, but they saw the change in Ruth happening under their eyes, starting at the beginning of the mother's third pregnancy.

Ruth's younger sister was now five. Dr Winnicott decided to try to cure Ruth 'of her compulsion to steal. To do this I must reach her own version of her deprived existence.' Ruth and Dr Winnicott played together the squiggle game. First the doctor made a squiggle which the child turned into a picture, then vice versa. After animals and aeroplanes and harps and heads Ruth made a whole picture herself. This was of a dream of

> Ships of olden times with water coming in. 'When my little sister was a baby in arms, I was running. It was before mother had bad legs. Water is rushing up. I am bringing things, baby food for the baby. They had got it because of the baby. The dream ended up nicely. Father came home with the car and went backwards into the garage. He bumped into the ship and smashed it all up and all the water went away. So it ended nicely.'
> There had been considerable anxiety in the middle of this description of the dream, before father came and saved the situation (p. 325).

In the picture 'the mother's mouth is curved, indicating a smile. The child is going towards the mother or is near her' (p. 326). Ruth has depicted a happy mother with herself as close by and hurrying towards her. But

> This dream was optimistic and in the end all went well, so there was a pessimistic version of the same dream somewhere. . . . I invited Ruth to draw the very worst. . . .
> This shows the mother with the baby, and *Ruth surprised herself as she drew*. 'Why! it's a little tiny midget!' She said that there was poison in the sea behind her which made the baby shrink up; mother would shrink up too. 'O look, I'm further and further away from mother!'(p. 327).

And mother has a straight line for a mouth. Here Ruth has depicted her sense of separation from her mother by means of physical distance. In the first picture she and her mother are together in the middle, in the second they are far apart, mother at one edge, Ruth lonely just past the middle, near to squiggles representing the poisonous sea. In his summary, Dr Winnicott comments that

> Ruth . . . was able to remember and relive the distress that belonged to the time of her becoming a deprived child and she was able to illustrate this in drawing. The experience was a therapeutic one for Ruth, and the changes in Ruth benefitted the whole family (p. 330).

It would be dangerous and inappropriate for a social worker to undertake work of this intense nature with a child unless she was confident of her ability to see the work through with both child and family, to be available to the child physically and emotionally and to manage whatever emotion and distress the child displayed. But there are many other perhaps less time-demanding occasions when other Ruths may show through the placing of themselves (or the symbols of themselves) in relation to other people what they feel in the depths which words have not before reached. It is part of the skill and responsibility of every social worker to know how to respond to such painful messages.

Symbol

Symbolism in painting is as old as painting itself. An animal may appear as a portrait of a creature or as the representation of some attribute associated with that creature, for example strength.

Children's drawing may include symbols whether of the children themselves or of people and things associated with them. Social workers need to be aware that symbols may be being used but they must never assume that this or that object does represent anything but that which it superfically appears to be. All round objects are not, for example, breasts.

Animals are popular with children as toys and pets, in stories and films and in drawing and they may serve as representatives of the children. Frank in the quotation above 'drew lively active pictures of animals fighting' and Julie (also quoted above) clearly invested the dog Goldie with much significance even if it did not in some way stand for herself. Mute Nadia drew legions of magnificent horses.

Jill Green (1974, p. 22) writes that in her playroom there is

> a meticulous drawing of a horse in a field with a man, woman and house outside the fence. It is entitled 'Just a Nice Place for a Horse to Live'. The child who drew this picture was an eight-year-old leukaemia girl who explained it to me. 'You see, the horse will live in the field for ever. His parents will come and visit and he can see where they live but he'll never leave the field.'

Dr Jack Kahn (1978, p. 66), child psychiatrist, also writes about significant and sad horses drawn this time by a girl of twelve. Or to be more accurate, sometimes not drawn. For in a picture of a gipsy caravan there are people and trees and a camp fire but

> When the drawing was complete, I said, 'This is a horse caravan. Where is the horse?' . . . She drew a piece of rope attached to a tree, and passing towards the back of the caravan. As she drew she said, 'The horse is behind the caravan.'

Later the horse did appear, this time in a circus.

> She completed the drawing and when I said, 'Well, tell me about it' she replied, 'Well, that's a horse, that's the clown, and that's the ringmaster'.

As she spoke, I noticed the whip and the carrot in the hands of the ringmaster. The theme of reward and punishment was immediately obvious, and so I said, 'Of course, the whip is for when the horse is naughty and the carrot is for when it's good'. Helen said, 'Oh no. This horse doesn't get punished when it's naughty. It's a funny horse. When it does something naughty, people laugh'. I said, 'Well, that's so with children too; when they are young, they are sometimes allowed to do naughty things and people think that it is funny; and later if children do exactly the same thing, people get cross and punish them.' Very seriously, Helen said, 'Yes, this is a young horse' (p. 66–8).

Helen's problems were connected with the death of her mother and various changes of home and, in consequence, of styles of upbringing.

In these extracts Dr Kahn suggests that he is fairly confident of his interpretation of the identity of the horse and of the other objects in the pictures. For example he says very definitely 'Of course, the whip is for when the horse is naughty' although in circuses the ringmaster's whip is not necessarily an instrument of punishment (it may, for example, represent status, authority, control or even noise; it could perhaps be seen as an image of emasculation since it is *not* used for whipping). From the whole article it seems evident that the doctor had such a rapport with and understanding of Helen that he was in a position to make such comments but social workers of less experience than Dr Kahn might prefer to express their apparent insights more cautiously.

The prognosis for Helen was good for her problems were such that the loving intervention of an adult could bring relief and freedom. All too often children can be helped only to become reconciled to their present life and, sometimes, imminent death. Jill Green's eight-year-old girl depicted herself as living forever in the hospital-cum-field; she knew that she would not go home, but she did not apparently know that she would leave the field for a graveyard. Susan Bach (1969) writes about children who, she believes, do know that they are dying and who accept this. She is convinced that this knowledge and the child's reaction to it can be expressed in and communicated through pictures which may, she hopes,

> serve as a warning signal when, in face of a 'lost life', we might feel tempted to try out new methods of treatment and so prolong a patient's life unduly when its natural span has clearly come to an end and we should stand by him and, if we can, let him go in peace (p. 65).

In her book Susan Bach describes with illustrations her diagnosis of the physical and emotional states of two young, dying children based entirely on her analysis of their paintings while in hospital and approaching death. She was given no medical details until after her 'blind' diagnoses from stage to stage. I do not think that this kind of work is within the compass or even the interest of most social workers not least because Susan Bach is a highly trained and experienced clinical artist working from a Jungian background. However her thesis is of great interest and I believe that social workers paying close attention to the drawings and paintings of sick and dying children might be able, perhaps with help from art experts, to learn a great deal about their thoughts, perceptions and feelings, particularly those which are too deep and appalling for verbal expression and the terrifying possibility of confirmation. An example of Susan Bach's approach (this time in direct contact with the child) follows. The girl, M. B., was eleven and a half and, although in bed, looked healthy and she was

> painting concentratedly, carefully choosing her crayons, stopping and then, as if rallying, continuing to draw. When she looked up I asked to be allowed to see her picture: a church turned to the left, slightly off-centre, standing on nothing. It had been outlined in pencil; the roof of the tower was filled in strongly, with 'burning' red, and so was the roof of the nave. Its five windows were empty (why five of them and why empty? was M. B.'s vision impaired?) Their frames, and that of the window in the tower, were overlaid with light brown that often reflects a state of decreasing earthiness, and the entrance door was filled in with the same colour. Finally, the walls of the whole building were shaded with pencil. As the girl was fully conscious, I wondered whether she suffered from headaches or fainting attacks. Or, physiologically, was her life under a shadow – the shadow of death? And why should she have chosen to draw a church, architecturally a union of body and spirit, of female and male elements, the place of worship where man terrestrial gathers himself to commune with soul eternal?
> While these questions were crossing my mind, the girl's mother, sitting by her bed, evidently felt she should entertain me and unfolded a whole package of photographs from home. There the girl was in the meadow, holding her favourite calf, her younger sister looking at her, the village church in the background with its Byzantine onion tower, so common in the Grisons. I said to the young patient; 'Oh, you didn't draw the village church?' whereupon she grew very angry and answered: 'I ought to have been told you wanted me to do that'. When I said: 'Oh no, not at all, we wanted you to do what you like' and, pointing at her pic-ture, added: 'This is *your* church, is it not?' she looked up at me startled, as if meeting with some unbelievable recognition. With a mighty effort, as though overcoming a resistance, she picked up the pencil, quickly put the black cross on the church tower and fell back on her pillow, looking exhausted but relieved. . . .
> At the time her prognosis was considered to be good. The operation a day later unfortunately revealed an inoperable, extensive malignant tumour The girl died five months later (cf. number of windows). Checking on the case history . . . I learned that she suffered from intermittently raised intercranial pressure with headaches and attacks of unconsciousness, and with marked loss of vision (cf. the shaded-in wall of the church and the empty windows) (pp. 24–5).

It is difficult and perhaps superflous to comment on this moving and mystical story; the reproduction of the pictures which accompanies the written account shows what can be seen as an ordinary enough church with grey walls, red roofs, brown door and un-coloured windows; and a black cross. All are colours which might be associated with any child's drawing of a building.

This story and picture leave me two legacies; sadness for the little dying girl and the unanswerable question, when is a church a symbol?

Order and disorder

Painting (indeed any art work) is important not only as a form of self-expression and means of communication but also as a medium for exploration and mastery. It is vital to development and education from the earliest years.

> The child who has been deprived of paint and clay, sand and water, in his early years, is slower to adapt to school life and is always more tentative in his reaction to new experiences. It is exactly the same as a child whose vocabulary is limited due to the lack of books and conversation (Scott, 1974, p. 11).

At first paint and clay and the other media of plastic and graphic creation are interesting to the child as objects in themselves, substances whose various consistencies provide various sensations to the skin. The eye too receives pleasure and stimulus from the colour, texture and shapes inherent in and resulting from the use of these materials. Exploration and mastery move from enjoyment of the substances alone to control and management of them into pictures and three-dimensional creations.

From an early age children are interested in order; they reveal a high degree of order and consistency

> even as young as three, four, or five. At a time when in much of their behaviour they appear whimsical, irrational, or easily distracted by the last thing to come along, their drawings reveal a great deal of order. In a sense, they proceed according to plan. To me, the discovery of this orderly sequence is as important and exciting as the finding that young children's language follows discernible rules (Goodnow, 1977, p. 59).

Jacqueline Goodnow considers that 'the apparent disorder in children's behaviour – its apparent lack of principles or rules – is due to our own ignorance of the principles they work by' (p. 60). This is demonstrated, for example, by the use of space by young children who often

> avoid overlapping space, and seem to prefer a sort of no-man's land between parts. All told, young children seem to operate with two general principles: to each its own boundary and to each its own space (p. 44).

Learning about oneself in relation to space is a perennial occupation of man. The child is learning, like Alice, that at one time the table top is way above his head, at another it is somewhere below his waist. Smallness and largeness are relative and growth confuses all. Even when the body reaches its more or less finished height there are still infinite explorations of the self in space, for example in a lift or on a mountain, a large but crowded store and a small but empty flat. And there is always space itself, eternity confined within a man-made rocketship.

The importance of these notions for social workers is that children in any kind of stressful situation need every possible means of discovering themselves in relation to their environment and of gaining control over both themselves and that environment. In hospital for example,

> In all creative art experiences the child . . . is encouraged to impose himself on the material, to change and control it. While this is as valuable for children in a normal playgroup situation it is crucial for the hospitalized child. His immediate need to come to terms with feelings of anger, frustration, confusion and fear as well as love and affection is urgent and demanding. His involvement with various art media is a valuable way of helping the hospitalized child cope with these feelings positively and creatively (Green, 1974, pp. 22–3).

Children who for physical, social and/or emotional reasons feel (and are) impotent need some way to be in control. This may be through the actual manipulation of the materials:

> For young children opportunities to explore paint and clay help to counteract the orderliness and cleanliness of hospital. Permission to find joyous release in finger paint helps children to accept and conform to the hospital's standards of hygiene. Some children are reluctant to join in. Their fear may be related to the unpleasantness of messy medical treatments. One active, imaginative four-year-old who had undergone many abdominal operations which resulted in a messy, open wound, refused to paint. With the encouragement of his mother he was gradually able to indulge in this activity without fear of losing control. Clean-up time is vital as it assures the child that no damage is done and all can be restored back to normal (Green, 1974, p. 22).

Or it may be through the subject of the drawing. Marianne, for example, was confined to bed convalescing after a serious illness. She acquired a magic pencil whose power was such that whatever she drew with it became real (or a dream, she was not sure which). In the drawing-world she met Mark, a boy suffering from a very grave illness who was known not to Marianne herself but to the peripatetic teacher whom they shared. At one point Marianne experienced terrific jealousy of Mark's relationship with the teacher and she expressed this in her drawing:

> Her eyes fell on the drawing book. She snatched it up. It opened at her page of the drawing of the house, with the boy, who had been Mark in her dream, looking out. Marianne picked up the pencil, which had been lying beside the book and scored thick lines across and across and up and down

over the window. 'I hate Mark', she was saying to herself, under her breath. 'I hate him, I hate him, I hate him. He's a beast, and he's spoiled my present. I hate him more than anyone else in the world and I wish he was dead.'

She scribbled viciously over the face in her picture, and felt as if it really was Mark she was destroying. The house had begun to look like a prison now, with thick crossed lines like bars over the window, and Marianne took an evil pleasure in heightening the resemblance. She made the fence round the sad little garden thicker and higher, so that it enclosed the house like a wall round a prison. Outside it were the great stones and boulders she had drawn before, reminding her of gaolers. They should watch Mark, she thought with angry satisfaction, keeping him prisoner under constant surveillance. Marianne drew in more stones, a ring of them round outside the fence. To each she gave a single eye. 'If he tried to get out of the house now, they would see', Marianne thought, 'They watch him all the time, everything he does. They will never let him out' (Storr, 1964, p. 55).

Mark's crime had been to give the teacher a huge bunch of roses for her birthday, innocently spoiling for Marianne her own gift of roses in, alas, a smaller bunch. Marianne imprisoned Mark in the picture-house so that he could not again, as she saw it, escape from her control and threaten her happiness by competing. The passion with which Marianne attacked Mark through her drawing was an overflowing of her frustation at being kept in bed and perhaps of anxiety about her illness and, since her teacher was involved, possibly also about her school work. In the story both Marianne and Mark regained health as the magic pencil led them into exciting adventures which developed both their physical and moral strength and their relationship. Even if social work agencies don't yet supply magic pencils, ordinary crayons may contain quite enough magic in the hand of a child with imagination, freedom, paper and need.

Did I ever do things like that?

Just as the materials and products of art can be used to express and control the present they may also be employed to record and recall the past.

> Drawings provide a record of change and of times past made from the child's own point of view. They are also a source of constant wonder to children as they grow older, leading them to ask: 'Did I ever do things like that?' (Goodnow, 1977, p. 7).

Social workers are responsible to try to offer children opportunities to discover, understand and manage their own backgrounds and past lives and the preservation of pictures made at various ages may be very valuable.

> The pictures that children draw can be a fascinating record of their development. It is saddening to see children who rush home eagerly with

a picture made at school only to have their efforts greeted perfunctorily and the picture quietly scrapped when tea is over. It is always encouraging to see those homes where children's art has pride of place in bedrooms and living rooms. From time to time children's pictures should be kept, the date and a brief comment written on the back and the picture put in the personal file (Jones, 1970, p. 23).

Or if children are making scrapbooks perhaps their own work could be included.

A picture made by a child is, like a photograph, proof that he really did exist at a time before today and that his existence was such that he made some physical impact either because his hand touched paper with paint and left his own mark or because his image was taken into a camera and given out again onto paper. Such things are very important to most people and especially to those who have some reason to be unsure of their own impact or even, sometimes, existence.

In order to preserve the past for their children social workers must both ensure that objects from the present are kept and work 'to retrieve the past' (Park, 1972, p. 142). Clara Claiborne Park endeavoured to reach the past with her small autistic daughter by means of drawing. The family was in England seeking treatment for Elly; her mother sought to recapture their American home for her (the latter part of this story is also told in chapter 6, p. 145):

> I would draw our house at home on a large sheet of paper, and see if through pictures I could bring Elly's memories out where they could be shared.
> Together, as so many times before, we sat on the floor. I drew the house. Elly watched with quiet attention; her empty stare was growing rarer now. It had not, of course, occurred to me to bring a photograph. Uncertainly I reconstructed the facade in my memory. What was the pitch of the roof? Should I make the chimney visible? What was the orientation of the windows and their relative size? While I thought, I had to be drawing, steadily and confidently even if incorrectly. Elly was watching and I must not dissipate her attention by fumbles. . . . Elly watched with noncommittal interest. . . . I started to fill in the downstairs window with the furniture of our living room, coffee table, couch. . . . . . At last, deep inside the room, floating above the other furniture, I drew the record player – the sliding doors, the turntable, the tone-arm, the needle, the record itself. Now Elly was more attentive. Tense and excited, she began to jump up and down, her signal for approval and delight. She got down again and put her finger on the crude circle that represented the turntable and moved it round and round. Then she began to sing (p. 149–50).

The song was a record which the family had had and which Elly had not heard for over a year. The idea had worked and proved to be successful at other times.

Communication depends on sense of identity, sense of identity on self-image and self-image on memory; pictures as aids to memory are unrivalled.

Social worker, RA?

Few social workers, like the children on their caseloads, will ever achieve the distinction of recognition by the Royal Academy but all must know the pleasure of achievement whether at passing examinations, obtaining a hoped-for post, or even feeling that some piece of work has been successful, or a client has been helped. Children known to social workers are often deficient in success, used to hearing how poor their work is, not how excellent.

Creating a picture or model can provide not only the satisfaction of the creation itself but also an object which may be noticed and praised by others, child and adult.

The child in hospital is, for example,

> so often infantilized by nurses, technicians and parents who are all on hand to care for him. . . . . Art provides . . . an opportunity to prove to himself that he is capable of independent activity and creating something of value (Green, 1974, p. 22).

If he can create of value he has a better chance of believing that he is himself of value, a belief which it is often difficult to hold on to especially when a low self-image is confirmed and even lowered by, for example, parents and teachers. For 'so many of our kids the experience of being a failure has been crippling developmentally – being a failure at reading, writing, language skills' (Petit, 1977, p. 48). Helen Petit at Brent Family Service Unit endeavoured to give these children the opportunity to achieve in an area of activity new to them and therefore unsullied by previous failure.

> With something completely new – like learning to print photographs – they have the opportunity to experiment without the risk of failure. There is no precedent for 'failing' or 'succeeding' in photography. They are dealing with images which they learnt to 'read' long before they learnt to read or recognize words. They are bound to start with a degree of visual literacy and I aim to develop this (p. 48).

The resulting photographs became objects to be shared and admired, bought (at 2p a time) and treasured.

The social worker understood how achievement would increase confidence and thus the motivation and ability to work positively and hopefully to develop successful ways of managing the problems of life. Nineteen-year-old Julie

> was living with her brother, depressed mother and her fourteen-month-old son in an alienating tower-block estate. . . . I saw that Julie, a bright, articulate person, needed to channel her creative energy in something positive. She was getting increasingly frustrated and depressed (Petit, p. 50).

Helen Petit taught her to use a camera and to develop the film.

> She became so skilled at printing that eventually she would come to the Unit and just get on with it in the darkroom on her own. Her prints, which

were of a really high quality, are around her flat, both on her bedroom walls and framed in the living room.

Such then was Julie's sense of achievement that she was proud to display her work saying in effect, 'Look, *I* did that' when before the social worker introduced her to the camera her sense of 'I' must have been very frail and grey.

Photography, like any art work, may be an excellent occupation for people who prefer to be on their own or with just one other person. Julie would just get on with it in the darkroom on her own and Helen Petit further comments that:

> Learning to do photography is something which withdrawn, inarticulate kids seem especially to respond to. There is a special intimacy about being in a darkroom for a couple of hours with one kid, lost in time. One volunteer who is doing a supervision order with a particularly introverted fourteen-year-old boy has found it an invaluable way to begin building a relationship with him (pp. 50–51).

While concentrating on the creation of photographs, especially in the dark when faces would be both unimportant and unlit, social worker and boy could forget the tensions of their different official relationship and enjoy together their activity and the pleasure of shared achievement. And the achievement would have been both the finished photographs and the growing relationship. The sense of achievement in a social worker – child relationship should not be all for the child alone!

Both social worker John Willis and twelve-year-old boy John found reward and achievement in their shared art work. The boy was a resident in a large hospital for the subnormal and the social worker was endeavouring to develop a relationship with him:

> One of the first things we attempted to do together was a wall poster. This involved us both in cutting and sticking small paper flowers onto a backcloth in order to make up his name. I attempted this so that John would see that I was in his classroom mainly for him. A lot of time was spent on it and he applied himself diligently until it was finished. It seems that many children in that situation suffer from a 'butterfly syndrome'. They are unable to concentrate on any subject for more than a very short time. John can be like this. A member of staff commented afterwards that maybe he had done this as a reward to me for my interest in him (Willis, 1978, p. 9).

It is surely impressive that a boy thought to be of very low intelligence, living in an institution and not expected to be able to relate to anyone, should not only cooperate so diligently with his social worker but also be thought to be rewarding that social worker for his interest in him. The flowering wall poster (whose subject was, importantly, the boy's *name*) reflects I think the flowering feeling between the two Johns, a feeling which could grow because each experienced some sense of achievement and each could offer the other some reward.

The Beck children were not interested in artistic creation at school and there were no materials in their home. I provided quantities of scrap paper and pencils for drawing and cereal boxes which at that time had cut-out models on the back. These gifts were received with great enthusiasm and the children derived pleasure and satisfaction from using them. Although drawings and completed models were unlikely to survive from one visit to the next the children expressed their considerable sense of achievement in their various creations.

Tell me about your painting

It is all very well to write about the possibilities of meaning and use of children's art work but it is not always easy for adults to know how to work with and respond to young artists. Henry Pluckrose (writing about playgroups and parents but with relevance to social workers) says:

> The role of the adult is to provide materials and indicate their use – but not to interfere by directing. To force conventional representation upon the young child can be quite disastrous. How many children have suffered from 'What a lovely picture. What is it supposed to be?' A sensitive adult would have elicited far more information about the child's thought by simply remarking, 'That's interesting. I like the way you've used the colour. Tell me about your painting' (Pluckrose, 1974, p. 7).

However even this question may lead to confusion and grief if it is not asked in a truly open spirit. Here is what happened when Barbara Dockar-Drysdale (1968, pp. 86–7) asked a boy in a residential special school to tell her about his picture. The boy was, she says,

> a 'frozen' delinquent who was just starting to feel guilt and conflict. He wished to give me a picture he had just painted; he was in rather a hurry, as we passed each other in the passage. The picture was of a sailing ship on a smooth sea; the sun shone, seagulls flew around the masts, and all looked tranquil. However, before I accepted this picture I asked the boy to tell me about the ship. He was a trifle reluctant to do so, saying: 'It's a picture for you'. At length, however, he revealed that this was a disguised pirate ship on the way to find some stolen treasure, hidden previously on an island. I was to be involved in this adventure, to be one of the crew, and to have some of the stolen treasure. When I refused to accept the picture or have anything to do with the pirates or the treasure, the boy was very angry; he tore up the picture and stamped off. Had I accepted the male role of a pirate seeking stolen treasure with him, I would have accepted a role which would have made it impossible for me to help him: in accepting the picture I would have unwittingly accepted the role.

While I understand the point the author is making and recognize the possibility of deep meanings and symbolizations in pictures, I find myself, each time I read that extract, hurt and annoyed on behalf of the boy. I am not surprised that he tore up the picture and stamped off. He may indeed have been furious that his plan to trap the author had failed, that she had escaped from his dastardly plot, that all was revealed. But might he not just as well have been upset that a gift, whether or not it had some nefarious purpose, had been rejected – and not only rejected but brushed off in the corridor? He might have been in a hurry (apparently) but should not the author have taken time with the picture and the boy? If she was suspicious of his intention should she not have asked him to see her at some calmer time to discuss the picture and his feelings (or if that would be too formal and threatening, managed another meeting informally)? And had she the right to be so sure that her interpretation of the picture and the boy's intention was the true or only one? She had asked the boy to tell her and then rejected what he offered; no doubt the boy experienced rejection in himself too at that moment. I do not mean that social workers would be drawn into collusions with children or feel forced to accept everything which is offered to them for this could lead to great trouble. But I do think they should be very very careful about how – and why – they reject offerings.

I think my reaction to this extract derives from my sense that the author did not treat him with respect (and as I indicate above I believe there would have been ways to reject the picture but show respect towards the painter). The social worker must show respect to the child, his activity and the eventual product.

Often children's art work is patronized and 'put down' by adults who see in it not its present achievement, interest and beauty but only that it is as yet childish, not adult, not realistic. Kenneth Jameson (1974, p. 1) has a definite opinion about this:

> The child's work is 'real' to him however unreal it may look to you. The child does not record reality. He uses his own childish symbols to represent what, to him, is reality. A good example is the little boy who banged his thumb and later drew a human-figure symbol with a thumb as big as the body, with a bandage tied round it. It was totally unreal in adult terms, but it was symbolically real to the child.

I would suggest that the child *does* record reality in that he depicts in a form which satisfies himself a representation of reality; what he does *not* do is accurately to *reproduce* reality.

It is easy to suppose that children either do not know what they are doing or that some strange effect in a drawing represents, as in the example of the little boy's over-sized thumb, something of great significance to the artist. Jacqueline Goodnow (1977, p. 48) warns that

> It is tempting, for example, to infer from bird-winged humans that the child is misperceiving, or to infer from over-sized hands that these have

special emotional significance. A simpler and likelier explanation, however, would seem to be the difficulty of anticipating the problems that each new use of line turns out to create.

In other words, drawing hands is difficult! Or to be more general, any diagnosis must take full account of the physical aspects and influences as well as the emotional, and normality must always be assumed and sought before the presence of abnormality is posited.

Children are often 'put down' and insulted by adults who do not realize that in their own field they may be expert and interesting. Seven-year-old Hugo was given some illustrated books on his first day at school:

> 'Must be fine to be able to draw like that. Only thing is, it all becomes so flat when it's just drawn. Not like when you carve, that's something you can take hold of' (Gripe, 1974, p. 59).

The teacher was flabbergasted and hastily tried to control Hugo. Like so many adults she could not hear that he was offering her something of interest from his own life; a really sensitive adult (and good teacher) would, I think, have said to Hugo, 'Tell me about your carving'.

Sometimes it may be the social worker's pictures which tell the stories. Jean Moore (1976, p.15) suggests that

> Pictures can be a very useful means by which children can interview the interviewer. A number of primary school children . . . have gained a lot of information about me by way of the pictures and mobiles in my office.

This social worker is not afraid of her child clients gaining information about her; she recognizes the essential interactiveness of social work and is prepared not only to receive but to give clues about interests, favourite themes and colours. Some of the pictures were made by other children and through these Jean Moore is able to communicate her major interest, that is, respect for both the artist and his artefact:

> A child would sometimes begin by making some scathing remark about a picture, and when I replied that I thought the artist had gone to a great deal of trouble the child client then knew that I would not disparage him either and might even value him.

Endpaper

This chapter has comprised some pictures of children making and using pictures. It has in no way been an attempt to show how children draw and model at this or that age. The social worker's preoccupation should be with how this child draws at this time and in this place. The child himself will soon show what he likes to do and any apparent retardation, precociousness or abnormality in his productions can quickly be checked with school teachers or art therapists. Social workers are primarily concerned with art work as a means of occupation, possible communication, shared activity and opportunity for achievement. And every social worker carries with her the basic materials for artistic creation: pencils and paper.

I end the chapter with two brief quotations. Helen Petit (1977, p. 48) introducing her article on her photography work says

I believe in doing things with kids which excite and grip *me*.

And Henry Pluckrose has the last word:

When the child's experimented and finished, what then? After the battle over who is to clear up has been finally resolved and the picture or model is the only reminder of the glory and frustrations of the afternoon, remember that it contains something of your child's vision and something of his growth. Respect it. (1974, p. 10).

Chapter 8
Keep in Touch

I was determined to include a chapter on the use of touch in social work with children even if it comprised only one page in the centre of which was the single word CUDDLE. In the event, the chapter on communicating without words uses about 6,000.

Don't touch

It may have been the accident of my choice of literature and live sources but I have not been overwhelmed with examples of social workers deliberately using physical contact to aid communication with their child clients. I wonder if this reflects the general underrating and compartmentalizing of the sense of touch in our society. The English bear a stereotyped image of reluctance to touch; all the window seats in a bus are filled before anyone will dare to sit next to a stranger and some of us are shy even of shaking hands with new acquaintances. Continental hugging and kissing 'even' between men is embarrassing. We are perhaps most comfortable in our cars, safe metal boxes which we can legitimately defend from being touched by any other box; and if our own box should be touched and defiled we can call on the law and the insurance company for redress. The human in his own metal box is protected from other humans' smells and conversation and the possibility of physical contamination. (No wonder we prefer to waste money, fuel and road space than to use transport which is all too 'public'.)

Physical contact is permitted between people within certain personal, private relationships. Mothers are supposed to make the comfort of their bodies available to their babies. Husbands and wives are supposed to seek and enjoy sexual contact, partly in order to make those babies, and marriages can be ended if 'conjugal rights' are withheld.

Many professional services depend on physical contact. Some such as hairdressing or chiropody we take for granted. Others such as medicine are governed by codes which intend to protect the patient who is forced to expose his (or more likely her) body to the potentially rampant operator from any attention other than that strictly required by the professional character of the contact.

Social workers are neither bound nor protected by any Hippo-cratic Oath and no amount of declaration that she has always respected her clients is likely to be of much help if a social worker is accused of sexually approaching a client. I mention this here because before I can discuss some of the possibilities of touch as a useful form of contact I must acknowledge that social workers are in a very vulnerable position and that it is no wonder if, the conventional behaviour of her surrounding society apart, she is reluctant to offer much in the way of hugs (and male social workers are even more vulnerable than female). In fact I think that social workers both male and female are often naive in their assessment of their physical impact on clients (and their clients' impact on them); sexual attraction and desire are perfectly possible and I suspect that most female social workers have a 'would you like to come to bed?' story tucked away in their memory, a story which may seem funny or even flattering but which could perhaps with no great difficulty have become a story of assault because the lady thought she was protected by her 'professional authority'. And it is not, as I write, very long since a male social worker was murdered by his client: another aspect of physical contact and one which I am surprised is not more often manifested, if not in the extreme of murder at least in the physical expression of the frustration which the social worker must so often represent and provoke.

Not only are social workers vulnerable themselves but they are often expected to supervise, control and even deny the normal physical interests and activities of their clients. Most of the worry about teenage girls centres around their sexual behaviour and the dangers of pregnancy and disease. There seems to be extant an image of a mythical girl, nubile, predatory, insatiable, interested only in flouting authority and 'having sex'. But normal teenage interest in sex is nothing to be afraid of. And the searching apparently for sexual relationships among the teenage girls who may appear on caseloads may be misleading. Angela Willans (1977, p. 114) suggests an interpretation:

> Once past the age to be cuddled and touched and treated tenderly by mother and father, there is almost no way in which a man or woman can find loving arms except in a sexual contact. We simply do not touch and hold and warm to each other non-sexually anything like as much as human nature needs. So at adolescence, there's a sudden drop in the emotional temperature and the only warm place to be found is in a sexual partner's arms. This, of course, is even more avidly sought if the temperature at home has always been on the chilly side.

It may be up to the social worker to show that warm places may be found in places and even embraces other than sexual. And if it really would be unwise and dangerous for the social worker herself to supply the hugging she must ensure that someone will be ready to offer cuddles for comfort. In saying this I am not forgetting that sometimes unhappy people of whatever age cannot tolerate physical contact and an over-zealous cuddler may be rebuffed; part of the skill of cuddling is knowing when to sit quietly, untouching and when to slip the kind arm around the sad shoulder.

Canes and cold shoulders

Physical contact can be used as much for punishment as for pleasure and comfort. All too familiar are the stories of severe abuse leading to injury and sometimes death. Some parents reject physical punishment within the home altogether, relying on verbal control (when I suspect there may be as many scars and agonies but hidden from the eye of the health visitor or school nurse). Most families, I suppose, work out their own system of retributive behaviour whether physical or verbal or both, and their children grow up accepting that breaking the rules leads to punishment and forgiveness. The importance of the form of punishment will depend on the context of the particular parent and child; a light slap on the hand in one household may betoken response to a 'worse crime' and greater displeasure than a hard crack on the head in another. And the hard crack could be perfectly acceptable if it suggested that a detected misdemeanor had been dealt with in a quick and consistent way; physical contact even in punishment *could* in some contexts be seen as beneficial to the relationship.

I cannot enter here into the controversy about use of physical punishment for crimes committed against such institutions as school or property but I refer to a recent incident in the House of Commons which suggests that there are still many people who are in favour of the precious sense of touch being used punitively. Robert Kilroy-Silk, MP (1979, p. 1), reported that the Bill to abolish corporal punishment for Handicapped and Deprived Children had been prevented from progressing by one MP who was later quoted as being 'strongly for corporal punishment in general' and who could 'see no reason why any protection should be given to the physically handicapped'.

It may come as a surprise to realize that, in Kilroy-Silk's words:

> while we have, rightly, abolished the use of the birch and the cat and other such refinements for even the most hardened and vicious criminals we can still, legally, take a cane to a young child – and a mentally handicapped or physically handicapped one at that – where it is illegal to beat adults but acceptable to beat children.

I wish here only to *raise* the question of physical punishment for children whether handicapped or healthy, at home or in school. It is, I think, a question on which every social worker must have an opinion for every child on every caseload will at some time or another be subject to disciplinary action and that will probably mean punishment of some kind: the social worker will have to be very careful in assessing her own attitude to that punishment. For example, I was present in a school staff-room in Scotland when the headmaster announced that two boys were to be beaten. I was shocked and distressed and despised the teacher who went to assist. (I was not helped by the friendly teacher who promised that I'd be able to hear the yells from the next room.) But when the drama was over I had to ask myself if my internal tears and anxiety were really for and about the two transgressing boys (whom I had never seen and would never know) or out of my own terror of being hurt. I was in no position really to assess what was happening to the boys when what I was actually reacting to was my own feeling.

As common as canes and blows are cold shoulders. The withdrawal of physical contact, the refusal to touch or to respond to touch can be deadly. Saying 'I love you' is nothing if the lips are cold and the body tense. Sixteen and a half-year-old Sally gives a vivid picture of such withdrawal and the power of its communication in her account of her short-lived cohabitation with Steve. She has brought her unemployed 'layabout' boyfriend to meet her well-off parents:

> When the Daimler turned up, Steve took my arm quickly. I could feel his hackles rising, half-afraid, half-ready to defend himself. I did something then, without thinking, that I'm a bit ashamed of – but it told me how I felt deep down about taking Steve home. I moved my arm out of his and drew away a bit as Daddy drew up. It was fatal, Steve said angrily, 'Be like that then'. . . . and stood there woodenly as I went up to the car (Willans, 1977, p. 33).

Children on social workers' caseloads are likely to be subject to such withdrawals and refusals very often; nurses and residential staff who move away because their notion of caring does not include providing an arm to hang on to, parents who push away because 'You're too big' or 'too naughty', social workers who 'say they couldn't have much physical contact because of fear of fleas and dirt'.

Benign control

Now that I have suggested some of the problems associated with touch I shall spend the rest of this chapter discussing some ways in which social workers may use it very positively.

Physical contact may be used to inflict pain in the name of punishment and control. But physical contact and control may also be associated non-punitively. An interesting example of this was presented during a discussion with workers at Newcastle FSU. They were talking about their work with groups of children and told of one group which was being run by students who were having difficulty in both controlling and interesting the children. The Unit leader (and group worker) discovered that she could neither understand what was going wrong nor bring into consciousness how she achieved success. The staff and students played the difficult group with the Unit leader playing herself.

Through this they discovered that the secret was in touch. Shouting was avoided because 'that's what goes on at home all the time, so the only way to indicate non-acceptance of behaviour is touch – holding, setting literal limits, physical bounds'.

Once the Unit workers realized what they had been doing they 'did it even more and the children went to great pains to *be* touched'.

Holding to control creates an environment of firm safety without roughness or hurting. The child is prevented by the stronger, calm adult (who, also, knows *how* to hold and isn't seduced or surprised into a wrestling match) from going beyond bounds which are acceptable within the context of the group (whether therapeutic, recreational, school or family). The holding may be no more than an arm around the shoulder symbolizing restraint and communicating kindness or it may entail a full-scale embrace or holding from behind. A light touch may suffice to help a careering child slow down, change direction; a firm full hold may be needed to allow a child time to swear and spit and fight and then relax. (Encouraging relaxation is vital; children known to social workers for whatever reason are likely to be very tense, emotionally and physically, and emotional relaxation may be stimulated by physical loosening.)

Controlling children who are small enough *may* be most effectively and comfortably done from a sitting position especially if achieving calm and relaxation looks like taking some time. A worker from Leicester FSU describes her work with Donald who

> refused to leave the Unit to go home but engaged in a variety of testing activities and then ran away in the side streets near the Unit. (As the worker described it) he was not so much 'running away' as 'asking to be chased'. A long period of negotiations was entered into before eventually limits were set by physically bringing him back to the Unit . . . then 'I pulled Donald on to my lap, he made another attempt to pull books (off the shelves) . . . and I took a firmer hold, though in fact Donald was quite relaxed and not fighting hard as I held him. I was anxious to let Donald know that I knew some of his reasons for being angry. But I also knew I must be firm and work round to seeing he knew he *must* go home' (Davies, 1975, p. 15).

To comfort and console

Touching and holding are almost always accompanied by speech of some kind. Adults tickling or cuddling babies usually make noises, creating a total environment of sensation, tactile, visual and auditory (and if feeding is involved, tasty as well); presumably the adult is smelly too (one way or another). The social worker holding Donald on her lap in the last extract also talked to him and I imagine the tone of her voice complemented the quality of her holding so that the words themselves were almost superfluous; the over-excited boy responded to the steady calm of the adult.

In this very verbal society we may overestimate the impact of speech at certain times, mistaking the importance of the sense of words for their value sometimes as 'musical' accompaniments to tactile communication. Clare Winnicott (1977, p. 8) says: 'In times of acute distress the actual physical holding of a child is likely to be the only means of bringing any relief.' And I suggest that at those times social workers concentrate on the holding, using words and silence as extensions of that. I think Harold Richman (1972, p. 47) understood this in his work with Tim who, terrified about his recent heart operation,

> came close to me and held my arm. I held him for a few minutes, told him I knew his fears were real and painful, and reassured him about the size of the knife. . . . No words or gestures however could soothe the starkness of his terror. I hoped that my presence and our mutual trust would lighten the burden of his fears.

Tim had been in peril of death; he had truly to fear the worst kind of tactile experience, attack on his body by a destructive weapon, in order to have any chance of that experience becoming wonderful and the weapon changing to an instrument of life. In his need he clung to the first and most universal form of communication, touch; he held his social worker's arm and was rewarded by being held as he faced the knowledge of his nearness to that greatest of all changes, the possibility of death. There is a strong old myth about being held through terrible change; the hero (or heroine) is enchanted and can be saved and returned to his normal form only through the courage and commitment of his lover who must embrace and hold onto him while he suffers a number of transformations, perhaps into a dragon, a worm, a fire, a flea, a glacier. One of the meanings is, I think, that the lover cannot be destroyed or daunted by the many aspects of the beloved, his moods, his faults, his problems, ambitions and fears; nor indeed by his inevitable physical changing as he ages. Catherine Storr has written a fascinating novel stimulated by this myth; Bee pursues and eventually literally holds her boyfriend Thursday as he suffers what may be a breakdown or may be enchantment (and is there any difference anyway?) The pursuit reminds me of Donald in the extract above, not so much running away as asking (or needing?) to be chased. The holding of Thursday is 'like embracing a stone figure, a statue' (Storr, 1974, p. 205). His rigidity is not very different from the terror of Tim, too weak to cry any more and lost inside himself from his fear of the hostile world; and it would be no easier to hold Thursday, rejecting with ice, than to hold Donald, wriggling in his angry worm transformation.

Bee held and rescued Thursday through the strength of her love within a still chaste relationship; Sally tells of the meaning of physical loving and holding for her boyfriend Steve:

> In private he was all for closeness and touching and hugging; it was as if he could never get enough of it. Sitting in the squat together in the evenings, with the radio on, he'd always have his arm round me or we'd hold each other if no one else was around . . . he wasn't all that sexy in the sense of forever wanting actually to make love. He'd want to cuddle and kiss at night but often he'd just want to fall asleep like that rather than go on to sex (Willans, 1977, p. 27).

Sally, whose home temperature was certainly on the chilly side, found Steve 'exciting and attractive and very loving in those early days' but when the glamour began to fade she had nothing to give to the comfort-needing boy she describes.

Social workers are concerned with the comfort needs of their children both directly and indirectly. If Sally and Steve had had a social worker their feelings about their intimacy might have been important to discuss in helping them understand their needs and relationship but I suspect that each would have given an impression of enjoying a 'fabulous' and very active sex life, ignoring, denying, perhaps even being ashamed of the tenderness and comforting.

It would probably have been a good deal easier for Jackie's social worker to learn about her need for comfort and the way in which it was met within her foster home. On her first night the foster parents' daughter

> cuddled her up . . . in bed, to help her feel the warmth and love. She fell to sleep immediately. Around midnight the screaming began, a terrifying cry for help. My husband and I went in to find Jackie lying in our daughter's arms fast asleep, but screaming in a most pitiful way. . . . The next day Jackie wanted no one except our daughter – she just clung to her like a leech (Theze, 1977, p. 14).

Jackie was lucky that her whole foster family understood so well and intuitively that she would need warmth and love and how to provide this, not depending on 'You'll be alright, love' or 'Stop that noise' or 'She'll soon forget and settle in' but *really* considering *this* child and responding to her unique need in their unique way.

Making contact

Contact, particularly with children perhaps, can sometimes best be initiated through touch. William Glasser (1975, p. 198), for example, writes of his help to the teacher of a very difficult, large and abusive epileptic mentally retarded boy. The teacher was rejecting the boy and said that he was far too busy for any personal counselling.

> I asked him if he could devote ten seconds twice a day to the boy to start a programme, a request so limited that he could not refuse. I suggested that

he put his arm around the boy's shoulder each day when he entered and when he left class, saying that he was glad to have the boy in class and asking whether he could help him to do the work.

The strategy was successful and

> Following my suggestion for one week, the teacher reported a remarkable change. The boy was pleasant, and his aggressive, abusive behaviour had almost stopped. A total investment of about two minutes had started the involvement and had begun the behaviour change.

Having achieved contact the teacher was able to help the boy a very great deal: (surely a salutary story for those who say 'Of course I believe in working with children but there just isn't time').

Making contact is not always so deliberate as in Glasser's example. The helping adult may wish to reach the child to help with an immediate problem and/or to start laying a foundation which may be of use later. One of the Newcastle FSU workers recalled an occasion when she had been babysitting for friends. The little boy was still suffering after a family tragedy and although the worker thought that he had great need to be cuddled she also guessed that 'he couldn't take the initiative – so I made it clear to him that I'd like him to sit with me'. At bath time be became naughty and dropped all the towels into the bath. The worker felt annoyed but decided that she must contain her feelings and brought a fresh towel. As she dried him the little boy was wary because he knew that she was cross so 'I dropped a huge bath sheet over his head and completely covered him and held him gently and felt him gradually relax into my body – then, he was so happy after that.'

Social workers may not have much chance to bath children (though it might sometimes be useful and appropriate for the social worker to bath and put to bed a child in residential or foster care or, indeed, within his own family) but there are many other opportunities of this kind for using ordinary small brief events to give essential messages of good will and invitations to trust.

Social workers are often inhibited from making direct contact with children because the parents are demanding and receiving all their attention. Even though the ears and voice are fully occupied with the adult involved, eyes and hands and laps can indicate awareness of and interest in the children. When Noel Hunnybun (1965, p. 81) narrates her work with David and his mother she describes the behaviour of the little boy as the adults talked:

> After a few minutes during which he sat quite still between us, I put my hand down and touched his head. He looked up with a most engaging smile to which I responded.

Even if the social worker is not working directly with or even primarily concerned about the child, if the child is present during interactions between social worker and adult he is bound to receive some message and that is likely to be about tension and anxiety. It is easy to overlook this and imagine that the child doesn't understand or isn't interested but I am sure that he is very interested and is likely to be convinced that the flurry and worry are connected with him in some way, especially if he hears his name. The simple acts of benign touching and smiling may be worth a great many words and may prevent a great deal of anxiety.

Sometimes parents try to inhibit contact between social worker and child; the reasons for this may be various but the effect is likely to be that the social worker feels embarrassed and does not like to persist and the child feels rebuffed and probably hostile to *all* the adults. The Newcastle FSU workers were very familiar with this:

> A child who's desperate to be cuddled climbs onto the social worker's knee and the parents say 'get down' and the social worker has to say 'it's OK, I like it' and to get the parents' permission.

The social worker is both giving and asking for permission to have this contact with the children. Not all social workers are willing to have close association with fleas and dirt and in any case it should never be assumed that every social worker is prepared to involve every part of herself in her work all the time. For example, I should never give permission for the close physical contact with their dogs which clients and foster parents seemed to consider to be an honour; why should the social worker be pawed and licked and be-haired? Acceptance can be shown in other ways than accepting assault, and acceptance is of value only if it is honest; I see no reason why it may not be qualified: 'I accept and respect you but not your alsatian or the attention of your baby to my handbag.' Receiving permission from parents for contact with their children is important too. Even when a court order is in force the social worker needs to engage the cooperation of all members of the family with courtesy and respect.

Sometimes contact may be made with just one part of the child's body.

> Peter . . . always seemed to have a running nose and to be miserable about it yet unable to find any comfort, so I took care of his nose over quite a long period. I brought handkerchief-tissues, and when I was not there I let him know with whom I had left a supply for him. I provided a little pot of cold cream to soothe the roughened skin: in this way I was able to take care of his nose and show him how much I was concerned about him, even when not present. The hopelessly running nose was a signal which I picked up, and really did mind about his poor nose; whatever we do for children must *matter to us* (Dockar-Drysdale, 1968, p. 78).

How often children present a minute cut or bruise for inspection, again and again seeking to be told not 'don't be silly' but in effect 'Even though this is a tiny hurt of course I care that *you* have been hurt at all and you can rest assured that if ever you are badly injured I will notice and attend to and heal the injury'. All that is not *said*; it is indicated by the spontaneous expression of interest and concern, by the gentle adult finger stroking the grazed knee and plastering the cut hand. For many people attention to some diseased or injured part of the body may be the only way in which they can attract physical contact and expression of care. To recall Angela Willans's (1977, p. 114) comment: 'We simply do not touch and hold and warm to each other non-sexually anything like as much as human nature needs'. Perhaps some children learn that only in illness can they receive care. Perhaps hospitals and doctors' waiting rooms are full of people for whom both sexual and non-sexual touching and holding and warming have failed and who resort to nurses and surgeons for contact with another human hand.

Touch line

One of the most socially acceptable arenas for touching is organized sport. Rugby scrums and wrestling, hugging footballers and embracing skating pairs come most easily to mind. (Ladies are still restricted mainly to games with some instrument to fend off direct physical contact, hockey and lacrosse sticks for example.)

Few active games can be played without physical contact and many social workers know the value of a game of football with the opportunity for hugging and horse-play with otherwise too-big-to-cuddle boys and of an hour in the swimming baths where inhibitions may be shed with clothes and social workers may offer comfort to tense children by supporting them in the water, suggesting by their strength and ability to keep their physical heads above water that they may be trustworthy and even able to help save emotional heads from drowning.

The Newcastle FSU workers deliberately played games with a high touch content with the children in their groups. They realized that the children largely avoided touching one another except for such aggressive contact as kicks. Thinking that the children might be fearful of touching one another in any affectional or self-exposing way they devised trust games so that physical contact could be experienced in a number of non-threatening ways. Hospital games were very popular for children had to be nursed and carried and covered up and operated on: 'Children were dropping like flies to be picked up, examined, carried to the "ambulance" car.'

Even if not running groups, social workers have many opportunities to play with children and to introduce games in which people who could not in normal circumstances touch one another are free to give and receive important messages through this subtle and important medium.

It is also important to be aware of the unspoken but none the less vivid communication between other people, often all too easily missed. Maureen Oswin (1978, p. 120) comments that in the Larch

Hospital (a long-stay hospital for mentally handicapped children),

> The staff had very little time to notice the possible development of friendships between the children, so they were likely accidentally to separate children who were relating to each other,

and she describes what she observed taking place

> between two blind boys, aged seven and ten, both of whom had been in Larch hospital for three years. They were lying together on a mat. Justin put his legs right across Stuart's face and chest and lay there for five minutes, quite still, then he rolled off. Stuart, stretching out his hand, found Justin's hand and held it, but Justin wriggled out of Stuart's way. Stuart groped and found Justin's hand again, then as Justin slipped once more out of his reach, Stuart caught hold of the cuff of Justin's jumper. There was a lot more wriggling between the two of them, some laughter, kicking of each other's faces, more laughter. Then for three minutes they lay still. Olive, a sighted child aged four, disturbed by all this romping on her mat, dragged herself slowly off and sat on the lino. Emma, also on the mat, began to kick herself around in a circle. Justin said, 'oh – m m m m' and Stuart said 'oh – d d d'. Justin rolled over and came face to face with Queenie, aged eight. Their faces were almost touching. Queenie, attracted by the nearness of Justin's face, smiled directly at him. Blind, he did not respond to her smile. She smiled again (p. 120–21).

These children working so hard to make contact and playing so happily might at the whim of authority be moved to different parts of the room to eat or sleep, might even, I suppose, be moved to different wards if that should be administratively convenient.

If adults do not expect children to be able to communicate they are unlikely to recognize communication even when it is blossoming under their feet. But not seeing or looking for the way children transmit messages without words may vastly distort any picture of those children and their ability to interact with their environment. Clara Claiborne Park (1972) learned more than enough about professional helpers looking at and constructing pictures of her autistic daughter. At one clinic Elly was subjected to a number of tests including playing 'among other strange children in the diagnostic nursery school' and much excellent attention was given to both child and mother. But

> I was not reassured when the very last day the social worker could still ask me 'Does she ever smile?' But that was my fault. I knew that their gentle caution had missed Elly's gay side; I had wanted desperately for them to see us romping together, to watch her delight in 'this little piggy', her laughter when her father threw her into the air. Every day I had determined to ask if they would watch us play. One day I even came in an old pair of pants; in our gayest game, I would lie on my back and lift her with my feet, high in the air. But they never learned the reason for my odd costume; I played no games with Elly there. Surrounded by that cool detachment, I just couldn't (p. 135).

I first used that quotation in an article in 1975 (Wardle) and make no apology for reproducing it here. How clearly and poignantly Mrs Park shows the serious committed professionals with the carefully thought-out and administered diagnostic procedures, everything translated into words. In all the intricate and expensive structure there is no room for the mother and child to behave naturally together. Mrs Park says that it 'was my fault' that 'the social worker could still ask me "Does she ever smile?" ' but surely it was for the social worker and her colleagues to recognize the importance of learning how mother and child (not to mention father and siblings) played and lived together. Surely skilled interviewing should have revealed the mother's wish and need to be seen romping and if the old pair of pants was an unusual outfit for Mrs Park's attendances at the clinic, surely someone in all that diagnostic factory should have taken note and found out if there was any reason for them. And having been let down by the inhibiting atmosphere and elements of insensitivity Mrs Park is left to bear the guilt for her own disappointment: 'that was my fault'.

Stroking and nuzzling

'Want a hold of this?'
From behind his back he brought the smallest untidiest scrap of white fur imaginable. It looked like something which might be found hanging from a barbed-wire fence or a gorsebush. But it had two pink eyes and two tiny curled-up black ears. . . .
He offered Donovan the sniffling scrap of fur on his flattened palm. He could see it was in Donovan's line of vision. But Donovan did not move. Keith held it there until his arm began to ache. Then slowly he put the white bundle down in Donovan's lap.
It is easy to ignore what is heard, or even what is seen; but it is virtually impossible, Keith knew, to ignore a three-week-old guinea-pig snuffling in your lap. . . . Donovan slowly took his hands out of his pockets and cupped the animal in them (Ashley, 1974, p. 16).

Keith is the son of the foster parents with whom the deeply withdrawn Donovan is being placed. This scene takes place in the social worker's car after both she and the foster mother have completely failed to make any contact with Donovan or persuade him to leave the car and enter the foster home. Keith alone remembers that there are more senses than hearing and sight.

Animals from guinea-pigs to horses are very important in communicating with children under stress. Part of their use is emotional. Donovan for example considers that the guinea-pig 'needed him as he needed it'; totally powerless and dependent children may be greatly helped by having contact with and if possible responsibility for some creature even weaker than themselves.

Some deprived children will turn to an animal rather than human beings, who in their experience have proved unreliable. A very close bond can grow between the suspicious youngster and a cat, dog, rabbit or bird. The animal is carried about, fed well with the child's own food, talked to, taken to bed and treated with devotion. It takes the place of a friend. An animal will not necessarily turn away because of a kick; it may allow the child to make up with double tenderness (Shotton Hall School, 1967, p. 34).

In the context of this chapter I want to stress the value of animals as comforting tactile objects. Children deprived or afraid of adults' cuddling may be safe to cuddle small soft creatures. Stroking fur is very soothing and an animal which receives affectionate attention is likely to respond in a very gratifying way, seeking further stroking by nuzzling and rubbing and following the stroker. Animals can be touched without the danger of developing a demanding human relationship. They can, if the child is not responsible for feeding them, be ignored with impunity.

Touch me, touch me not

There is a beautiful wild flower called *noli-me-tangere* or touch-me-not because apparently the flowers fall off if the plant is touched. The flowers of intimate relationships flourish when the people are touched but in many areas of human contact there are perhaps fears that the flowers will fall if any but verbal communication is attempted. Social workers who must understand and be able to practice all modes of communication need to know both the virtues and dangers of touch and to recognize their own attitudes towards and inhibitions about that subtle sense.

Part Three

Being Together

Chapter 9

The whole Place was Part of the Group

Family Service Units children's groups

Joan in a long low-cut sparkly evening dress is thinking, 'Should I wear this in front of "ogling" Mr James?'

Alison is gyrating her hips and clicking her fingers, a one-woman backing group to Elvis Presley.

Now they are marching up and down with a home-made juvenile jazz band, the mace 'disguised' as a broom handle.

Now running through a local park anxiously imagining the headlines, 'Two Social Workers Lose Three Children in Jesmond Dene!'

All in the course of a normal day's work they are, in Alison's words, 'joining in, being relaxed, having fun', working in some of the numerous childrens' groups which have run and sung and acted and marched and played in and around Newcastle Family Service Unit.

Most of the ideas and information in this chapter are from Newcastle FSU including transcriptions from some conversations with the workers there, but reference is also made to work by the Units at Leicester, East London and Bishop Auckland.

I have chosen to write a chapter on the work of FSU with children's groups because not only is it excellent and exciting in itself but also it perfectly exemplifies ways of being and communicating with children which are available to field social workers in any kind of social work agency. Although some of the workers I shall mention are group workers with specialized training and experience, others are generically trained field workers and groups have been led or helped by students and volunteers. The three essentials seem to be the energy and initiative of the workers, the tolerance and support of other staff and a roof to keep off the rain.

A new method of intervention

During the past few years Newcastle FSU has run three kinds of children's groups; sibling groups, family groups and school groups.

Sibling groups

These started because workers visiting families at best once a week realized that the parents' needs were usually so huge that visits were devoted entirely to the adults. The children would hinder the proceedings, constantly seeking attention, roaming, sitting, climbing on knees, interrupting. No one was being satisfied, visits were all a bit fruitless. And the behaviour of the children did nothing but emphasize for the parents their own inadequacies and problems.

The children

> actually didn't know what to do – they were aimless and not happy with that – for example, they were never allowed out because their parents worried about what would happen if they went out.

They were

> desperate for affection, caring, mothering, cuddling – in no way going to be able to get that with their parents. We noticed that the oldest often acted as, say, a father so we maximized on that.
> The parents didn't have enough to go round, basically – and the parents knew it and wanted to be different.

In response to their observations of the needs and longings of both parents and children the workers invited the children of some families to become groups. For example:

> The Brown family, consisting of two parents and six children, were all living in a three bedroomed council house, always on top of each other. Mr Brown is a very quiet man, unable to take an active role as the father of the household. Mrs Brown, a woman of low intelligence, found the daily coping with the children an extreme strain on herself. All six children, one of whom is severely subnormal, have developed into isolated individuals, each straining to fulfil their unmet emotional needs in competition with the other family members. Their mother had been overwhelmed by this and became more withdrawn from the children as they grew older.
> In setting up a sibling group for these children, our aim was two fold:
> 1 to enable the children to handle a group situation including school groups, etc., as well as their natural group. This would entail improving their self-image and confidence, and developing a positive attitude towards themselves and others
> 2 to develop their internal resources in order to cope with boredom, frustration, competition, etc. This would entail stimulating their imaginative capacity and increase their level of tolerance etc.
> The group was to be time limited – sixteen sessions of one and a half hours duration. There would be a leader and two co-leaders in the group: the groupworker, the caseworker and a volunteer. This is a high ratio, but one that proved to be necessary in order to be available for much-needed individual attention initially, and to contribute to the hard task of achieving some group cohesion (Smith and Brooke, 1978).

As with any group (indeed any social work at all) work could not even begin let alone be effective unless all concerned gave consent. At Leicester FSU,

> the offer of a group to the boys was discussed fully with the parents . . . : the response was generally favourable, if only because it would relieve mother of the children for a few hours each week. The boys were also told of the group and asked if they would like to come. . . . Verbally the boys gave the exercise the benefit of the doubt and decided to come (Davies, 1975, pp. 16–17).

Contact with parents was maintained 'throughout the life of the group'. The Newcastle workers 'discussed observations with the mother' but confessed that

> It was a salutory lesson to us to discover how much we had underestimated her capacity to understand the emotional needs of her children at the various stages of their development and to convert her understanding into changed attitudes and positive action to the best of her ability (Smith, 1978, p. 50).

Family groups

The Newcastle workers realized that there wasn't going to be any future without including the parents. So some families, parents and children together, became groups with the same basic aims and activities as the sibling groups. Fundamental in both sibling and family groups was the belief that in their normally overcrowded and stressful family lives neither parents nor children could discover much that was good or enjoyable about one another: 'the kids were a drag and there wasn't a chance to see the positives in the kids and in each other'.

Sometimes the group sessions took place in the family's home but more usually at the Unit: 'they (the parents) came or you went for them and *they were part of the playing*' (emphasis added) Children will never be free to play (in any sense of that enormous word) while their parents, themselves playless in childhood and adulthood, are frustrated. By enabling the parents to be part of the playing the workers thoroughly recognized and acknowledged both the individuality and the corporateness of the family members.

School groups

During the summer term of 1976 two groups of about ten children each were set up in response to

> recognition that in the area there was a pretty good attendance and level of achievement in local infant and junior schools and a tremendous drop in attainment and lack of achievement – and unhappiness – in the comprehensive schools.

The FSU workers and local junior-school teachers cooperated to compile a list of children who

> for a variety of reasons might have particular difficulties in adjusting to comprehensive school, for example being too introverted, not sticking up for self, not asserting self – or – too aggressive – a kick, a thump and a fight every time

and who might benefit from membership of a group. The children were from families not formally known to the Unit. The aims of the groups were

> to do with self-confidence, self-control, being taken seriously, treated seriously, learning other options of how to react, to deal with difficult situations.

It has not been possible to assess the effects of the groups, not least because there were no control groups, but the FSU workers do think that another time it would probably be better to select membership of each group according to the school to which the children would be going; the 21 children of the 1976 groups went to eight different comprehensive schools and friendships which had been formed within the group and might have helped in the new schools were, largely, lost. Any future groups would probably span the summer holiday in order to help bridge the leap from junior to comprehensive school.

Although these groups comprised children who were thought to be potentially at risk of a particular social problem, rather than members of one family, once meetings had started the school factor was found to be of no further importance and the philosophy and activities were indistinguishable from those of the sibling and family groups, rather to the surprise of the workers.

Family Service Units throughout the country run these and other kinds of children's groups and I refer here to two further examples.

The Tuesday group

This group for six girls aged eight to ten started in the East London Unit in December 1968. It met for one and a half hours after school on Tuesdays and the worker was assisted by one or two volunteers. The purpose of this and the other two children's groups in the Unit

> was defined as helping children from deprived home backgrounds who exhibit behavioural problems and experience difficulty primarily in peer relationships, but also to some extent in adult – child relationships. The aim, therefore, was to provide an activity-orientated programme in a secure and accepting group setting. Within this, individuals could be encouraged to interact constructively with each other and behaviour could be tolerated which would meet with disapproval outside the group (Bennett, 1974, p. 42).

Bishop Auckland FSU home education project

In November 1976 two teachers were employed under the Job Creation Scheme to set up and work on a project arising from a survey which showed that there was approximately twice the national average of ESN children in the area served by the Unit.

> FSU felt that a project designed to work with pre-school children and their parents, in those recognized families, might prevent other siblings attending special educational schools, or to recognize at an earlier stage those children likely to encounter learning difficulties. . . .
> The workers formulated three broad aims:
> 1 to improve parent/child relationships through play.
> 2 To provide a play experience for the child (and mothers/parents).
> 3 To help with the transition between home and nursery/school (Langan and Daynes, 1978, pp. 13–14).

Much of the work took place within the children's own homes but in July 1977

> we set up two small play groups operating for half a day each week for mums and children. The mums were in a separate room from the children, but in the same building. The aims of the children's group were to socialize the children as part of the preparation for nursery and to offer a different play situation (p. 17).

Whatever the stimulus for starting these groups, whether, for example, to help to overcome problems relating to school or to assist intensive work with a disintegrating family, the aims of all seem clearly summarized by Joan Smith (1978, p. 45) in her account of work with the Sheraton family:

> to help the children develop their caring capacities, enjoy themselves and each other and relieve some of the pressure from the children and the mother.

Portraits of the children

> the group was . . . concerned with them as individuals.

One of the strongest points to emerge from both the conversation and the writing of the FSU workers is that each child (and parent) was always regarded and related to as an individual for whom the experience of the group would be unique. To illustrate this and to introduce the real children for and with whom the groups were created I shall simply reproduce some of the portraits for these are clear and alive and say all that is necessary.

One of the (four) Sheratons: Susan (aged eight)

> The eldest, never allowed to enjoy childhood. She had too many adult responsibilities on her shoulders, including shopping, going to the

launderette, rocking the cot when baby cried, making tea, helping to dress and wash children, delivering and collecting the younger child to and from the Nursery, reading correspondence to her mother – and so on. Not achieving well at school despite much improved attendance.

Physically quite well developed; good coordination, pretty face surrounded by thick black hair, lovely smile. Often smelled of urine and head usually quite heavily infested. Reasonably well dressed despite the 'second hand' look of her clothes.

Wanted to please and do things for you. She was quick to criticize younger children and attempted to invite adults to show their disapproval of them. She had adopted the same attitudes as her mother towards the children in that she was at times grossly impatient, domineering, dismissive, critical, easily exasperated and quickly resorted to ·slaps, pushes, kicks and thumps. The younger children got in the way of her doing things, e.g. cooking, cleaning, serving meals, shopping etc., (as observed in role play). The group helped her learn to be a child, loved for her own sake, not for what she does. She learned not to be too serious all the time, she had fun, laughed, cried, showed off, got angry, etc., without being reprimanded. She also learned to relax with, have more fun with, be more gentle with, not feel too threatened by her siblings.

In order to reach the prescribed stage, she had to regress to baby-hood with accompanying baby talk, thumbsucking, floppiness (inability to sit up, walk, etc.) and spoon feeding. (A frightening experience for the leaders, but seemingly necessary for Susan) (Smith, 1978, pp. 45–6).

Donald Cunningham (aged nine)

Neighbours and family constantly complained about him and to the worker he seemed at times to be totally at the mercy of conflicting feelings, yet ultimately relieved and calm when limits were set for him. He attended large groups at the Unit (i.e. ten to twelve children with four to six workers), with a mainly recreational focus, for two years; he had constantly emerged as the most troubled and difficult child to handle. It gradually became obvious that Donald's deeper needs were not going to be met in this rather diffuse group.

Nor could he be met by a worker at his real point of need in the context of the family casework relationship. Certainly at times important positive confrontations took place between Donald and the worker. For example, there was an incident when Donald was at the Unit with his mother following angry episodes at home, with mother fairly near to the end of her tether. Donald refused to leave the Unit to go home but engaged in a variety of testing activities and then ran away in the side streets near the Unit. As the worker described it, he was not so much 'running away' as 'asking to be chased'. A long period of negotiations was entered into before eventually limits were set by physically bringing him back to the Unit. The worker described what took place eventually.

'I pulled Donald on to my lap, he made another attempt to pull books (off the shelves) . . . and I took a firmer hold, though in fact Donald was quite relaxed and not fighting hard as I held him. I was anxious to let Donald know that I knew some of his reasons for being angry. But I also knew that I must be firm and work round to seeing he knew he must go home. . . . I emphasized to Donald that his mother wanted him home and at times his mother and father and at other times teachers and sometimes we at the Unit had to say 'no' to him, and had to tell him to do things or not to do things. He could ask why we said 'no' – but he must accept at times that such people had to do things for him. He seemed not to object to this.' (Davies, 1975, pp. 15–16). . . .

Two . . . significant incidents tell something of what Donald had achieved. Shortly before the start of this group, his reply to a casual greeting from a worker who passed him on the ground floor of the Unit was 'f--- off'. This was accompanied by a look of fear which indicated a need to attack before he was attacked. If it is true that an individual's behaviour influences and creates his environment as well as vice versa, then the outlook for Donald seemed bleak. Almost exactly a year later in a similar situation, he replied to a greeting from a worker with a 'hullo' and an interested glance before returning to his own thoughts as he lay along the banisters on the ground floor of the Unit, peacefully preoccupied, whilst briefly withdrawing from the action of the group.

Perhaps more important is an example of changed behaviour in his own home. The local police were making some enquiries about a minor offence and visited his home to question Donald. His mother reported that he replied calmly and confidently to their enquiries. After the departure of the police, he returned to his play, apparently unruffled by events. Guilty or innocent, a far more stormy response would have been predicted a year before (p. 22).

One Tuesday girl: Mary (before)

Mary is aged eight years, and the middle child in a family of five children. The family is financially poor, although the father works regularly, and the children's material well-being is sub-standard. Mother is of low intelligence, rather vague and neglectful and spends a good deal of time out of the home. The children are therefore left to occupy themselves for the majority of the time and although the parents want to give their family a happy life, they are unable to provide them with adequate material care or stimulation for growth and development. The children tend to be rather scruffy and dirty and Mary is particularly sensitive to the comments made about her appearance by other children. In spite of this and her small size, Mary is an attractive, lively friendly child who is highly strung but usually amiable and happy. She is the most intelligent child in the family, curious about everything and quick to learn new skills. This inevitably causes some resentment and isolation in an otherwise backward family. Mary tends to be deprived of the stimulation which she needs and therefore appears young for her age. She relates very well to adults, eager for their attention and the opportunity to form a close relationship. With peers, however, she is very cautious, having been rejected constantly due to her background and dirtiness. She tends to avoid peer relationships and is therefore rather a loner, being quiet, shy and withdrawn in the presence of other children.

Referral to the group is therefore aimed at helping her to interact with peers, and make satisfactory relationships with them, in a stable, accepting environment. It is also hoped to provide stimulation for her through activities to aid her development.

After

Mary remains the quietest member of the group, but is quick and eager to try new skills and ideas. After initial shyness she relates very well to the group leader or adult helpers on a one-to-one basis, and sometimes chatters incessantly. In the presence of peers however, she is still inclined to withdraw but a marked improvement occurred in this respect a couple of months ago. At the outset of the group meetings she was reluctant to join the others in any activity but this changed over time to a peripheral participation. She was then pleased to be asked by the others to join them but never pushed herself forward to be included in any activity, nor argued with any decision made by the others concerning herself. A couple of months ago, however, she began asserting herself as an individual with a mind of her own and was able to argue and fight with Cathy over possession of an item of equipment. She defeated a startled Cathy and since that time has been able to make her presence felt during group meetings quite successfully. It may be that Jane's increased awareness and open comment concerning firstly Mary's quietness and secondly her competence in various activities, gave Mary the self-confidence which she needed in order to express herself. The leader and helpers have naturally given Mary every praise and encouragement in all the activities but it has been the admiration and acceptance of peers which has been lacking in Mary's life. Hopefully this gap is now being filled and the confidence to express herself will continue to grow (Bennett, 1974, pp. 56–7).

Thomas R of Bishop Auckland (aged four and a half)

Thomas has never attended a nursery and started school in January. He is the only boy in the family of five; his sisters are all teenagers and attending secondary school. Not unnaturally Tom has been spoiled by all members of the family.

Thomas has never had to share with anybody, having an abundance of toys for himself. He has grown up in a very adult environment and been the centre of attraction. He has had little contact with children his own age and when confronted by them does not know how to play alongside them or share the toys.

I have been visiting Thomas for a year, during which time he has made a lot of progress. At first Thomas was very impatient – wanting all the toys out at once and not really playing with anything. He tended to be very destructive and abuse the toys. He was extremely difficult to motivate and lacked concentration to spend even short periods with one particular toy. He was very inhibited and thought that playing was silly, especially imaginative play. Even stories were 'lies' to him because they were make-believe.

Since those first few weeks, Thomas has learned that play can be fun and has received a lot of enjoyment out of the more creative play, e.g. painting, plasticine and modelling. He has shown a lot of imagination and skill in using scissors, paintbrushes, etc . . .

Thomas's lack of concentration has made progress slow in cognitive areas of shape and colour. More progress could have been made if the parents had been more cooperative and given more support and encouragement (Langan and Daynes, 1978, pp. 22–3).

These four children are as varied as any in a caseload (although Susan, Donald and Mary are close in age). From these accounts, all seem to have considerable problems and all to have benefitted from the attention of their social workers and involvement in their various groups.

Joan welcomed them at the door

As in the previous section I am going to let the FSU writers speak for themselves, this time about what happened when the Susans and Donalds and Marys were assembled and –

> Joan welcomed them at the door and saw to coats-off, etc. She had already set out a room for activities, including: paints, brushes, paper, gummed paper pieces, chalk, Wendy House tidy and well equipped, same with 'shop', lots of cushions around. She had also hidden 'band instruments' in a cupboard and placed orange juice, biscuits, plates, cups, mopping-up cloth, etc. on the mantlepiece out of reach.
>
> The first few minutes were spent allowing the children to decide for themselves, by themselves, what to do, which activity to pursue, for as little or as long as they liked, while the leaders observed, listened, responded and generally tried to get in touch with the mood of the children.
>
> When the children had settled, the leaders attempted to join in the play at the child's level. This was easier to do from the Wendy house and 'shop' where Susan or Anne were usually 'playing'. We would be children, neighbours, shopkeepers, whatever was appropriate, developing the characters quickly and manipulating the story to some 'incident'. This was usually an 'accident' of some kind, with the victims needing care, attention, comfort through ambulance men, nurses, doctors, visiting parents, etc. (n.b. it was usually one of the *children* who developed the story to the 'accident' stage, after which the leaders, in whatever role, responded *to*, emphasized the need *for* and encouraged other characters *to show overtly* their *concern and care* for the victim.) Within this sort of role-play the children could get in touch with all manner of feelings and express them quite safely.
>
> When the role-play naturally concluded (it could last half an hour to one hour) the leaders introduced an activity which the children had initiated during the first session and which they loved. It also helped everyone to get out of role. This was to emulate the Juvenile Jazz Bands with an assortment of noisy, if often unmusical, instruments; a brush shank, a strict march tempo, and pathetically few tunes. Up and down we'd march, making as much noise as possible, no doubt to the dismay of workers upstairs.
>
> Next there was tea. This was very formal. Nothing was served until everyone was seated at table. Jobs were shared and carried out *well* – or no tea! Polite manners were required. At first the leaders served tea to the

children, offering a model of polite sharing. After the second session the children always served each other and the leaders. The routine was quickly established and tea developed from an unruly, messy brawl over who had more juice or biscuits, to: 'Would you like a biscuit, Susan?' 'Yes please, John.' 'Can I have a biscuit John?' 'What do you have to say, Anne?' 'Please' 'Here you are.'

There was a quick tidy-up if time permitted, otherwise it was toilets, coats-on and time to go home (at about 5.45 pm). The journey home was an important part of the group session. Both leaders took the children home. These children had pleasant singing voices, loved to sing together and were encouraged to do so for the entire journey, irrespective of who and how many were crying (Billy was usually tired out by this time and whingey). This ritual singing was tremendously important in many ways and, on the occasion of Susan's regression to babyhood, it was the familiarity, ritual and pleasure which brought her out of it in order to join in the singing.

Towards the end of the group's life, and with the coming of the warmer weather, the sessions were sometimes held outside, when 'tea' became 'picnic' and activities took place in parks or by the river banks or on the sea shore. By this time the leaders did not need to join in their play so much and there were definite signs of a big improvement in the children's capacity to share and enjoy playing together both during the group and at home (Smith, 1978, pp. 49–50).

Donald and a hammer

The Group offered many opportunities for this learning and with experience groupworkers became increasingly skilled in making use of them. The following is an extract from a process record of one such interaction between Donald and John, one of the group-workers.

On arrival at the Unit Donald immediately ran to the cellar, keen to get on with the den we had worked on previously. He skipped there but was overwhelmed as soon as he arrived by the enormity of the task facing him and his reaction was to despair.

'Will you help me with the den, John?'

'Yes Donald, what would you like me to do?'

We were in the smallest cellar where the den was being constructed. Donald had already hammered some pieces of wood to the wall but had had some difficulty in getting nails into the brick wall. He started again with the hammer. One of the nails he was using bent and he got very angry. 'These nails aren't any good; it's useless.'

I said I would look for more larger and stronger nails that were scattered around the floor of the large cellar. I left Donald and began searching. Donald continued hammering but with little success, partly because he found it difficult to persevere and partly because the task was really difficult. He began a destructive hammering and eventually came out to the larger room brandishing the hammer. I stopped picking the nails up from the floor and concentrated my attention on him.

'We'll never get the den done; it's useless. You don't want to help either.'
So saying Donald then smashed a hole in the plaster ceiling.
'What do you want us to do, Donald?'
'I don't know.'
He had another swing at the ceiling.
'I want to help you Donald, but you must tell me what you want me to do.'
'You're not interested in the den, you would rather stay here.'
('Here' being the other part of the cellar away from the den.)
'I am interested Donald but you remember the boat we tried to build last week? I helped you there but you got fed up with that. When I made suggestions it was easy for you to get angry with me if things went wrong. Now I want you to make suggestions.'
Donald then went on the rampage, smashing anything the hammer would come into contact with. I felt, partly for my own safety, that I ought to intervene. Donald was also getting beyond his own limit but needed, I felt, some control from me at that time.
'You're very angry aren't you, Donald?'
'No.'
'I know you are because you are using the hammer to bang the table.'
I then moved around behind Donald and took the hammer away from him. He did not resist. I stood with the hammer by the table and in my anger and frustration hit the table myself. Realizing this I said, 'You see Donald, I have become angry too.'
Donald then shuffled around the room mentioning that at home he had had the equipment that was needed. I said maybe we had to use what we had. That we had nails and wood and that maybe if we use these things we would find that we had enough. Just because things were not on a plate for us did not mean that we couldn't do anything. Maybe we had to overcome these difficulties.
I needed to get away from the situation just briefly but I knew that I must not let Donald think I was leaving him.
'I'm just going upstairs to get a cigarette Donald, then I'll be back down again.'
When I returned Donald said, 'It's all right for you, you can have a smoke.'
He obviously meant that it was easier for me to withdraw from the situation. Donald then began stacking wood and taking it back into the cellar where the den was. I immediately made a positive move to help him.
He put some nails in and then the den began to take shape. Donald now seemed to have an idea of what he wanted. He was able to relax and leave after a period of work to join the others for orange and biscuits. During the snack he told everyone that he and John had a 'secret' – his way of saying that something important had happened.
Something important had happened. Donald survived frustration and anger and had come out the other end with a positive achievement (Davies, 1975, pp. 20–21).

A Tuesday bake *(extract from full description of group meeting)*

Today's choice is cooking. London Buns to be precise.
The mixing bowls laid out in readiness, catch the eye of one girl, who

leaps to claim hers and is rapidly pursued by the others anxious not to be left out. Amid much clamouring and beating of spoons in bowls, the recipe is read aloud slowly and the ingredients given out. Accusations are voiced that one has more than another but closer examination reveals that all is fair. Favourite perches are then mounted, be it table, chair or canteen counter and the serious work of mixing commences. Perfect peace. Not a murmur. Deep concentration. 'Is it all right?' 'Mix mine for me, my arm's tired.' The silence is short-lived. A stir here, more flour there and words of encouragement to all are a spur to further effort. A couple of girls sit quietly, slowly mixing the ingredients with astonishing thoroughness and patience, while the others are rushing on, eager to have their cakes in the oven. The first is already fashioning small cakes on a tray. The others follow in turn, each electing to mould the mixture in a variety of sizes and shapes, and on completion the trays disappear into the oven.

Attention is then immediately turned to the question of the next activity. The natural leader of the group enthusiastically suggests, 'Let's do a play'. This proposal is seized upon by a couple of the others and the trio rush excitedly into the hall to select their attire from the dressing-up clothes. A fourth member reflects on the idea momentarily before she, too, decides to join in and sets off in hot pursuit of the others, bemoaning the fact that the best garments will have already been claimed. The remaining two opt to stay in the canteen and chat happily to the leader whilst painting paper doillies. The relative peace in here is suddenly disturbed by a figure in long flowing robes and high-heeled shoes, who totters hastily across to the oven, opens the door and peers in. Finding that her cakes are only half cooked, she retraces her steps and disappears once more into the hall. The duo in the canteen follow her, curious to know what the others are doing and soon find themselves participating. The leader quietly withdraws into the background, keeping one eye on the precious cakes and the other on the interaction of the group as they organize themselves. Each member is involved in varying degrees in the proceedings, some issuing instructions, some carrying them out, others disputing the ideas and offering their own instead. The total effect is of a loud, happy noise with six gaily clad figures acting their own part, sometimes in conjunction with the others, sometimes in isolation. 'Come and watch' is the invitation shrieked across the room. The leader is told where to sit and the chief organizer rallies the others, endeavouring to get them all acting the same scene. Everyone eventually cooperates and the performance begins. Not to the satisfaction of the director, who calls for a re-run. Some agree to start again, others ignore her and continue; two scenes are performed simultaneously. It doesn't seem to matter. Everyone is contentedly playing in their own fantasy world, acting out their chosen characters. Interest in this activity wanes for a couple of participants and it is suggested that they might prepare the tea. One responds enthusiastically, the other indifferently, but both vanish into the canteen and, suddenly remembering their cakes, ask eagerly if they are ready yet. They are, and are on the counter awaiting collection. Immediate consumption is the usual practice, although invariably some are taken home to show Mum. Today is no exception (Bennett, 1974, pp. 44–5).

The Newcastle Browns

Sessions were often chaotic. In theory there was some structure provided: the session would begin with everyone sitting on the floor in a circle holding hands when dialogue and/or games were attempted; activities were selected from a choice of three or four and would last for about 40 minutes; orange juice and biscuits would be shared; washing up; another attempt at dialogue, then home in the van. In practice the children argued, fought, vied with each other, grabbed whatever they could for themselves whether this be food, objects or attention. They were quite isolated from each other in many ways. They seemed to prefer any room to the 'group' room and were often found rummaging amongst the 'goodies' in other rooms, sometimes attempting to steal toys, etc.

The leaders had to strongly resist being too controlling. Instead we tried to be more honest with the children in expressing our feelings, i.e. we would *tell them* when we were angry, fed up, disappointed etc., but we were also alert to expressing pleasure and giving praise at every opportunity. We repeatedly attempted dialogue with them about the purpose of the group. Eventually they were able to grasp the concept of the group as simply 'doing things together' and the need for rules in order to achieve this, i.e. 'if individuals wander out of the room we cannot operate as a group'.

By the fifth session there were three interesting and important developments:

1 The children began to express positive feelings towards each other when using the tape recorder. This was particularly beneficial to Michael, who could hear on tape the nice things said about him, and accept them. His behaviour changed almost immediately.

2 The sitting-in-a-circle beginning became a means whereby each child could test out his or her importance to the group. It developed from Michael's reluctance to join the circle until the others began to chant 'We want Michael'. Over the weeks each child deliberately stayed out of the circle joining in only in response to the chant.

3 They were beginning to overcome their inhibitions and join in a few games which brought them into close physical contact with the members of the group including the leaders. (these games were used to specific purpose, e.g. to develop mutual trust; help let off steam, help increase awareness of each other and self, overcome fears and verbalize their positive feelings for each other.)

After the eighth session the leaders were aware that somehow progress had to be speeded up. Objects were still a major distraction, a fact which led to the comment that ideally the group should be held in a padded cell with no toys, books, paints, etc. available.

It was quite fortunate that the group room was being decorated the following week and not available to us. We seized this opportunity to create a situation whereby the group would have to rely completely on its own resources. An alternative room was selected, giving access only to stairs and toilet, barren of furniture apart from a necessary table and a few chairs.

The situation was fully explained to the children, followed by an outline of the programme and the leaders' expectations of the group: 'Today we are all going to join in the games, some for fun, some to complete a task, like trying to lift each member (including leaders) high up in the air using only our hands. Then we will act out a story before we have our orange juice and biscuits'. This proved to be the most successful and enjoyable session so far.

We continued with the same programme for the next three sessions, beginning with a circle game in which each told the group of something they liked. At first the children were only able to name favourite food: 'I like ice-cream', chocolate, cakes, biscuits, etc., long after the leaders were naming individuals in the group. Each child found it comparatively easy to say they liked Sarah (the sub-normal sibling) and the leaders, but it took four sessions for them to be able to name each other!

By the end of these four sessions their feelings about themselves and each other had changed considerably: they were much more confident, relaxed, considerate and trusting of each other, able to share and involve one another in their improvised games which became increasingly imaginative and enjoyable.

There followed three outdoor sessions when we visited a pleasant stretch of riverside, suitable for paddling, swimming, picnicking, etc. By this time the leaders were keeping a very low profile, leaving the children to their own devices, while keeping a watchful eye on them for safety reasons, and encouraging their adventurous play. Their capacity to enjoy themselves, explore new situations and share together, continued to increase.

The final session was spent indoors at the children's request: the leaders provided food for a party, followed by a concert planned and performed by the children with no help from us. It was superb! (Smith and Brooke, 1978).

An all-time low

While there is plenty of fun and achievement in working in such groups as these it is not all buns and jazz bands; the cost to the workers is great and the work can be undertaken and maintained only if they receive constant and firm support.

The team who worked with Donald and his siblings 'prepared themselves for a demanding task and they were not disappointed!' (Davies, 1975, p. 16). At the climax of Donald's testing out 'morale of all the workers sank to an all-time low and the support of the other Unit members was essential in keeping workers to the task' (p. 18).

Cooperation, support and care for colleagues characterizes the work and philosophy of Family Service Units and enable workers to undertake tasks and ventures which may, indeed do, involve anxiety and exhaustion.

Support is sometimes sought from outside the Unit. For example, the Bishop Auckland Project had as consultant a lecturer from a counselling course; this Unit served a large council estate both physically and socially rather remote from the small parent town. Strains of working in this kind of isolation are great at the best of times especially when, as here, the Unit was of recent foundation. Setting up and working on a special project is likely to be even more

stressful and an outside consultant can offer not only encouragement but also evaluation of problems and progress. In fact the
Bishop Auckland workers not only worked with their own consultant but also

> felt that it was necessary to have contact and visit places where similar
> schemes were already in operation. . . .
> We were able to discuss and exchange ideas about this type of work and
> also seek advice (Langan and Daynes, 1978, p. 14).

Work with groups involving not only much staff time and energy
but also use of the agency premises can be undertaken only with
the freely given permission of the whole staff group (including sec-
retarial and cleaning members). The Newcastle workers recalled
that the

> whole agency gave permission for noisy play, for example the Sheraton's
> 'juvenile jazz band' – humming tunes, marching up and down the room,
> and everyone else in the building had to permit the noise. This was very
> important to the workers. *The whole place was part of the group* (emphasis
> added).

Although only two or three workers may be working directly with
a group, the whole staff group may be involved in not only tolerating
the noise but also learning and understanding what is happening.
For example, one of the Newcastle groups was being led by
social-work students who were experiencing great trouble in holding the interest of and controlling the children. No one could
suggest a solution since Joan Smith and her colleagues realized they
did not know what they did to manage the groups. So all the staff and
students role-played the problematic children's group with Joan
Smith playing herself and discovered that the answer was physical
contact. The hitherto unformulated philosophy of the Unit was to
avoid shouting (because that was the all-too-common home experience of the children) and to control by gentle and firm physical
restraint, being consistent and clear about boundaries and as
positive as possible. A colleague said, 'Joan gives a brilliant smile
while saying "no" '.

Enjoy yourself

One of the most vital elements of working with children at all and
with groups in particular is the enjoyment and satisfaction of the
worker. A worker who is not (apart from those low spots) enjoying
herself and committed to the whole enterprise will communicate
little but her own boredom and disengagement to the group. The
Newcastle workers put this firmly: 'Don't attempt to do anything
with a group you won't enjoy yourself.' The worker who is herself
happy will communicate her enthusiasm and involve the children.

What the group gave

Earlier in this chapter I have referred to the experiences of individual children. To conclude, here is the summary of what the group gave to the Brown family of Newcastle.

What the group gave to the family was an ability to communicate and share with each other rather than struggling in isolation beyond the coping ability of the parents. Visits to the house after the group was finished demonstrated the change in the family as conversation was possible without a constant stream of requests for attention from the children. For the first time the children could play together and join in playing with other children. Outside the home it was with great pleasure that the news came about the children using the summer playhouse when previously these children could never join in anything organized in the area. Within the house the parents could now hold a conversation with themselves, a visitor or one of the children. This family is a closely-knit loving cluster that had been cut-off from fully appreciating each other (Smith and Brooke, 1978).

Chapter 10

Not by Treatment but by Love

The Northorpe Hall Trust

> At Northorpe we try to heal the wounds between adults and the children, not by 'treatment', but by love (Northorpe Hall Trust, 1978).

For more than ten years I had been afraid of the boys of Northorpe. It was all very well to be a member of the management group and discuss policy and problems but during the six years of my membership I managed never actually to see a boy. One on his own might have been all right but a group of eight or ten would, I was sure, be overwhelming and would expose my suspected inability to communicate with numbers of proven delinquents. As the present director, Peter Harrison, says, 'ten, even five years ago, fieldworkers were scared of coming out from behind their desks and meeting eight people on their own territory'. He is right about me at least.

But at last I was forced to meet them, these boys who are thought by some people to be on the verge of contributing to the appalling future envisaged by the Chairman of the Northorpe Trustees in 1973 (although I do not think his opinion is shared by the staff of Northorpe Hall):

> Is anarchy too strong a word to use when contemplating the possible state of the Nation in, say, another generation? That respect for law and order is much less than it was is not denied but some fail to realize that the effects of this are gradual and unless there is a reversal one cannot resist the fear that anarchy can overtake us (Hiley, 1973).

At last I had to go to Northorpe Hall on a Saturday when the boys would be there. And they were so little; thin and pale, etiolated children. Perhaps some boys in other groups are well grown and tough but I am sure that the physical appearance and reedy voices of the boys I met reflect the truth that these are not people to be afraid of, to punish and shun but children to be cherished and fed and given the food of both body and spirit of which they have been kept short. They and their parents have been wounded and the Northorpe Hall Trust endeavours to offer healing. This chapter is about the ways in which the staff of Northorpe Hall work with the boys and their families. It is based on conversations with staff and associates of Northorpe Hall some of which are transcribed below, and draws on their writings and an article by Bob Payne of Sheffield Family Service Unit. Readers who wish for further information about the philosophy and work of the Northorpe Hall Trust are advised to write to The Director, Northorpe Hall Trust, Northorpe Lane, Mirfield, West Yorkshire, WF14 OQL.

The staff of Northorpe Hall come from a variety of backgrounds and trainings (including the ministry) and they combine work in both residential and field work. Although the setting and particular combination of work is unusual I believe that the philosophy and practice of child care at Northorpe Hall has the greatest possible relevance to social work in all settings.

Why and wherefore

The Northorpe Hall Trust was established in 1963 on a basis and pattern which have been maintained throughout its life. (The work had in fact been started under the auspices of Children's Relief International shortly before and the separate trust was established for financial reasons.) Bruce Duncan (1968, p. 88), the first director, described the work thus:

> ... group work with the boys during their visits, a process of bringing a small group of delinquent and disturbed boys together and observing and dealing with their reactions to one another and to the staff and family case-work, which covers the mid-week work of the staff with the boys in their own families.

I suspect that today's staff might find the words 'observing and dealing with' rather cold but I think this is really only an accident of semantics for the real philosophy as expressed by Bruce Duncan is in no way cold and is as thoroughly alive and in practice now as it was when he first invited boys in trouble to come from Leeds, a dozen miles away, to the Elizabethan farmhouse in Mirfield for a monthly weekend.

> My first objective was to provide an accepting, homely atmosphere where the boys could feel at ease, relax, let off steam and recover from the tensions and unhappiness present in one form or another in all their homes. Second, to provide a situation where the boys could learn to live happily and amicably in a small community, with the responsibilities, freedom and 'give and take' that is necessary. Finally, to create conditions under which mutual trust and friendship between the staff and boys could develop, with the consequent lowering of defensive barriers on their part and increased awareness of their needs and problems on our part (p. 85).

In 1974 the third director, Peter Hopkins, and his staff added:

> *Our Objectives* are to increase self-confidence, self-awareness and to help boys improve relationships with both adults and peers. In short, our aim

is not to produce boys who conform to a set pattern, but to have boys leave
us thinking more rationally and reasonably about themselves and their
impact on others.

To increase the validity of our work at weekends, it is of the utmost
importance to relate the boy's progress at Northorpe to changes in his
home environment and to achieve this end, family casework is undertaken by the same staff team (Hopkins and Feeny, 1974, p. 1)

and this statement was incorporated into the 1978 staff paper on
Northorpe Hall.

Annual Reports for several years began with the statement that

Northorpe Hall maintains a radically different approach to the problem
of juvenile delinquency, its overall aim being that of enabling boys to live
well adjusted lives in their own families. To achieve this the Trust
operates an intensive family casework service within the boys' homes
and invites the boys for regular weekend visits in groups ... All that is
possible is done to strengthen any beneficial ties that a boy may have with
his home and environment (Northorpe Hall Trust, 1972/3/4).

Not all the boys are subject to court orders and referral is strictly
related to the need of each boy and his probable ability to benefit
from connection with Northorpe Hall:

The most suitable boys are those who are not so grossly disturbed as to
need full-time residential treatment away from their own home, but can
benefit from the therapeutic programme we offer. Such boys are those
whose experiences have been so limited that their emotional, and/or
intellectual growth is stunted. They may be unable to make satisfactory
relationships with peers, and/or adults. They may lack self-confidence in
emotional, verbal, social and physical spheres, or they may be boys with
anti-authority feelings. .... The age for a boy to start ... is between twelve
and fourteen years. We find it unlikely that a boy will benefit much if he is
severely subnormal, immersed in a life of crime, or the youngest in a
family with a problem of delinquency (Northorpe Hall Trust, 1978, p. 4).

There are as many objectives as boys on the scheme; before each
weekend staff talk together about each boy, his needs and what *each*
weekend should provide for him. For example Kevin, a loner, lives
alone with his father and the overall aim for him is to help him to
learn to relate to other people and sharing a room with other boys is
a useful contributor to this. But Kevin snores and at a weekend when
the group is small it is tempting to place him in a room on his own for
the sake of his colleagues. Not only his colleagues but also Kevin
himself would prefer this for he likes to be apart from the group (for
example he 'hides behind comics'). This kind of dilemma, where the
problem is one of ordinary daily life and the solution must in some
way contribute to the development of each boy's self-respect and
ability to cope with the area of life in which he has most struggle, is
typical of the concern of Northorpe.

The staff are guided always by the principle that the boys must be
helped to manage ordinary life in the ordinary community. The

boys are themselves extra-ordinary in that they are deemed to be in need of such help (and may possess any number of idiosyncrasies of personality and behaviour): Northorpe Hall is also extra-ordinary for it is not very common to spend weekends in an ancient and beautiful house with trips to rocks and sports centres, on boats and bicycles and in company with several contemporaries, and a number of adults whose attention is all focused on the visiting children. Boys whose trouble is concerned with conforming to the demands of conventional life may enjoy the tension-breaking experience of such extra-ordinariness but it can be of real help to them only if firmly related to life in everyday Leeds. The activities

> are important, in that they must be stimulating, enjoyable and rewarding; more important is their function as a vehicle for the development of relationships and trust between the individuals involved. Activities are used as imaginatively as possible and it is recognized that any interaction can become a very positive experience. . . . The activities are not, there-fore, exceptional or extraordinary. They are normal activities which we try to use to their maximum potential (Northorpe Hall Trust, 1978, p. 6).

An ordinary experience of living together

Life at Northorpe Hall is as far as possible

> an ordinary experience of living together, but for many of the boys it is, in fact, an extra-ordinary experience, an alternative society; and the staff must help the boys to come to terms with it (Northorpe Hall Trust, 1978, p. 6).

Many field social workers reading this chapter may be thinking that it is all very interesting but rather remote from their own work. Field social workers don't live with their clients, by definition. The staff at Northorpe Hall have the opportunity to combine sharing two nights and days with each group of boys every four weeks (plus longer holidays), and field social work with their families; but the 'living togetherness' is essentially a quality within their contacts, underlying and completely woven into those contacts. Their work is charac-terized by the belief that 'Living together makes tremendous strides towards communication' but living together is 'not necessarily sleeping in the same house . . . it may be three hours every Wednesday evening'. For example, Peter Harrison (1978) suggests that a social worker with four boys on supervision orders might to do better to see all four together, regularly, for two hours than each boy individually for only half an hour, and to create within the two hours some quality of being, living, experiencing together. Perhaps this can be expressed in another phrase, *being fully alive together*, a quality in interaction which does not depend on numbers or environment or length of contact. Peter Harrison considers that 'barriers between professional worker and client must be reduced to the absolute minimum'; if the social worker can have access to information about, for example, a boy's income so may the boy know about that of the social worker: 'they're going to know about my personal life in the way I know about theirs'. There is an important difference between a social worker offering a client information about herself and her private life and expecting a client to bear the burden of any problems she may be experiencing. But 'really knowing the worker is an important step between loss of fear and the development of trust' and it is a sign of health and maturity in both parties if a client is able to offer concern and consideration and the social worker to receive it. 'Charity' is an unpopular word, probably because of its associations of patronage, the rich giving to the (deserving) poor, those poor valued only as the vehicles for those rich to feel and show virtue.

A child who learns that an apparently powerful adult can be affected by his behaviour is in a powerful position which may lead him to abuse that power but may equally, and particularly if the adult has treated the child with respect, lead him to develop control of himself and consideration for the adult. When Peter Harrison ran a youth club in south London he found one evening that the children had been pestering his wife, trying to gain entry to the house although Mrs Harrison was ill. At the beginning of the club session Peter Harrison told the children what their behaviour had meant to both himself and his wife and how he now felt about it and them. The children responded by saying that they would forgo the session so that he could look after his wife; in other words when they were treated in an adult manner they were able to offer mature thought, consideration and action, and their relationship with their adult leader was strengthened. Living together in any community, whether a family, street or residential establishment entails the development of limits and controls, clear messages about what behaviour is and is not acceptable. It is no good complaining that Mrs Jones is forever calling just when you're sitting down to listen to *The Archers* if you have never told Mrs Jones that Archers time is sacred and asked her to come fifteen minutes later. So Peter Harrison suggests that living togetherness in social work implies not perpetual availability in an unrealistic way but the development of normal interactions between people, some of whom may be clients and some social workers. If a client calls on a social worker at a bad time it is up to the social worker to say so with adult-adult respect; and after all, social workers often expect right of entry to their clients' homes.

This is, I think, a very difficult issue; social workers with large caseloads might reasonably expect to protect their own homes and private lives, to expect to be able to retreat from the stress and anxiety of work. Service to clients can be offered in so many different ways within the general idea of social work that I believe each social worker should be empowered to make her own decision about availability to her clients, whether she opens her home, always or at particular times, gives weekend and evening time to visiting and arranging expeditions, works strictly within a five-day week and the office and her clients' own homes or whatever. I do not believe one can prescribe for conditions of service. But I do believe that it is important for social workers to discover what their own barriers are and then to reduce and if possible dispose of them. If 'the private self is excluded from the relationship there is too much distance' and there is no relationship; a boy cannot relate to an animated role.

Living together at Northorpe Hall has both the quality and the substance of sharing. Boys and staff together cook and eat and wash up:

SUNDAY 'Morning lazy bones'
'Change your sheets this morning'
Wet ones and dry ones pile up on the floor
Washing mashine spins before the water comes in!
Boiled eggs.
Billy hasn't washed up
'Won't'
'Must'
Does eventually (Northorpe Hall Trust, 1978).

Through ordinary life and work in the house and gardens as well as in leisure activities outside, communication can lead to trust, trust to communication and both to the development of a sense of personal respect and responsibility. For example,

a worker became involved with two boys in the garden digging: a spontaneous conversation developed within which these two boys were able to comment on and discuss their own personal situations. The fact that everyone was engrossed in what they were doing, tended to alleviate any tension or embarrassment which might have existed had they been sitting face to face in a rather more formal situation (Northorpe Hall Trust, 1978, p. 6).

Few people are really comfortable or encouraged to communicate 'sitting face to face in a ... formal situation' whether they are chronologically child or adult and particularly if, as with Bob Payne's group of boys at Sheffield Family Service Unit, they lack verbal skills and are inarticulate. Bob Payne (1975, p. 20) learned that

it was because of this that the communication between worker and boys and between boys, was expressed in physical gestures, the offering of sweets, or the sharing of precious cigarettes.

Another sharing is of planning and therefore of responsibility for what happens during a weekend. This includes deciding how to spend the £10 which is available to each group each weekend and which is kept in a jam jar on top of the television set in the living room. If the money is ever stolen that is a matter for the whole group's concern for the money belongs to the group and therefore its loss means that everyone suffers. The boys are learning to take responsibility for their own actions instead of merely responding to (or reacting against) external rules and restrictions. A typical example of planning is illustrated by the weekend when a group arrived with the firm intention of going to Blackpool. Groups do sometimes visit Blackpool but on this occasion the staff suggested that such a trip would not be a good idea; if the boys were coming only for treats there would be no help towards any change. The boys discussed further with the staff and then chose to have an expedition to some crags a few miles away. This visit was successful because 'they were all living together in a way not possible at Blackpool . . there they'd all be off in ones and twos'. The staff members were not being kill-joy or paternalistic in suggesting that Plumpton Rocks would provide a chance of a better experience than Blackpool, for their attitude was based on knowledge and thought about the members of the particular group and the recent history of the group: during the previous weekend, (four weeks previously), two very dominant members of the group had been absent (at a detention centre) the remaining members had made and enjoyed a more satisfying weekend than usual. Now they were nervous that, with the return of the two dominating boys, they might not be able to 'keep the good feeling' and chose Blackpool partly as a way of escape from working to maintain the progress and satisfaction; 'the feeling of the group was being tested'. The experience of the Plumpton Rocks outing confirmed that they could continue to be 'together' without the protection of heady (and expensive) distractions. Throughout every experience at Northorpe the boys are being helped 'to control their behaviour and to choose what to accept what to reject, when to conform, when to deviate' (Balbernie, 1972, p. 11) and this control is learned through the endeavour

> to give them *security* which, tragically, some of our boys have never experienced. This security is generated by clear boundaries and controls, by consistent behaviour from the adults and by a directness and honesty in discussion. This includes giving opinions about boys, even though at times this will prove painful. . . . From this secure base of rational and consistent limits, a boy can gradually learn self-control, self-discipline (Northorpe Hall Trust, 1978, p. 6).

This vital learning is enhanced and made real because it takes place within the everday life of the boys in their ordinary contact with one another and the staff:

> Real situations arise so we can use these together; if contact takes place only in an office it is always in some way abstract; for example if a boy steals at Northorpe we can deal with *that*, not just with a report.

Northorpe is therefore about a real person doing a real thing at the prsent time rather than, as Peter Harrison suggests, a part of a boy with a part of a social worker in an abstract context trying to discuss behaviour which took place elsewhere and at a different time. 'The way a boy behaves in a weekend is the way he behaves in the outside world'. An illustration of this is the occasion on which one group, after a very positive and good weekend during which the members had worked hard on the property of Northorpe, went silly on the roof and broke a tile. One of the boys was particularly upset about this and the staff realized that this reflected his behaviour at home, doing something well and then undoing it. Peter Harrison said simply to the boy, 'That's what you do at home' and the boy answered 'Yes'. It was felt by the staff that this incident and brief verbal exchange contained much depth of insight and communication for although it looks very simple in print, the usefulness of the few words depended on considerable contact, understanding, awareness and trust between the boy and the staff. It also depended on knowing that children don't go in for long conversations on difficult topics: the worker needs 'to drift in and out . . . depth can be caught quickly'.

Things could get sorted out when he came

'I enjoyed Mark coming round, but can't stand social workers, they go on and on. But when Mark came he just talked and sorted things out. But social workers never believed me; they believed what my Mum said much more; but Mark listened to both points of view and that's why things could get sorted out when he came' (Harrison, 1978).

Mark Feeny (the assistant director) became for Frank a 'friend'; although his work with Frank's family was that of a field social worker he was perceived to have qualities which differentiated him from social workers. Frank's parents commented that 'social workers do no good, they come and go; they talk but they don't do anything'. Since those social workers have no opportunity to comment on their contacts with this family it would be wrong to dwell on these criticisms; the important point seems to be that in some way Mark Feeny achieved with both Frank and his family a deep and positive rapport which depended on his real care and respect for each member of the family and his implementation of the philosophy of living-togetherness, of true sharing of self and work.

During all the time that Frank was at Northorpe, Mark visited the family regularly and became a friend to them. When he first came, he was, in their eyes, someone trying to do something with Frank, something which was failing, but they never doubted his good intentions. At times they have become very depressed with the way things went for Frank and Mark's visits were often for them times when they could talk over difficulties with him and Frank.

One of the most difficult parts of Mark Feeny's achievement was gaining the trust of both the boy and his parents. Frank's criticism of social workers centred on their apparent siding with his mother: 'The social workers never believed me; they believed what my Mum said much more' and his positive use of the facilities of Northorpe depended greatly on his belief that 'Mark listened to both points of view':

> Frank . . . learned to trust Mark and be open with him, knowing that Mark would be straight with him – the 'distance' between adults and boys has always been kept to a minium.

Peter Harrison believes that the work of Northorpe is 'validated by meeting in the boys' own living rooms or meeting them from school'; if only a residential experience is offered he thinks that it is possible 'to build it up and protect it so that it is virtually useless'. For example, Alan, the oldest boy in the Beck family (mentioned in previous chapters), was placed in a residential special school where he made good progress in the eyes of both the headmaster and myself (and, indeed, of his parents). So good was the progress that the headmaster pressed me to receive Alan into care in order that he would not deteriorate during holidays at home; the headmaster was completely uninterested in the notion that Alan was a member of his own family and that my job was concerned with helping to hold together the various strands of his life. To that headmaster, apparently, the child existed and had validity only within the context of the physical boundaries of his own institution and of any other institution which might deputize during holidays. Almost, perhaps, the child was expected to conform to and serve the requirements of institutions rather than the (explicitly therapeutic) institution serving the needs of the child.

Northorpe Hall is concerned with the care and development of *whole* children in the context of their normal lives within the community which houses their parents and siblings and the workers seek always to help the boys bring the various aspects of their lives together; Northorpe is not split off as something 'good', an unreal place of escape: rather it is offered as a haven from pressing worries in which each boy may gain strength, essentially *to return to* his own family, and essentially *supported within* his own family by his particular worker from Northorpe. Liz Jeffery (1978) describes her work with Bill and his family. Mrs Jackson, his mother, is bringing up six children on her own:

> She is worn out with the effort of keeping going, and trying to control the children and frequently threatens to walk out. She usually makes use of my visits to 'let off steam' and usually gets things out of her system. I see my role in the family, primarily in terms of supporting Mrs Jackson in caring for the family, reinforcing her in the things she does well, and pointing out some of the things the family is good at – e.g. their consistently good school reports. Also I occasionally offer advice, when

asked, about how to control the children and set reasonable limits on their behaviour. This week we concentrate on this, and afterwards, when Bill has arrived home from school, I talk with him about areas of his life that he sees as problematical. He agrees that he doesn't often help at home, or get on with his brothers and sisters, and we talk about what he can do to improve this. Hopefully, if he remembers what we have said and does try to carry some of it out, this will have a beneficial spin off for mum.

Bill is able to see that the social worker is concerned about and trusted by his mother, that she is not afraid of his home and therefore does not reject the part of him which lives in that home (unlike Alan Beck's headmaster). Moreover she does not change between Northorpe and his home but consistently cares about and communicates with him, helping him to relate his Northorpe self with his home self, to carry home any good changes, to be thoroughly *known* without the risk of rejection because some part of him is unlovely.

Perhaps the prime implication of this for field social workers is concerned with visiting residential establishments. Children on caseloads very often find difficulty in achieving any sense of consistency or cohesion in their lives and the social worker may be the only person in touch with both the individual child and all his scattered important people; only the social worker may stand in the middle and hold for the child the strands of his identity, the clue to his wholeness. And these clues may be essentially physical, depending on the social worker herself being seen in the places of significance to the child (as was Liz Jeffery with Bill) or ensuring that the child may himself be in an important place; for example a boarded-out child may need to return to a nursery or children's home, perhaps in order to ensure that he really has left it (demonstrated by actually leaving it again at the end of the visit), to see people with whom he has shared his ordinary life, maybe for years, to remember the self or part of self which he has left behind as part of self is always left in a moved-from place. Bob Payne (1975, pp. 20–21) says that

> The visiting of old familiar haunts . . . was a means the worker employed to develop a sense of not only identity, but a sense of the past and personal history. For to be without a conscious knowledge of one's past is to be in a perpetual state of immaturity, acting and reacting only in the present.

Social work with children is surely pre-eminently about helping to develop a sense of identity, a knowledge of self, integration of the fragments of life for children in a society which fosters fragmentation.

Up Snowdon and out to sea

Activities, says Peter Harrison, are a 'red herring'; their importance is in the opportunities they offer for boys and staff to *be* together, *whatever* they are *doing*. There is no paradox in the belief that any activity must also be enjoyable and of some value in itself. Swimming may be an ideal way to offer play and the demonstration of the staff members as trustworthy in the water, but however much communication and trust are fostered, the swimming itself must be worthwhile. Some activities offer the experience of taking risks with oneself and of achievement which can lead to increased confidence and therefore self-respect. Bob Payne's (1975, p. 10)

> first group outing was curtailed by heavy snow. ... The attitude of the group members was typical of under-achievers and at later meetings frequent reference was made to their own ability to triumph over the difficulty, 'It were smart that snow, weren't it Bob?' What had been subjectively a cold, wet, unpleasant experience had been used by the group members as a boost to their low self-esteem.

Here the sense of achievement was corporate, the boys and staff had endured the experience together and the sharing of experience strengthend their trust in one another. Sometimes the achievement is for an individual:

> Phil, whilst fooling around on a ruined jetty on the beach, was bet 50p by one of the instructors that he would not run out into the sea and touch one of the rusting supports of the jetty before the waves returned. He did touch it and got soaked in the process and duly won his 50p. The significant thing is that he talked about this for the rest of the weekend and on subsequent meetings of the group. The reference to this exciting and rewarding little adventure had a lot to do with the reliability of the adult figure in keeping his word and handing over the bet. Phil basked in the attention and treated the rest ... to chips on the way back (p. 14).

Exertion, risk and achievement are not confined to the 'client' members of such adventures. Soon after Len Goad joined the staff at Northorpe he found himself climbing Snowdon with

> two strong, strapping sixteen-year-olds. They were extremely nice lads who patiently waited 200 feet above while I dragged my sagging fifteen-stone frame up to them. ...
> On reaching the summit of Everest ... my positive thinking and my ideas of full involvement were certainly in question. The two lads ... were impatiently waiting to get back to camp. Thinking that I should be doing something, I stalled for time, attempted to drink a scalding cup of tea and look as if I was enjoying myself. Shouldn't I have been using this opportunity to get to know the boys? At that moment ... I couldn't even remember their names. Not having the strength to talk, I let the boys take the initiative. I wasn't sure if it was them caring for my welfare or their laziness when they suggested we should go back down by train. Well, thinking I should be a tower of strength and not wanting to admit I was just a broken lump of humanity I pleaded poverty and set off down the mountain (Goad, 1978).

Here the adult's achievement was not only in surviving the encounter with a mountain but also in recognizing and so humanly dealing with his feelings, for example the conflict between his need for complete rest and his ideas of professional behaviour – 'Shouldn't I have been using this opportunity to get to know the boys?'

Space and success

Snowdon and Plumpton Rocks and the garden at Northorpe Hall provide plenty of physical space for moving and breathing, working and having adventures. But Northorpe also, and perhaps even more importantly, gives its boys emotional space. The boys who need Northorpe Hall live in cramped houses and flats in fume and dirt-filled streets and their emotional life and environment is also cramped and dusty. The staff respect the boys and this means that they can give them time and space to grow at their own pace. Harry, for example, lived with a mother who combined both possessive and rejecting behaviour; at Northorpe Hall he chose to be known as Andy, a name which was used nowhere else, thus indicating that he wanted to be himself in a new way. The staff made no comment on this until one day someone said, 'You're Andy here but Harry everywhere else; when will you be Harry here?' and Harry/Andy answered, 'Not until the autumn'. The boy understood what he was doing and, given peace and space and respect, he worked in his own time towards putting together his private Andy-self with his public-Harry-self.

Whatever the *doing* at Northorpe Hall the *being* is all about believing that the boys are all important worthwhile people, for there is no such thing as an unimportant worthless person. The boys may have committed offences, they may believe those around them who persistently tell them that they are rubbish, they may think that love is nothing but a word in girls' comics; at Northorpe Hall they meet respect, concern and love without sentimentality or collusion, "stern love". Communication from the staff is clear and direct, humorous and human, expectations are realistic and consistent, activities are related to relationship and the true encounter between individuals. The staff are not afraid to admit that they have problems, negative feelings and failures but neither are they afraid to confess to success. To conclude this chapter, and indeed the whole book, here are pictures of two boys described in a hopeful, honest paper by social worker Liz Jeffery.

Success is . . . elusive, abstract, insubstantial: an ideal that we aim towards but rarely allow ourselves to feel we've achieved. . . . I feel *it is important that we are aware of our successes* – if only to help us through those periods when we feel particularly hopeless, and success seems very remote. Perhaps my personal definition of success can best be illustrated by . . . Philip and Jo.

Philip

Philip comes from a large family living on a large council estate. He, and his family, like so many of their neighbours, have very anti-authority feelings and are suspicious of social workers. The area sees nothing wrong in truanting from school and a bit of thieving on the side – so long as you are not caught. Philip was, therefore, very distrustful of us when he started coming about eighteen months ago and his family were never open to us. This attitude has in the last few months changed significantly and doubtless this was partly the result of Mrs Gray attending our Parent's Party. Anyway, for what ever reasons, Philip and the family are very much more open to us and welcome our intervention. Certainly barriers are coming down and attitudes beginning to change.

Jo

Jo was a very odd boy when he came to us a year ago. He was unable to take responsibility for himself or his possessions and needed a full time nanny to help him through some of the most obvious activities, such as going swimming with a group. In addition we noticed his strange behaviour in many little mannerisms and his aloofness from other boys. Another strange characteristic was the way he would often use words quite incorrectly. We discovered that he had an interest and liking for doing pin and thread designs and soon he became competent and able to teach others. This was one of the ways in which he built up his confidence and a year after starting to attend Northorpe he is now totally different – well able to take responsibility for himself and increasingly taking a responsibility for the group as well. His general bearing, his relationships and his attendance at school have all improved (Jeffery, 1979). (emphasis added)

Northorpe Hall is a special place with special facilities but the staff members are ordinary social workers (not all social-work trained) whose philosophy and practice of working with children might be found in any social-work department or establishment. Philip and Jo and all the other boys can be helped and healed through love because the caring staff learn how to recognize and overcome their own fear in order truly to communicate with the children.

Part Four

Post Script

Chapter 11

Peace and Silence

I have finished writing this book and the manuscript is almost ready to send to the publisher. And at this point I realize that I have omitted a whole important medium of communication. Silence.

In the Quaker Meeting yesterday someone spoke about living silence and I hear now how the book is full of noise and activity, although, reading through again, I see a number of passing references to silence.

Elijah in the wilderness could hear the 'still small voice' because he was throughout his whole being silent, really listening (I Kings, 19 12). Social workers cannot thoroughly hear the communications of their clients unless they too still the noises both outside and within. Perhaps many clients and social workers are seeking (whether to offer or receive) help and enlightenment in the 'great and strong wind' of activity instead of 'a quiet, still centre, where we are most vividly aware of ourselves as individuals, and also of our relationship to others' (Gorman, 1978, p. 31). People in need of social-work help are almost certainly in distress and the social workers' first concern is perhaps to help their clients 'to be calmed by the stillness at the centre of [their] being' (Gorman, p. 14).

In the deepest of our feelings and confusions words and actions often cannot reach us; we may need to be *encompassed* (to recall Clare Winnicott's word from chapter 2) by the accessible unpressurizing silence of people who respect and can tolerate our feelings. The silence is itself the communication of understanding, caring, gentle waiting. The silent helper demonstrates that she does not need words when no words are needed.

Children may often use silence in communication: I have never before thought to analyse this! But I am sure that there are many occasions when a social worker could offer a troubled child relief from pressure by naturally slipping with him into a period, maybe quite short, of silence. And perhaps older children and adolescents might also, in particular circumstances, join with their social workers in deliberate quietness in order to seek themselves 'as individuals' and their 'relationships to others,' in order to share an experience of peace, an escape from confusion and anxiety, an opportunity simply and wholly to *be* both as individuals and together.

List of Abbreviations

ABAFA	Association of British Adoption and Fostering Agencies
BASW	British Association of Social Workers
BSMT	British Society for Music Therapy
CCETSW	Central Council for the Education and Training of Social Workers
DHSS	Department of Health and Social Security
ESN	Educationally Subnormal
FSU	Family Service Units
HMSO	Her Majesty's Stationery Office
NAWCH	National Association for the Welfare of Children in Hospital
NAYPIC	National Association of Young People in Care
NCSS	National Council of Social Service
NHT	Northorpe Hall Trust
RCCA	Residential Child Care Association
TSCF	The Save the Children Fund

Bibliography

ABAFA 1976: *Planning for Children in Long-Term Care*. London: Association of British Adoption and Fostering Agencies
— 1977: *Working with Children who are Joining New Families*. London: Association of British Adoption and Fostering Agencies
Abbatt, P. 1967: Toys and Play. In Lambert, D. (ed.) *Play in Child Care*. Ossett, W. Yorks.: Residential Social Work (RCCA)
Adams, R. 1973: *Watership Down*. Harmondsworth: Penguin
Alvin, J. 1967: Music and the Maladjusted Child. In Lambert, D. (ed.) *Play in Child Care*, Ossett, W. Yorks.: Residential Social Work (RCCA)
— 1969: *Music Therapy for Severely Subnormal Boys*. London: British Society for Music Therapy
— 1971a: Individual Therapy with Psychotic Adults and Children. In BSMT, *Individual Music Therapy*, London: British Society for Music Therapy
— 1971b: Study in Depth of an Autistic Child. In BSMT, *Individual Music Therapy*, London: British Society for Music Therapy
Amende, Erica 1974: *Moses the Mouse*. (unpublished) School of Applied Social Studies, Bradford
Aries, P. 1973: *Centuries of Childhood*. Harmondsworth: Penguin
Ashley, B. 1974: *The Trouble with Donovan Croft*. London: Oxford University Press
Axline, V. M. 1947: *Play Therapy: The Inner Dynamics of Childhood*. Boston: Houghton Mifflin
— 1971: *Dibs: in Search of Self*. Harmondsworth: Penguin
Bach, S. 1969: Spontaneous Painting of Severely Ill Patients, A Contribution to Psychosomatic Medicine. *Acta Psychosomatica* 8
Balbernie, R. 1972: *A Future and Differentiated Model for Specific Residential Work with Young Offenders*. Annual General Meeting of NHT (unpublished paper)
Barclay, P. 1960: Music Therapy for the Mentally Deficient Child. In BSMT, *Music Therapy in the Education of the Child*, London: British Society for Music Therapy
Barnes, G. G. 1978: Communicating with Children. In CCETSW: *Good Enough Parenting*, London: Central Council for the Education and Training of Social Workers
Baskin, B. H. and Harris, K. H. (eds) 1976: *The Special Child in the Library*. Chicago: American Library Association
— 1977: *Notes from a Different Drummer*. Epping, Essex: R. R. Bowker Co.

BASW 1977: Children in Care: A BASW Charter of Rights. *Social Work Today* 8 (25)

Bennett, A. 1974: The Tuesday Group. In Smith, D. M. (ed) *Families and Groups: a Unit at Work*, FSU Monograph no. 2, Bristol: Bookstall Publications

Berg, L. 1972: *Look at Kids*. Harmondsworth: Penguin.

Berger, N. 1971: The Child, the Law and the State. In Hall, J. (ed) *Children's Rights*, London: Elek

Berne, E. 1968: *Games People Play: The Psychology of Human Relationships*. Harmondsworth: Penguin

Bernstein, J. E. 1977: *Books to Help Children Cope with Separation and Loss*. Epping, Essex: R. R. Bowker Co.

Bettelheim, B. 1978: *The Uses of Enchantment: The Meanings and Importance of Fairy Tales*. Harmondsworth: Penguin

Brandon, D. 1976: *Zen in the Art of Helping*. London: Routledge & Kegan Paul

Bristol, H. 1945: Play Therapy. *The New Era*, May

Britton, C. (Winnicott) 1945: *Children Who Cannot Play*. The New Era, May

Brown, J. 1972: Casework with Young Children in Care. In Holgate, E. (ed) *Communicating with Children*. Harlow, Essex: Longman

Brown, M. 1974: Jackie Goes to Hospital. (unpublished) School of Applied Social Studies, Bradford

Bruner, J. (ed) 1976: *Play*. Harmondsworth: Penguin

BSMT 1960: *Music Therapy in the Education of the Child*. London: British Society for Music Therapy

— 1969: *Music Therapy for Severely Subnormal Boys*. London: British Society for Music Therapy

— 1971: *Individual Music Therapy*. London: British Society for Music Therapy

Bugler, J. 1977: The Genius of Nadia. *Observer*, 27 November

Carroll, L. 1948: *Alice through the Looking Glass*. Harmondsworth: Penguin

Cass, J. 1962: Children and Books. In Lambert, D. (ed) *Play in Child Care*, Ossett, W. Yorks.: Residential Social Work (RCCA)

CCETSW 1978: *Good Enough Parenting*. London: Central Council for the Education and Training of Social Workers

Chadbourne, S. P. 1977: *Bibliotherapy: An Overview and the Librarian's Role*. U.S. Department of Health, Welfare, National Institute of Education (microfiche)

Cohen, A. and Garner, N. 1967: (eds) *Readings in the History of Educational Thought*. London: University of London Press

Crompton, M. 1978a: *The House Where Jack Lives*. London: The Bodley Head

— 1978b: When is an Adult not an Adult? When He's an Adolescent. *Community Care*, 12 April

— 1978c: Harp-Assisted Casework: Music as an Aid to Communicating with Children. *Social Work Service* 17, October

— 1979: Bibliotherapy in Social Work with Children. *Social Work Service* 21, November

Curtis, C. J. and Boultwood, H. E. 1953: *A Short History of Educational Ideas*. London: University Tutorial Press

Davies, H. 1975: Donald: A Child in a Social Work Group. In FSU, *Time to*

Consider; Papers from a Family Service Unit. London: The Bedford Square Press of NCSS

Day, P. 1972: *Communication in Social Work*. Oxford: Pergamon-

De Costa, L. 1976: Brief Intervention with Bereaved Adolescents. *Social Work Today* 8 (6)

DHSS 1976: *Report of the Enquiry into the Care and Supervision Provided in Relation to Maria Colwell*. London: HMSO

— 1976: *Report of the Expert Group on Play in Hospital*. London: HMSO

De Mause, L. (ed) 1976: *The History of Childhood: The Evolution of Parent – Child Relationships as a Factor in History*. London: Souvenir Press

Denney, A. H. (ed) 1968: *Children at Risk*. London: Church Information Office

Dickinson, C. 1976: *Last Straw*. London: Macmillan

Dockar-Drysdale, B. 1968: *Therapy in Child Care*. Harlow, Middx.: Longman

— 1973: *Consultation in Child Care*. Harlow, Middx.: Longman

Donaldson, M. 1978: *Children's Minds*. London: Fontana

Donley, K. 1975: *Opening New Doors*. London: Association of British Adoption and Fostering Agencies

Duncan, B. 1968: Northorpe Hall for Boys. In Denney, A. H. (ed) *Children at Risk*, London: Church Information Office

Eikenberry, D. 1972: A Story for Mary. In Holgate, E. (ed) *Communicating with Children*, Harlow, Essex: Longman

Erikson, E. 1965: *Childhood and Society*. Harmondsworth: Penguin

Frank, J. 1977: Children's Books and the Literature of Human Understanding. In Schultheiss, M. *Humanistic Approach to Teaching*: A Look at Bibliotherapy, U.S. Department of Health, Education, Welfare, National Institute of Education (microfiche)

FSU 1974: *Families and Groups: A Unit at Work, FSU Monograph No. 2*. Bristol: Bookstall Publications

— 1975: *Time to Consider: Papers from a Family Service Unit*. London: The Bedford Square Press of NCSS

Gillis, R. J. 1978: *Children's Books for Times of Stress: an Annotated Bibliography*. Bloomenston: Indiana University Press

Ginnott, H. G. 1965: *Between Parent and Child*. St Alban's: Staples Press

Glasser, W. 1975: *Reality Therapy: A New Approach to Psychiatry*. Bedfont, Middx: Perennial Library

Goad, L. 1978: First Impressions Can be Deceptive. *In Northorpe Work is Family Work*, NHT Annual Report

Golcher, J. 1978: Child's Play: A Social Work Responsibility? *Social Work Today* 19 (25)

Golding, W. 1954: *Lord of the Flies*. London: Faber

Goodnow, J. 1977: *Children's Drawing*. London: Fontana

Gorman, G. 1978: *Introducing Quakers*. London: Friends Home Service Committee

Green, J. In TSCF, 1974: *Every Side of the Picture*. London: The Save the Children Fund

Gripe, M. 1962: *Hugo and Josephine*. London: Pan

Gydal, M. and Danielsson, T. 1976: *When Gemma's Parents Got Divorced*. London: Hodder & Stoughton (transl. C. Ellis)

— 1973: *Olly Goes to Hospital*. London: Hodder & Stoughton (transl. C. Ellis)

Hadfield, J. A. 1962: *Childhood and Adolescence.* Harmondsworth: Penguin

Hall, J. (ed) 1971: *Children's Rights.* London: Elek

Harding, V. and Walker, S. 1972: *Let's Make a Game of It.* London: The Save the Children Fund (reprinted from *Nursing Mirror* 22 December 1972)

Harrison, P. 1978: Peter Harrison meets an 'Old Boy' and his Family. *In Northorpe Work is Family Work*, NHT Annual Report

Harvey, S. and Hales-Tooke, A. 1972: *Play in Hospital.* London: Faber

Herbert, M. 1975: *Problems of Childhood.* London: Pan

Heywood, J. 1978: *Children in Care.* London: Routledge & Kegan Paul

Hiley, J. 1973: *As Our Chairman Sees It.* NHT Annual Report

Hill, S. 1974: *I'm the King of the Castle.* Harmondsworth: Penguin

Holgate, E. (ed) 1972: *Communicating with Children.* Harlow, Essex: Longman

Holgate, E. and Neill, T. 1978: In Practice. *Community Care*, 4 January

Holt, J., 1970: *How Children Learn.* Harmondsworth: Penguin

Hopkins, P. and Feeny, M. 1974: *Northorpe Hall: a Scheme of Intermediate Treatment.* Northorpe Hall trust (unpublished)

Hunnybun, N. K. 1965: David and his Mother. In Younghusband, E. *Social Work with Families*, London: Allen & Unwin

Ingram, E. 1967: A Home is a Place to Play in. In Lambert, D. (ed) *Play in Child Care*, Ossett, W. Yorks.: Residential Social Work (RCCA)

Ingram, K. 1975: A Casework Study of a Disturbed Child and his Family. In FSU *Time to Consider: Papers from a Family Service Unit*, London: The Bedford Square Press of NCSS

Jacobs, T. C. 1972: Casework with Very Young Children in Hospital. In Holgate, E. (ed) *Communicating with Children.* Harlow, Essex: Longman

Jameson, K. in TSCF 1974: *Every Side of the Picture.* London: The Save the Children Fund

Jeffery, L. 1978: Liz Jeffery Looks Back over the Last Few Days. *In Northorpe Work is Family Work*, NHT Annual Report

— 1979: *What is Success?* NHT Annual Report

Jewell, P. 1978: Learning to Live with Client Max. *Social Work Today* 9 (35)

Jolly, H. 1976: Why Children must be able to Play in Hospital. *Play for Children in Hospital*, NAWCH Newsletter, Summer

Jones, W. 1970: Keeping the Memories of Childhood. *Social Work Today* 1 (5)

Kahn, J. 1978: Recollected Grief. *Journal of Adolescence* 1 (1)

Kastell, J. 1962: *Casework in Child Care.* London: Routledge & Kegan Paul

Keat, D. B. 1974: *Fundamentals of Child Counselling.* Boston: Houghton Mifflin

Kerr, J. 1974: *When Hitler Stole Pink Rabbit.* London: Armada (Collins)

Kilroy-Silk, R. 1979: An Objectionable Objection, Comment. *Social Work Today* 10 (28)

Knight, F. 1960: Music Therapy with Maladjusted Children. *In Music Therapy in the Education of the Child*, London: British Society for Music Therapy

Kydd, R. 1967: Communism or a Property-Owning Democracy? In Lambert, D. (ed), *Play in Child Care*, Ossett, W. Yorks. Residential Social Work (RCCA)

Lambert, D. (ed) 1967: *Play in Child Care.* Ossett, W. Yorks: Residential Social Work (RCCA)

Lambert, J. and Pearson, J. 1974: *Adventure Play Grounds.* Harmondsworth: Penguin

Langan, L. and Daynes, L. 1978: *Bishop Auckland FSU Home Education Project.* FSU Quarterly 15

Lee, J. 1978: *Play in Hospital.* (unpublished dissertation) Newcastle University

Lenhoff, F. G. 1970: *Let's Try and Try Again.* Harmat Hill, Shrewsbury: Shotton Hall Publications

Littner, N. 1975: *The Strains and Stresses on the Child Care Welfare Worker.* Newyork: Child Welfare League of America

Lloyd, A. K. 1965: Helping a Child adapt to Stress: the Use of Ego Psychology in Casework. In Younghusband, E. (ed), *Social Work with Families.* London: Allen & Unwin

Lovell, A. 1978: *In a Summer Garment.* London: Secker & Warburg

Lynes, A. 1976: 'Suffer the Little Children . . .'. *Social Work Today* 8 (8)

McConnell, M. 1979: *A Group in Transition.* (unpublished dissertation) Newcastle University

Mahy, M. 1974: *Stepmother.* London: Franklin Watts

Mann, T. 1962: *Buddenbrooks.* London: Secker & Warburg (transl. H. T. Lowe-Porter)

M. C. 1893: *Everybody's Book of Correct Conduct.* London: Saxon & Co.

Ministry of Health 1958: *Report on the Welfare of Children in Hospital* (The Platt Report). London: HMSO

Minns, H. 1976: Children Talking – Teacher Learning. *English in Education* 10 (1)

Moore, J. 1976: The Child Client. *Social Work Today* 8 (3)

Morris, A. and McIsaac, M. 1978: *Juvenile Justice?.* London: Heinemann

Moustakas, C. E. 1959: *Psychotherapy with Children: the Living Relationship.* New York: Harper & Bros.

Nash, P. 1968: *Models of Man.* New York: John Wiley & Sons

NAWCH 1976: *Play for Children in Hospital*, NAWCH Newsletter. London: National Association for the Welfare of Children in Hospital

Neill, A. S. 1968: *Summerhill.* Harmondsworth: Penguin

Newcastle FSU 1978: *Annual Report*

Northorpe Hall Trust: *Annual Reports*, 1972, 1973, 1974, 1978, 1979

Nordoff P. and Robbins, C. 1971: the Children's Tune. In BSMT, *Individual Music Therapy*, London: British Society for Music Therapy

Omwake, E. B. and Solnit, A. J. 1961: 'It isn't Fair': The Treatment of a Blind Child. *The Psycholanalytic Study of the Child* 16

Oswin, M. 1978 *Children Living in Long-Stay Hospitals.* Spastics International Medical Publications, London: Heinemann Medical Books

Page, R. and Clark, G. A. (ed) 1977: *Who Cares? Young People in Care Speak Out.* London: National Children's Bureau

Park, C. C. 1972: *The Siege.* Harmondsworth: Penguin

Parry, J. 1968: *The Psychology of Human Communication.* New York: Elsevier

Payne, B. 1975: *An Experience of an Intermediate Treatment Group.* FSU

Petit, H. 1977: *Images and Self-Images.* FSU Quarterly 13

Phillips, J. 1979: *Give Your Child Music*, London: Elek

Plank, E. and Horwood, C. 1961: Leg Amputation in a Four-Year-Old. *The Psychoanalytic Study of the Child* 16

Plank, E. 1971: *Working with Children in Hospital.* Cleveland: The Press of Case Western Reserve University

Pluckrose, H. in TSCF 1974: *Every Side of the Picture*. London: The Save the Children Fund

Prestage, R. 1972: Life for Kim. In Holgate, E. (ed), *Communicating with Children*, Harlow, Essex: Longman

Pringle, M. K. 1975: *The Needs of Children*. London: Hutchinson

Rey, M. and H. A. 1967: *Zozo Goes to Hospital*. London: Chatto & Windus

Rich, J. 1968: *Interviewing Children and Adolescents*. London: Macmillan

Richards, E. 1971: Working with the Inner World of Children. *Social Work Today* 2 (15)

Richman, H. 1972: Casework with a Child Following Heart Surgery. In Holgate, E. (ed) *Communicating with Children*, Harlow, Essex: Longman

Robertson, J. 1969: *John*. London: Tavistock Institute of Human Relations (film)

Rutter, M. 1975: *Helping Troubled Children*. Harmondsworth: Penguin

Schultheiss, M. 1977: *Humanistic Approach to Teaching: A Look at Bibliotherapy*. U.S. Department of Health, Education, Welfare, National Institute of Education (microfiche)

Scott, G. In TSCF 1974: *Every Side of the Picture*. London: The Save the Children Fund

Selfe, L. 1977: *Nadia: a Case of Extraordinary Drawing Ability*. London: Academic Press

Sereny, G. 1972: *The Case of Mary Bell*. London: Eyre Methuen

Shapiro, P. 1965: Children's Play as a Concern of Family Caseworkers. In Younghusband, E. (ed), *Social Work with Families*, London: Allen & Unwin

Shipman, N. D. 1972: *Childhood: a Sociological Perspective*. Slough: NFER Publishing Co.

Shotton Hall School 1967: The Disturbed Child and Play. In Lambert, D. (ed) *Play in Child Care*, Ossett, W. Yorks.: Residential Social Work (RCCA)

Sloss, J. 1978: Play Therapy for Maladjusted Children. *Social Work Today* 9 (46)

Smith, D. M. (ed) 1974: *Families and Groups: a Unit at Work*, FSU Monograph no. 2. Bristol: Bookstall Publications

Smith, J. 1978: The Sheraton Family: *FSU Quarterly* 15

Smith, J. and Brooke, T. 1978: *A Sibling Group*. Newcastle FSU Annual Report

Smith, S. 1975: *Collected Poems*. London: Allen Lane

Storr, C. 1964: *Marianne Dreams*. Harmondsworth: Penguin

— 1974: *Thursday*. Harmondsworth: Penguin

Szasz, T. S. 1974: *The Ethics of Psychoanalysis*. London: Routledge & Kegan Paul

Theze, S. 1977: Jackie, Consumer's Viewpoint. *Social Work Today* 8 (32)

Thomas, J. 1977: Communicating with Children. *Social Work Today* 8 (25)

Timms, N. W. 1969: *Casework in the Child Care Services*. London: Butterworths

Tizard, B. 1976: Phillips, J. and Plewis, I. 1976: Staff Behaviour in Pre-School Centres. *Journal of Child Psychology and Psychiatry* 17 (1)

Tolkien, J. R. R. 1954–5: *The Lord of the Rings*. London: Allen & Unwin

Truax, C. B. and Carkhuff, R. 1967: *Toward Effective Counseling and Psychotherapy: Training and Practice*. Chicago: Aldine

TSCF 1974: *Every Side of the Picture*. London: The Save the Children Fund

Tucker, N. 1975: Can Literature Solve Problems? *Where?*, September

Tuters, E. 1974: Short-Term Contracts: Visha: Brief Intervention in Family Mourning. *Social Work Today* 5 (8)

Uttley, A. 1940: *Little Grey Rabbit's Christmas*. Glasgow: Collins

— 1976: Field Toys. In Bruner, J., *Play*, Harmondsworth: Penguin

Walton, R. 1979: Charter of Rights: the End or the Beginning? *Social Work Today* 10 (19)

Warburton, Y. 1967: Six Little Girls from School. In Lambert, D. (ed), *Play in Child Care*, Ossett, W. Yorks.: Residential Social Work (RCCA)

Wardle, M. 1975: (Crompton) Hippopotamus or Cow? On not Communicating *about* Children. *Social Work Today* 6 (14)

Webb, L. 1969: *Children with Special Needs in the Infants School*. London: Fontana

Weinstein, S. H. 1978: *Bibliotherapy for Children: Using Books and Other Media to Help Children Cope*. U.S. Department of Health, Education, Welfare, National Institute of Education (microfiche)

Willans, A. 1977: *Breakaway: Family Conflict and the Teenage Girl*. London: Maurice Temple Smith

Williams, B. J. 1978: *The Value of Play in Communicating with Children*. (unpublished dissertation) Newcastle University

Willis, J. 1978: *John: a Mentally Handicapped Boy*. (unpublished dissertation) Newcastle University

Winnicott, C. 1964: *Social Work in Child Care*. Hitchin: Codicote Press, Bristol: repr. Bookstall Publications

— 1966: Casework Techniques in the Child Care Services. In Younghusband, E. (ed) *New Developments in Casework*. London: Allen & Unwin

— 1977: Face to Face with Children. *Social Work Today* 8 (26)

Winnicott, D. W. 1971: *Therapeutic Consultations in Child Psychiatry*. London: The Hogarth Press

— 1974: *Playing and Reality*. Harmondsworth: Penguin

— 1978: *The Piggle*. London: The Hogarth Press; 1980: Harmondsworth: Penguin

Wolff, S. 1973: *Children Under Stress*. Harmondsworth: Penguin

Wyndham: J. 1964: *The Midwich Cuckoos*. Harlow, Essex: Longman

Younghusband, E. (ed) 1965: *Social Work with Families*. London: Allen & Unwin

— 1966: *New Developments in Casework*. London: Allen & Unwin

Zwart, C. 1976: NAWCH's Contribution to Play in Hospital, *Play for Children in Hospital*, NAWCH Newsletter, Summer

Zwerdling, E. 1974: *The ABCs of Casework with Children: a Social Work Teacher's Notebook*. New York: Child Welfare League of America

Index

Author Index

244